T0208406

A Sheltered LIFE

DARRELL HAZLE

WESTBOW
PRESS®
A DIVISION OF THOMAS NELSON
& ZONDERVAN

This book is a work of non-fiction. Unless otherwise noted, the author
and the publisher make no explicit guarantees as to the accuracy of
the information contained in this book and in some cases, names of
people and places have been altered to protect their privacy.

WestBow Press books may be ordered through booksellers or by contacting:

WestBow Press
A Division of Thomas Nelson & Zondervan
1663 Liberty Drive
Bloomington, IN 47403
www.westbowpress.com
844-714-3454

Interior Image Credit: Carlos Angon, Owasso, Oklahoma 74055

Scripture taken from the NEW AMERICAN STANDARD BIBLE®,
Copyright © 1960,1962,1963,1968,1971,1972,1973,1975,1977,1995 by The
Lockman Foundation. Used by permission. www.Lockman.org

Scripture quotations taken from The Holy Bible, New International Version® NIV®
Copyright © 1973 1978 1984 2011 by Biblica, Inc. TM. Used
by permission. All rights reserved worldwide.

ISBN: 978-1-6642-0021-0 (sc)
ISBN: 978-1-6642-0020-3 (hc)
ISBN: 978-1-6642-0022-7 (e)

Library of Congress Control Number: 2020916901

Print information available on the last page.

WestBow Press rev. date: 09/02/2020

To my mother, Zelma, and my
grandfather A. L. Hazle.
To my mother for the graceful way
she lived with depression and to
my grandfather in appreciation for
dedicating his life toward helping me.

To my Lord and Savior Jesus Christ,
for His healing power and my
salvation and eternal life.

Contents

Preface

I nstead of continuing the revision of my book in chronological order, I have decided to begin with my third major depression in chapter 1. There are several reasons for this, but it is primarily because of the importance of events that led to a major change in my spiritual life during the eighteen months of depression and anxiety from February 2017 until August 2018.

After the first twenty years of my life I lived a self-centered, prideful, and secular life for fifty years. I now believe I was on my way to hell and didn't know it because I also believed that I was living a Christian life. I had wondered for many years how it would feel to have Jesus in my heart as well as in my head. I was a Christian but not a Christ-centered Christian. I praise God for giving me the adversity of a third depression for eighteen months because it gave me a chance to become a more mature Christian. I now understand what my grandfather meant in a recording of his life-changing experience when he was forty-seven years old, which I recorded in this book. He said, "I didn't know about the love, peace, and hope that lives in the hearts and minds of other Christians. I didn't know that God had given us the Holy Word and Holy Spirit to direct our living—to tell us things we should do and should not do." I now have the joy of having Jesus in my heart as well as in my head and know I have the Holy Spirit. Praise God

I am now eager to serve Jesus and others. I thank God for all the counseling by Terry Devitt, the preaching by pastor Ted Johnson, and the prayers and compassion for me by all my friends at the Bible Church of Owasso that made this possible.

What's New in This Version

C hapter 1 is the most important addition, as it describes the adversity of a third depression, which God gave to me for eighteen months to make me a more mature Christian.

In chapter 4, I added a new subtitle, "**Esketamine, A New Drug for Depression.**" Esketamine is an antidepressant that works immediately instead of taking two to four weeks to be effective.

In chapter 9 a new help section, "**Discussion of Alcohol, Tobacco, and Other Drug Abuse**" (ATOD) was added. A section on oral cancer prevention with symptoms for early diagnosis is included with tobacco abuse under the subtitle "**Nicotine the Most Abused Drug in America.**" The promising treatment of alcohol and nicotine addiction, and anxiety and depression during cancer treatment with psilocybin is discussed.

Another drug discussed is in the subtitle "**Benzodiazepines and Unexpected Problems.**"

At the end of chapter 10, "Guidance and Protection," for my mother's older brother, Herbert Hawkins, I have mentioned some of his accomplishments and more complimentary comments about his life well lived instead of just stating that he attempted suicide in his late seventies in a new subtitle, "**Another Favorite Uncle.**"

A new subtitle---"**Becoming a Friend of Gideons**"—has been added to the end of chapter 11, **"The Gideons and Becoming a Christian."**

In chapter 13, to make the new version more attractive to hunters, I have added memoirs of eighteen interesting stories of **"My Most Memorable Hunting and Fishing Trips."**

Acknowledgments

I would like to give a posthumous thanks to Donald E. Knapp for all that he did for me while I was at the University of Kentucky College of Dentistry (UKCD).

Dr. Knapp was a popular thirty-six-year-old pharmacology instructor at the UKCD.

He was a pharmacist, dentist, and pharmacologist with joint appointments to the UK Colleges of Dentistry and Medicine. As my mentor and the supervisor of my honors program research project on protein synthesis and the recovery of peripheral nerve from local anesthesia he taught me creativity, research attentiveness, inquisitiveness, and a respectful consideration for the ideas of others. Had it not been for Dr. Knapp, I would never have had the opportunity for developing an interest in neurotransmitters and emotions and been able to write this book.

Dr. Knapp rose through the academic ranks in the College of Dentistry to become professor and chairman of the Department of Oral Biology in 1969. He was responsible for instruction in pharmacology and oral biology in the college and was especially active in both teaching and research in the application of pharmacology to dentistry. It was a great loss of knowledge, creativity, and friendship to humanity when he died in 1971 at the young age of forty-one.

I am grateful for the conversations with my uncle Charles "Red" Hazle about his life and especially the Korean War stories.

I thank him for being a close friend all my life. Also, thanks to Phyllis, his wife, for her good memories about Red's stories and about my mother. She also had knowledge about my grandfather Hazle and the Hazle family. Thanks to my mother's twin sister, Thelma Webb, who at ninety-five still drives to town for shopping and has never had depression. She has enlightened me about Mom's playfulness and adventurousness during her early years at home.

Thanks to Glenn Hawkins for the information he provided about his father, Herbert Hawkins.

I would like to thank my wife, Donna, for editing my manuscript, offering suggestions for changes in the content, and for just being my loving wife since 1967 and mother of our two loving daughters, Wendy and Angie. Thanks to my daughters for their helpful suggestions and editing.

I would have gone nowhere without my energetic publisher, Carlos Angon, pushing me to get the book ready for publishing. This bright young man with many computer software and hardware skills made it easy for me to get published. Thanks for his patience through all the changes required because of my inexperience.

Thanks to Terry Devitt, a pastor at Bible Church of Owasso, for treating me as a believer while counseling me during the eighteen months of my third depression.

Thanks to Dr. Stephanie Christner for recommending discontinuing Sinemet for Parkinson's, my medication, which put my third depression into remission.

Thanks to physiologist Ken Dormer, for making recommendation about the sections on alcohol and nicotine abuse.

Thanks to Starbucks in Owasso, Oklahoma, for allowing us to meet there while preparing the manuscript.

One

MY THIRD DEPRESSION

I published a book, *A Sheltered Life*, at the end of December 2016, which was a time of great joy and celebration of an accomplishment I had desired for many years. This was after I had attempted many times through agents and publishing companies to publish a manuscript titled *Happiness Chemistry* in 2002. The significance of what I believe was God's plan for not allowing me to publish that book will be discussed later. I was excited about the new book I had self-published with the help of Carlos Angon. With his work experience, he also helped me develop a functional and attractive website for promoting and selling the book. But my joy was short-lived.

By February 2017 I had become withdrawn and lethargic without any motivation to accomplish anything. I lost confidence in pursuing planned activities for promoting the book. My experiences as a captain in the US Public Health Service (USPHS) had prepared me well for promoting the book, but my anxiety and fear that others would sense my inadequacies inhibited me from doing it. I also didn't want to sell the books because of the requirement for packaging and mailing them as well as keeping accounting records of income and state sales tax collected. I was fearful of not being able to accomplish all those things. I also began to worry about many situations that had no rational basis for worry. I was fearful and anxious about every new experience and even older experiences like driving a car. The other depressions had also occurred at times when I was happy and feeling successful in my career. However, when my brain changes with depression, fewer options are available for problem-solving and creative thinking.

Being out of options to me was the result of a decrease in numbers of or function of neurotransmitters in the brain, which results in the absence of adequate transmission of sensory input for creating options, making good decisions, and being happy. This also seems to be a major reason for the suicidal thoughts that have accompanied my three major depressions. It's as if my higher level of brain function was decreased, and I was left to function with fear. I was also out of options that would normally provide reasonable alternatives to suicide. It's a hopeless state that should not exist for a believer in Christ. I would ask myself, *Am I living in an evil place?*

MY DEMENTIA AND PARKINSON'S DISEASE

In January 2016 I was diagnosed with dementia by my primary care physician after he had a tech give me several tests. That day I was only able to recall a limited number of animals, which I assume was not adequate to pass that part of the test. I failed to repeat a sequence of numbers forward and in reverse order. Then later the tech blindsided me with questions about earlier test questions. If I had been aware of this process, I might have tried better memory tricks to recall that earlier information. After the diagnosis, I was more aware of errors in my memory and thought I might really have dementia. I had started writing a book shortly before being diagnosed with dementia and had doubts about completing it. During my third depression, I really felt that I had dementia. When others asked me how I was doing, I would usually just say okay. Other times I would say, "Fine except for the dementia, depression, and Parkinson's."

More than two years before being diagnosed with Parkinson's disease (PD), I noticed a pill-rolling tremor, a rhythmic tremor of my thumb occurring when resting my hand on my leg and attempting to lift my thumb up from my leg. I had noticed this happening to my grandfather when I was talking to him one day in the late 1960s before he had been diagnosed with PD. I mentioned to him that I had learned about the tremor being an early sign of PD in dental school and suggested that he be checked out for Parkinson's. He was soon diagnosed with PD. I had no other symptoms except some occasional drooling. But toward the end of January, I noticed some upper body shaking when sitting on the couch watching television. Since my grandfather had been diagnosed with PD, I was concerned enough to see a neurologist.

The neurologist questioned me and did some physical testing such as observing my gait while walking five yards away and spinning to walk back to him as well as watching me walk heel to toe and standing on one foot. He also observed my hand and arm movements while repeatedly touching my nose with my eyes closed. He watched my hand tremor while stretching my arms out in front of me and rotating my hands slowly. He stood behind me and abruptly pulled me back and caught me to observe my balance. He concluded that I had PD and started me on Sinemet March 1, 2017. A more definitive test for PD exists, but it costs several thousands of dollars, and I don't believe it is readily available at present. Six weeks later he started me on Primidone, an antiseizure medication, for my essential tremor. It was about four months later, after I had complained about numbness in my feet, that he tested nerve conduction in my feet, ankles, and legs. He diagnosed me with peripheral neuropathy.

It was shortly after being diagnosed with PD that I began

to have severe leg cramps. I also began experiencing sleepless nights from the cramping and anxiety. The sleepless nights would sometimes continue for two or three consecutive days. That was really wearing me down. I first tried to prevent the cramping by eating bananas and drinking more fluids. That wasn't working, so I tried drinking V8 juice, which has 850 mg of potassium in eight ounces. That worked well enough most of the time, but when it failed, I learned that taking two heaping teaspoons of yellow mustard would instantly stop the pain when I woke up with leg cramps. I was always careful to rinse down the mustard with water to reduce the possibility of GERD-like pain in my esophagus. My psychiatrist started me on 0.5 mg of alprazolam XR before bedtime, and that helped sleepless nights and anxiety to a limited extent; at least those problems were more tolerable. I eventually got off the V8 after about a year, and today, praise God, my leg cramps are rare.

OTHER WORRIES

In March 2017 I began receiving messages on my iPhone reading, "Email cannot be delivered, check settings." Carlos had created an email inbox that was published in my book and posted on my website. I tried changing my settings but could never receive the emails. Finally, I canceled the book's email address on my iPhone so the messages would stop. In retrospect, I should have just consulted Carlos about how to start receiving the emails. Not having done that would be a source of more worry later. Maybe I didn't consider that option because my brain was affected by the depression. This continued to be a concern, but it was not until the end of May that I called Carlos and requested that he take down the website for the book. I at least had considered the fact that some people might be trying to buy my book from the website, and PayPal could have been trying to send me mailing labels for people who had purchased my book.

It was also about April that my pastor at Bible Church of Owasso (BCO) began preaching about being a better disciple for Christ in Luke chapters 9–14. After listening to several sermons, I became convicted that I had published a book that was a condemnation of my Christian life. I had not been a good disciple for Christ for the last fifty years of my life.

After the age of twenty, I lost focus of my reason for living a Christ-centered life, which was, up until then, to be a disciple for Christ and obey the great commission in my life. I had been taught through my elementary school years about the great commission in the Royal Ambassadors at my country church, Barren Run Baptist Church. Matthew 28:19–20 (NASB) states, "Go therefore and make disciples of all the nations, baptizing them in the name of the Father and the Son and the Holy Spirit, teaching them to observe all that I commanded you; and lo, I am with you always, even to the end of the age." This is a commandment for all Christians.

The last time I remember attempting to witness to someone about Christ on a personal level was when I was a freshman at the University of Kentucky. My English comp teacher was a young man who looked like Ernest Hemingway to me. We were reading *Catcher in the Rye, Lord of the Flies,* and *The Sun Also Rises,* which certainly didn't promote Christian values. I thought my professor was an atheist, and I wanted to witness to him. When he asked the class to write a term paper about our reason for living, I wrote about the great commission as my reason for living. I can remember that he gave me a surprisingly good grade but offered some reasonable alternatives as reasons for living.

Oh, from the age of twenty I continued going to church and doing all the things Christians do including giving to the church and singing in the choir. I became a Gideon in 2000. I sang in the church choir wherever I was a member, including thirty-six years at Memorial Heights Baptist Church. In 2013 we moved to Broken Arrow, Oklahoma, and joined BCO, which didn't have a church choir. I was losing my voice from disuse atrophy from not talking much as well as from the effects of PD, which weakens the voice.

After my depression had continued into June 2017, all I was doing was sitting at home and worrying about everything that popped into my mind. I had no energy or motivation to do anything and experienced more difficulty making decisions. I quit working as a Linnaeus Gardener volunteer at the Tulsa Garden Center. This was after I had taken fourteen weeks of training by Barry Fugatt in 2015 to become a Linnaeus Gardener and volunteered for two years. I worried about getting a new roof placed on our fourteen-year-old house with some blown-off shingles. Even after the new roof was completed, I worried about an eight-inch flu vent that was leaking into the attic through a crimped seam in the vent. The roofers returned several times and finally sealed the seam. I worried about my beautiful yard being overtaken by weeds and annual bluegrass (poa annua). I hadn't placed any preemergent crabgrass killer or weed killer on my yard; the crabgrass and more dandelions would surely be coming soon.

Many of my one-foot-square pavers along one side of the house had been covered with dirt by drainage and the lack of sod on my neighbor's side of the fence. Weeds and annual bluegrass were sprouting between many pavers and even on the top surface of some of them where dirt had collected. Some small weeds were growing seed heads, and the weeds were spreading. Ants seemed to be everywhere around the house foundation and some inside even though we had a pest control service to spray every other month. I hadn't sprayed my crepe myrtle for scale with horticultural oil during the February window that was recommended, and the scale would show up again during summertime to chew on the bark for the second consecutive year. That could potentially kill them. No new annuals had been planted except for the few my wife had managed to plant. My wife was also mowing the yard for me. I felt worthless.

MY DOUBTS ABOUT MY SALVATION BECAME A MAJOR WORRY

Besides these minor inconveniences and all my needless worrying, which added to the stress of my inability to accomplish anything that would eliminate my concerns, one persistent problem was more of a major concern—that was about my salvation. It was for this reason that I contacted one of my associate pastors at BCO in June for counseling. Terry Devitt was exceptionally accommodating for me and even came to my home. Terry's counseling was reassuring because he approached me as a Christian believer, which I had always thought I was since I had a salvation experience with God in the presence of my pastor and grandfather at the age of nine. I described that event in detail in chapter 2 of this version of *A Sheltered Life*. I vaguely could remember having problems with my faith during my first two depressions in 1975 and 2004 and thought maybe I was just feeling like an unbeliever because of my depression.

However, I later noted that David, one of God's chosen men, had a similar fear of the loss of the Holy Spirit after his sin with Bathsheba and the murder of her husband. "Do not cast me away from your presence and do not take Your Holy Spirit from me" (Psalm 51:11 NASB). He was petitioning God for restoration when he said, "Create in me a clean heart, O God, and renew a steadfast spirit within me" (Psalm 51:10 NASB). Also knowing that we do not need to fear a loss of the Holly Spirit when we sin because as believers in Christ, we are saved and sealed with the Holy Spirit. "Now He who establishes us with you in Christ and anointed us is God, who also sealed us and gave us the Spirit in our hearts as a pledge" (2 Corinthians1:21--22 NASB).

But I still wondered how I would know when God had created in me a clean heart and renewed a steadfast spirit within me? I had been asking for forgiveness.

Three years earlier, I had paraphrased a scripture and printed it on the front cover of a personalized hand-crafted leather cover for my old King James Version Bible. Using John 10:28, I had printed, "Jesus gives me eternal life and no man shall pluck me out of His hand." However, something had changed during this current depression. All the negative comments I read in the Bible about unbelievers seemed to apply to me. I had lost my security expressed in John 10:28, which I had so proudly displayed on my Bible cover for three years. Rob Holler was teaching the book of Jude to our flock each Sunday, and I worried that I was an apostate.

Terry emphasized that I shouldn't rely on my feelings for determining my salvation but that I should remember all God's promises, among which was, He would never leave me. "God is our refuge and strength, A very present help in trouble" (Psalm 46:1 NASB). Isaiah 41:10 (NASB) states: "Do not fear, for I am with you; Do not anxiously look about you, for I am your God. I will strengthen you. Surely I will uphold you with my righteous right hand." I knew those promises but needed to be reminded. I saved the texts of many of God's promises on my iPhone voice recorder so I could listen to them often. Terry recommended reading *Trusting God* by Jerry Bridges.

I kept telling Terry about my past problem of believing in evolution, and even having attempted to publish a book in 2002 called *Happiness Chemistry*, largely based on how evolution influences our behavior. I couldn't get evolution out of my head because of my past involvement. I had justified my belief in theistic evolution by believing that God had still created man and the world but through evolution. I had prepared small, attractive plastic wallet-sized cards about the "Sad Brain," "Happy Brain," "Mean Brain," and the "Contented Peaceful Mind," all based on

Dr. Paul Maclean's book *The Triune Brain and Evolution*. I had called him at the National Institutes of Health (NIH) in Bethesda, Maryland, to discuss his ideas and obtained written permission to use his graphics of the triune brain. I had handed out some of these cards when presenting alcohol, tobacco, and other drug (ATOD) use prevention programs to high school students. I kept telling Terry that I couldn't get evolution out of my head even though I had asked for God's forgiveness of this sin. I told him that I wasn't sure of God's forgiveness. I knew this was erroneous thinking because I also knew of God's grace and his promise to forgive me if I confessed my sins. "If we confess our sins, He is faithful and righteous to forgive us our sins and to cleanse us from all unrighteousness" (1 John 1:9 NASB).

But I still had the fear and anxiety from the depression that kept me from feeling the joy of having Jesus in my heart. I read *Trusting God* and gave attention to the chapter on the reasons God gives us adversity in our lives. The book agreed with what Terry kept telling me: "God gives us adversity to make us a more mature Christian." The scripture in James 1:2–4 (NASB) reads, "Consider it all joy, my brethren, when you encounter various trials, knowing that the testing of your faith produces endurance. And let endurance have its perfect result, so that you may be perfect and complete, lacking in nothing." It made me realize that in the first version of my book, *A Sheltered Life*, I had used the term "providence of God" many times, but only in reference to all the good events in my life. Never once had I thanked Him for the adversities of my first two depressions.

Since I had asked for forgiveness of all the sins that I could think of and had begun thanking Him for the adversities given me during this depression, why was it taking so long for me to know God's forgiveness and know the joy of having Jesus in my heart? Then I read some verses that David wrote in Psalms about waiting on the Lord that made sense to me. Psalm 27:14 (NASB) reads: "Wait for the Lord; be strong and let your heart take courage; Yes, wait on the Lord." Psalm 37:9, 11 (NASB) reads: "For evildoers will be cut off, but those who wait for the Lord, they will inherit the land. But the humble will inherit the land and will delight themselves in abundant prosperity." "Indeed, none of those who wait for You will be ashamed …" (Psalm 25:3a NASB).

Waiting on the Lord for renewal of strength puts us in our proper place to follow Him---physically strengthening us by resting. "Yet those who wait for the Lord will gain new strength; they will mount up with wings like eagles; they will run and not get tired, they will walk and not become weary" (Isaiah 40:23 NASB).

MORE HOUSECLEANING REQUIRED

A few other things were required for pleasing God and clearing my own conscience. I had listened to a sermon by John MacArthur that Terry had sent me about believing in theistic evolution and the Bible at the same time. I could never find the sermon again but did find an interview discussing the age of the earth and evolutionary theories (Google "John MacArthur and the Geochristian"). In the interview John Macarthur argues against believing in old-age-earth theories and evolutionary theories. He expresses doubts that a committed Christian could believe in those theories and the Bible at the same time and must choose between scripture and the opinions of men. Theistic evolution is the belief that God created man through evolution. You can read more about theistic evolution in an article by Gregg Allison, (Feb. 9, 2019), called "Can Christians Believe in Evolution?" in John Piper's desiringGod.org, by selecting "articles," selecting "more articles," then selecting "authors," and then selecting Gregg Allison. I decided that I had to choose one or the other. I choose to believe the Bible.

Pleasing God and obeying his commandments required finding all my old manuscripts—about thirty pounds in one box—that had anything to do with evolution, and I trashed them. I also threw away Darwin's *Origin of the Species*, a book that was one of my favorite possessions because it was so old. I could have given it to someone who appreciated it, but I reasoned that if I wasn't going to use the book, I shouldn't give it to someone else to read and maybe encourage belief in evolution.

Don't ask me how to explain why there is no evidence of human remains found with the dinosaur fossils or why the many rock formation layers in the Grand Canyon seem to be very old. I can't ignore that evidence exists suggesting humans were widespread in North America twenty thousand years ago—maybe longer. Although I can't find explanations for questions about these things in the Bible, I can find many prophecies in the Old Testament that came true as explained in the New Testament. I can now tell everyone who asks me about evolution that the only reference I have about creation is the Bible. I now believe that Dr. Paul MacLean discovered what God created and that those behavioral traits he associated with reptiles and animals may be true but not because of evolution. If they're true, it's because that's the way God created us. That's how God got evolution out of my head!

FINANCIAL STRESS

It was in July 2014 that Donna and I flew to Salt Lake City, Utah, for a few days to meet with officers and staff for discussing the operations of a company called The Falls Event Center (TFEC). Over the next couple of months, we invested about a third of our savings in TFEC. In June 2017 we were made aware that the company was in financial trouble. TFEC and the CEO, Steve Down, were being investigated by the Securities and Exchange Commission (SEC).

According to subpoenas issued by the SEC in 2016, regulators were investigating the possible sale of unregistered securities to investors, allegedly using "schemes to defraud." On May11, 2018, Steve Down was ordered by US District Court judge Jill N. Parish to pay the SEC a civil penalty of $150,000. He was also restrained from the offer of sale of any security to obtain money by means of an untrue statement. The company was building event centers in several western states using shares and notes to raise capital, with plans to eventually sell the company for a profit in which investors would share. The fourteen event centers were losing money, according to the chief financial officer, and he had informed Steve of this in 2017. But Steve had continued to promote them as profitable at high quality, free continuing dental education courses like the ones I had attended in Oklahoma in 2014 through 2016. It is a long story of a series of events that resulted in TFEC declaring Chapter 11 bankruptcy in July 2018.

It wasn't until January 2019 that most of the 339 investors probably realized that reorganization was not likely going to happen, and liquidation of the company was more than likely a reality. That meant that the remaining event centers would have to be sold off and some given back to the creditors because loan payments and taxes had not been paid by Steve and TFEC. Steve had overborrowed, overinvested, and overspent for TFEC. Steve purchased Oregon's Evergreen Aviation and Space Museum for $10.9 million in McMinnville, Oregon in 2016—exclaiming what a great deal he had made. The site consisted of the museum's two buildings, an adjacent water park, a chapel that was converted into a lodge, nearby farmland, eleven vintage warplanes, and the Spruce Goose built by Howard Hughes Jr. in 1949. It even appeared that Steve might have used some TFEC money to support several other ventures.

When bankruptcy was declared in July 2018, TFEC had a debt of $9 million, but by December 31, 2018, the negative equity was $57 million, including $1,061,610 in lawyer and accountants' fees. TFEC was losing $54,700 per day with the remaining event centers. That meant the investors would probably recoup very little if anything out of their investments. Donna and I had filed three proofs of claim with the bankruptcy court in November 2018 for $452,000. During my depression I probably worried about our financial situation more than I should have. I had not worried when the stock market crashed on September 29, 2008, and lost 7 percent in one day and 50 percent of its value over the next few weeks. My brain was healthy and creative with plenty of options and creativity. My faith in God was strong. Now in 2019 there are no worries because I am healthy again; I am resolved that this was just another adversity that God gave us to strengthen our faith in Him and make us more mature Christians. I have forgiven Steve Down, and I pray for him. He still calls and wants to meet to discuss his newest venture, but we have declined.

During my depression I had learned to believe the answer to one of *The New City Catechism*[23] questions: "What is God?", which we had been memorizing at BCO since September 2017. The answer is: "God is the creator and sustainer of everyone and everything. He is eternal, infinite, and unchangeable in his power and perfection, goodness and glory, wisdom, justice, and truth. Nothing happens except through him and by his will." I had acknowledged God's sovereignty as James 4:7a (NASB) reads: "Submit therefore to God." I rejoiced in knowing the scripture of Philippians 4:6–7 (NASB): "Be anxious for nothing, but in everything by prayer and supplication with thanksgiving let your requests be made known to God. And the peace of God, which surpasses all comprehension, will guard your hearts and your minds in Christ Jesus."

It was very embarrassing at first to have been taken by Steve Down, but even the embarrassment from others having knowledge of my investment loss has vanished; our financial situation is fine. I still have the embarrassment that I was not a good steward of God's money, which could have been used to glorify Him in many ways. That loss could have been prevented if I had been more

Christ-centered and followed His commandments in 1 Timothy 6:10–11 (NASB): "For the love of money is the root of all sorts of evil, and some by longing for it have wondered away from the faith and pierced themselves with many griefs. Flee from these things, you man of God and pursue righteousness, goodness, faith, love, perseverance and gentleness." I am sorry for being wise in my own eyes, contrary to the scripture in Proverbs 3:7 (NASB): "Do not be wise in your own eyes; fear the Lord and turn away from evil." I was glad that God had prevented me from publishing the book based on evolution in 2002. At least I wasn't embarrassed by having published that nonspiritual reasoning for public viewing. Thank God, that was by His will.

A SHOCKING EVENT

Another disturbing event happened on February 28, 2018. That day I received three calls from Seattle, Washington. I would not answer the call because I wasn't expecting any calls from Seattle, and I suspected it was a scam call. However, the caller—a recording—left a message. The message was the same each time: "We've been trying to contact you for six months. You are being sued for fraud by the United States, and if you do not call our office for more information, your case will be downloaded to the courts." Initially I shrugged off the three calls because I couldn't think of any reason someone could be suing me for fraud, but it did concern me that they had called three times in one day and never called again. I feared maybe they really had initiated the process of "downloading my case to the courts."

After not receiving any more calls for several days I thought about the possibility that people might have been trying to purchase my book through my website. The call began to seem more believable because I had been also receiving calls from "United States" for about six months, which I would not answer because I thought it was a scam call, and they never left any messages. I began to believe that it could have been a US Attorney's office trying to call me. People could have been making purchases of my book by just selecting "buy book" on my website and paying through PayPal; I had not been mailing books to anyone. At that moment I was shocked when I realized that I could have committed fraud by false advertising and failure to deliver the product. I began to worry, and this caused more restless, sleepless nights. I wondered, if people had been purchasing books and paying through PayPal, why hadn't PayPal called me? Everyone that I told this story just laughed and said it was probably a scam. Even my tax accountant thought it was a scam. His comment offered more reassuring relief than those coming from others, but I still waited for a summons or knock on my door with someone telling me to appear in federal court.

I later tried several times returning the call number left on my iPhone from "United States" and only received a recording that said, "Goodbye." It was also reassuring when I finally answered one of the calls from "United States." A voice said, "This is your grandson, and I have a broken jaw and a broken nose." I just hung up because Donna had received a similar call claiming to be our grandson, Jake, who lived in Georgia, stating that he was in New York and had a broken jaw; the caller was requesting money. They were both scam calls. It's been more than two and a half years since the first three calls, and I haven't heard more about any fraud suit. What a relief! Praise God!

HOW GOD FINALLY HEALED ME

It's an amazing story of how God finally lifted my depression and anxiety. It all started when after one year of not improving and having lost forty pounds, my daughter and wife helped me find another psychiatrist. Through a good friend at BCO they heard about the improvement of a female patient of Dr. Stephanie Christner. This patient who attended Tulsa Bible Church had been severely depressed for two years, but after being treated by Dr. Christner her depression went into remission. They wanted me to see her, but I was resisting changing physicians partly because I hated change in my depressed state. Even though I felt that my present psychiatrist didn't have the answer for stopping my depression, I was dragging my feet.

My daughter, Angie, called Dr. Christner's office and made me an appointment, so I had to go. When Donna and I went to her office, which looked more like a home, I started up the stairs to the second floor and saw a counter about eight feet long that was covered with white plastic bottles of supplements. I became skeptical and begin to wonder why I was at that place. When the receptionist took us to a small room to wait for Dr. Christner, I sat down next to a desk that had a book on it titled *Natural Healing Medicine*. I saw schematics of human bodies hanging on the walls with lines drawn to various parts of the body and a description of their significance. I grabbed Donna's arm and said, "I've got to get out of here. This is not for me!" But she convinced me to stay.

When a young Dr. Christner came in, she greeted us in a friendly manner. I was upfront with her in the beginning and told her that I had never believed in supplements and natural healing medicine. She just said calmly and confidently, "Well, I didn't either until ten years ago; and I changed." She listened to my medical history, and soon began to mention that she associated the beginning of my depression with the time I began taking Sinemet for Parkinson's. She suggested that Sinemet could deplete vitamin B-6, which could cause depression. This wasn't completely correct because my depression had begun about a month before being diagnosed with Parkinson's.

I had brought the results of a recent panel of forty-seven blood tests from my primary care physician, which were all normal except for one indicating slightly low protein. However, Dr.

Christner wanted me to have more blood tests, saying, "I like to get to the metabolic basis of problems." I agreed and when dismissed after some refill meds were prescribed, I went into a small lab where the receptionist came in to draw my blood. It took her fifteen minutes---with the needle in my arm---to draw five vials of blood using a small-gauge butterfly needle. Never before had I experienced taking that long to draw blood. That made me even more skeptical about seeing Dr. Christner.

At the next visit, Dr. Christner reviewed the results of eighty-four lab tests that she had requested. Her review reminded me of a biochemistry or physiology class. She was very knowledgeable about the detailed biochemistry of the human body. Most of my tests were within the normal range, but a few deficiencies were identified. She discussed options for which ones I should consider addressing with supplements soon and possibly others in the future. I left the office that day with some Pure Genomics multivitamins, clinician's preference oils, liposomal B-12, and super liquid folate. I agreed to increase the CoQ-10 that I was already taking and stopped at Sprouts to buy some Vitamin B-6 100 mg capsules. Her push for supplements was not as extreme as I had expected, and she agreed to continue renewing my present medications of bupropion XL 300mg, alprazolam XR 0.5mg, and olanzapine 5 mg. The only change that she requested was for me to get a prescription for Wellbutrin instead of the generic bupropion, which I had taken for fifteen years, because she said she thought it was better. She called in the prescription for Wellbutrin to my local retail pharmacy.

I stopped at the Walgreens pharmacy, and they had filled my prescription with bupropion. I had previously been receiving all my prescriptions from Dr. Aarquisola through mail order from Express Scripts Pharmacy since I had TRICARE for Life. I asked the pharmacist why they hadn't given me Wellbutrin as the doctor had prescribed. She said that TRICARE would not pay for the brand-name drug. I thought maybe I might just pay for it myself until I found out that a thirty-day supply would cost $2,400. Even though Dr. Christner had given me a coupon for a few dollars discount, there was no way I was going to give up taking the generic drug costing me only $7 for a three-month supply, which had worked well for fifteen years. My thought was that Dr. Christner was out of touch with reality. It was just another event that made me wonder why I had switched to this doctor!

At the next visit I was more distraught, and she asked me if I had thought about suicide. I said yes. She asked me if I had thought of how I might do it. I said, "With a gun." Because I had been admitted twice before in my life with suicide thoughts, I knew what was coming next. We discussed whether I should be admitted to a hospital, and we decided that Donna would remain with me 24/7, and she would remove all guns from the house. After some discussion, Dr. Christner agreed to that. When we got home, I found my two pistols; Donna hid them, and she contacted a neighbor about keeping the ten other long guns for a while. We later sent all the guns with my older daughter when she came to visit me from Georgia.

I stuck with Dr. Christner, and I'm glad I did. She kept telling me that I should consider discontinuing the Sinemet. She said she could give me the supplement L-DOPA if I still needed something for the Parkinson's. She said that Sinemet also had carbidopa in it that could deplete vitamin B-6. I was skeptical because I thought maybe she just wanted to sell me another supplement—L-DOPA. My neurologist didn't think discontinuing Sinemet was a good idea and said that he had never heard of it causing vitamin B-6 depletion. I delayed about three months before tapering off the four tablets of Sinemet per day over a five-week period. Within one or two days of taking the last Sinemet tablet, I had a good day on August 1, 2018, like I hadn't had for eighteen months.

I had elevated mood, energy, and motivation to work in my yard. The first thing I did that day was spray my crepe myrtle for scale with Neem oil on a very hot day. For two weeks I had a few bad days between good days. By bad days I mean exactly like I had been feeling every day for eighteen months. The bad days faded the second week, and for the next two weeks I had only one bad day each week. Since then, praise God, I have not had a bad day—at least not any bad days as I had during the eighteen months of depression. I was praising God for sending me to Dr. Christner and healing me. I was thanking Him for the adversity He had given me that had made me a more mature Christian. God transformed me. By God's grace I knew the joy of having Jesus in my heart as well as in my head.

God does things in His own time. I just had to be patient. The same was true for me as David had written: "I waited patiently for the Lord; And He inclined to me and heard my cry. He brought me up out of the pit of destruction, out of the miry clay, And He set my feet upon a rock making my footsteps firm. He put a new song of praise to God; Many will trust in the Lord" (Psalm 40:1–4 NASB).

I WAS WELL AGAIN

I began doing all the yard work I had put off for eighteen months. I spread preemergent crabgrass killer to prevent any more annual bluegrass from sprouting because I knew in the middle of August it would begin sprouting again. I sprayed weed killer and fertilized the yard. I trimmed shrubbery, cleaned my gutters, and began to relieve my wife from mowing the yard. I began exercising three times each week using the exercise machines and treadmill at Planet Fitness. I also went to the Broken Arrow Senior Citizens Center for singing out of the *Baptist Hymnal* twice each week to build up my voice. Several months later I began volunteer work again at the Tulsa Garden Center as a Linnaeus Gardener.

I started going back to the Saturday morning Gideon prayer breakfasts, monthly Gideon dinner meetings, and Bible distributions that I had missed for four months. I had felt hypocritical doing those things during my depression. God lifted all that bad reasoning and negative feelings I once had about my salvation. I knew that I could take communion again without fearing God's wrath. I knew that I wasn't an apostate. I also no longer felt as if I would be excommunicated from BCO—as I had feared when I was depressed.

I called a good friend, Lindel Adair, asking him about going dove hunting on opening day, September 1. Lindel had called me several times during my depression inviting me to go fishing with him saying, "Dr. Hazle, you need to get out and get some sunshine." Jason's brother was going to Georgia in August, and I arranged for him to bring back one shotgun so I could go dove hunting.

Lindel arranged for a dove hunt on his son's land opening day. We didn't kill many doves, but it was another refreshing event after my recovery, doing what I had enjoyed in the past with one of my best friends. We had hunted and fished together on many trips to Kansas, South Dakota, and Lake Texoma since 1978. Lindel passed away in December 2018, and I was glad to tell some good stories about him at his funeral. Lindel was a Christian. He set a good example for all of us and enjoyed life. I never saw Lindel intoxicated on any of our many trips together.

I shot more doves in October with another duck-hunting friend, Bob Newlon. He had driven to Dumas, Texas, for opening day in September and had a very successful hunt for five days shooting three hundred collard Eurasian, whitewing and mourning doves. Bob and I drove six hours to Dumas and stayed at his son-in-law's farmhouse. We shot forty-five doves the next day, and Bob was disappointed because he and his friend had killed sixty each day on his last trip; I thought it was great. We could shoot that many because collard Eurasian doves were abundant, and there was no limit on them. Very few mourning doves remained because Dumas had a snow two weeks earlier, and the mourning doves had migrated south. We had an enjoyable trip even though it rained part of a day, and men were working in the area next to the feed lot where we had the best hunting on our first day. We had no luck hunting at another feed lot, so we returned home earlier than planned. Although Bob said he would never hunt doves there again in October, we did return opening day September 1 in 2019 and had outstanding hunting.

After my recovery I respected Dr. Christner more for helping me in a way my other psychiatrist had not. The next visit—my last visit with her—was a joyous occasion. We were both so happy I believe we both were teary-eyed. I thanked her profusely and gave her a copy of my book; I told her that I would always mention her in my testimony. I was doing well without having to take any L-DOPA supplement. She added 0.25 mg tabs of alprazolam for situations when I anticipated that my tremor and anxiety would be worse—like playing pickleball or public speaking. She also gave me a bottle of L-DOPA in case I needed it. Our reunion was short-lived; she had decided to retire from clinical practice and enter a more research-oriented position.

In December I was forced to look for another psychiatrist. I had my first appointment with Dr. Bradley McClure on February 25, 2019, at the Laureate Clinic in Tulsa. He took a thorough medical and family history. I explained how I had lost forty pounds but gained back thirty-two since August 1, 2018. He reviewed my past meds and sent prescriptions for bupropion, alprazolam, and olanzapine to Express Scripts. I have confidence in Dr. McClure and am very comfortable with him. I gave him a copy of my book with all the documentation of my first two depressions and extensive family history as well as other memoirs of my life and the science of neurotransmitters and depression. He gladly received it.

A CHANGE OF HEART

My spiritual revitalization and confirmation of my earlier salvation experience at nine years old, after my recovery, is best summed up by God's reassurance in 1 Peter 1:3–9 (NASB):

> Blessed be the God and Father of our Lord Jesus Christ, who according to His great mercy has caused us to be born again to a living hope through the resurrection of Jesus Christ from the dead, to obtain an inheritance that is imperishable and undefiled and will not fade away, reserved in heaven for you, who are protected by the power of God through faith for a salvation ready to be revealed in the last time. In this you greatly rejoice, even though now for a little while, if necessary, you have been distressed by various trials, so that the proof of your faith, being more precious than gold, which is perishable, even though tested by fire, may be found to result in praise and glory and honor at the revelation of Jesus Christ; and though you have not seen Him, you love Him, and though you do not see Him now, but believe in Him, you greatly rejoice with joy inexpressible and full of glory, obtaining as the outcome of your faith the salvation of your souls.

Yes, God had used my experiences during my adversity to reassure me that I was saved, for which I am grateful.

I know that my future is what God told the Jews while in exile in Babylon recorded in Jeremiah 29:11 (NASB): "For I know the plans that I have for you, declares the Lord, plans for welfare and not calamity to give you a future and a hope."

THE CREATIVE URGE

It was early morning on March 14, 2019—at 3:00 a.m.—when I woke up with thoughts that I wanted to write down—thoughts and ideas about my book. That feeling was one that I had experienced at various times since the mid-1970s—that I had to get up and write my ideas down before I forgot their clarity and couldn't remember exactly what I wanted to say. I believe that creative urge to get up and write down my ideas was created by not taking my medicine that evening before I went to bed at ten. It had happened two nights before for the same reason; I had forgotten my bedtime meds. I had been thrown out of my routine for taking my nighttime meds because we started using the guest bedroom and bathroom while some painting was being done in the master bathroom where my meds were kept. That change in routine had caused me to skip my bedtime meds, which included Zyprexa (olanzapine) and Xanax (alprazolam)—a benzodiazepine that works in a similar way as alcohol and results in a similar rebound effect when discontinued.

When this happened, it reminded me of exactly what used to happen in the springtime in the mid-1970s when I lived in Tahlequah, Oklahoma. After drinking one glass of wine at 6:00 p.m. I would wake up at two thirty in the morning, wide awake with creative ideas for a book I was working on at that time.

I believed then that this was the result of a rebound effect from the mild central nervous system (CNS) depression caused by the wine taken the previous evening. Much more is known about this phenomenon today, and drinking alcohol before bedtime is not recommended for people having problems sleeping through the night. Because I believe insomnia can promote anxiety, depression, and psychosis, drinking alcohol in the evening can't be repeated frequently. It could be possible that this rebound effect represents an unperceived benefit, especially for musicians, singers, artists, writers, and actors whose survival depends on creativity, but it also may account for more alcohol dependence in these groups. Read more about this on in chapter 9.

This is not an endorsement for drinking alcohol, because drinking any alcohol puts one at risk for drunkenness and dependence on alcohol. I've had pastors and others tell me that the word "wine" used in the Bible refers to grape juice. That seems unlikely to me considering all the references in scripture that associate wine with merriment or drunkenness. Grape juice does not produce those effects. Why did Jesus turn water into wine— as described in John chapter 2—at Nathanael's house during a wedding celebration, which was attended by Jesus, his mother, his disciples, and John, if it was forbidden to drink wine? When a servant took some of the water, which had become wine, to the headwaiter, he was pleased with the quality and called it "good wine" (verses 9–10). Grape juice has no reason for being described as "good wine" or "poorer wine"; grape juice is just grape juice.

The Bible condemns abuse of wine and drunkenness in the scripture on numerous occasions. In I Timothy 3:3, 8 (NASB) Paul described the requirements for deacons and bishops using the terms, "not addicted to wine or pugnacious" and "Not double-tongued or addicted to much wine." Proverbs reads: "Wine is a mocker, strong drink a brawler, and whoever is intoxicated by it is not wise" (Proverbs 20:1 NASB). "And do not be drunk with wine, for that is dissipation, but be filled with the Holy Spirit" (Ephesians 5:18 NASB).

Other scripture does not condemn the consumption of wine, "And wine which makes man's heart glad, so that he may make his face glisten with oil, and food which sustains man's heart" (Psalm 104:15 NASB). "Go then, eat your bread in happiness and drink your wine with a cheerful heart; for God has already approved your works" (Ecclesiastes 9:7 NASB).

The only sure way to prevent alcohol abuse and addiction is total abstinence. If you don't drink, don't start. Multiple factors are involved—including genetics—that predispose a person to alcohol dependence. Not many people consider their risks for addiction to alcohol the first time they use it; addiction just happens with frequent consumption over time. If you do drink alcohol, God commands us not to drink to excess or drunkenness; our laws require us not to drink and drive. Don't drink on a frequent basis, because that can produce more tolerance and the need for more alcohol to have the same effect.

The connection between my skipping Xanax, a prescribed antianxiety benzodiazepine, is that the benzodiazepine works in a similar way on the CNS as alcohol to produce a rebound effect. When I was in dental school in the 1960s, I was told that Valium, a benzodiazepine, was not addicting. However, additional knowledge and experience has changed that attitude today; it is a drug that is addicting. Millions of housewives and stressed men were prescribed Valium for anxiety beginning in the early 1960s, became addicted, and had difficulty quitting. It is more difficult to quit than heroin and has withdrawal effects when larger amounts are stopped abruptly. The same is true for all benzodiazepines (benzos). A more extensive discussion about benzos is presented later in chapter 9.

A NEW HEART AND A NEW SPIRIT

The adverse experiences during the eighteen months of depression are some of my greatest examples of God's providence and protection in my life—just as He protected David when Saul was trying to kill him as recorded in chapter 23 of Samuel. God led me through adversity with Terry's counseling, then directed me through people to Dr. Christner and healed me when He was ready.

Ezekiel chapter 18 (NASB) is a story of repentance, forgiveness, and joy that Ezekiel gave to the Israelites. Israel had been blaming their forefathers for their sins as recorded in verse 3. But God told them they would be held responsible for His judgment of their own sins—not their forefathers', as described in verse 4. Ezekiel told them God would hold each individual accountable for pursuing righteousness in Ezekiel 18:3-32.

For my life during my depression the important message begins in verse 28: "Because he considered and turned away from all his transgressions which he had committed, he shall surely live; he shall not die." In verses 30b--32 Ezekiel said, "Repent and turn away from all your transgressions, so that the iniquity may not become a stumbling block for you. Cast away from you all the transgressions that you have committed and make yourselves a new heart and a new spirit! For why will you die O house of Israel? For I have no pleasure in the death of anyone who dies," declares the Lord God. "Therefore, repent and live." (NASB)

When I asked God for forgiveness of all my sins, including doubting my righteous justification, and I destroyed all my previous references to evolution, he did forgive me and give me a new heart and a new spirit.

THE IMPORTANCE OF GOD'S GRACE

I now believe that the difference maker in my grandfather's life—as described by his testimony in chapter 5 of this version of *A Sheltered Life*—was his understanding and acceptance of God's grace. He never used the term "God's grace" in his testimony, but he referred to the Holy Word and Holy Spirit. He said, "I didn't know about the love, peace and hope that lives in the heart and minds of Christians. I didn't know that God has given us the Holy Word and Holy Spirit to direct our living, to tell us the things we should do and should not do." I mentioned this to Terry Devitt, and he said it is interesting that the Holy Spirit is often referred to as the Holy Spirit of Grace. It is now evident to me that my grandfather understood the value of grace in his life.

That was the part that I never understood when I wrote in the first version of my book, "I'm not sure I understand it all yet." His testimony is one about experiencing the grace of God in his life.

God's grace can be taken for granted. When we hear the statement that "you are saved through faith by the grace of Christ," we tend to gloss over the word grace without considering the full value of grace in the statement. I would like to add some descriptive words that will increase your value for this word that I recently heard from Terry Devitt in a presentation while teaching our Sojourners Flock at BCO on March 31, 2019.

God's grace affects our salvation from the beginning to the end. We are called by grace as noted by Paul: "I am amazed that you are so quickly deserting Him who called you by the grace of Christ, for a different gospel" (Galatians 1:6 NASB). "For by grace you have been saved through faith and not that of yourselves, it is the gift of God; not as a result of works, so that no one may boast" (Ephesians 2:8–9 (NASB). We are converted by grace as Paul notes, "he greatly helped those who had believed through grace" (Acts 18:27 NASB).

We are justified and sanctified by grace as noted in the following scriptures. Paul said, "for all have sinned and fall short of the glory of God, being justified as a gift of His grace through the redemption which is in Christ Jesus " (Romans 3:23–24 NASB). He also demonstrated sanctification when he said, "And God is able to make all grace abound to you, so that always having all sufficiency in everything, you may have an abundance for every good deed" (2 Corinthians 9:8 NASB). We are glorified by grace, which will ensure eternal life—needing this grace, or we will not make it until the end. "The Law came in so that the transgression would increase; but where sin increased, grace abounded all the more, so that, as sin reigned in death, even so grace would reign through righteousness to eternal life through Jesus Christ our Lord" (Romans 5:20–21 NASB). We can't keep ourselves saved; only God can do that through grace. We should ask for grace through Jesus. Grace that comes through Christ is what produces love for Christ and for others.

Among the fruits of grace are humility and hard work. Support for humility is found in Romans 12:3 (NASB): "For through the grace given to me I say to everyone among you not to think more highly of himself than he ought to think; but to think so as to have sound judgment." About hard work Paul says, "But by the grace of God I am what I am, and His grace toward me did not prove vain; but I labored even more than all of them, yet not I, but the grace of God with me" (1 Corinthians 15:10 NASB). Our speech should edify God. "Let no unwholesome word proceed from your mouth, but only such a word as is good for edification according to the need of the moment; so that it will give grace of those who hear" (Ephesians 4:29 NASB).

We are given advice on glorifying God through His grace. "To this end also we pray for you always, that our God will count you worthy of your calling, and fulfill every desire for goodness and the work of faith with power, so that the name of our Lord Jesus will be glorified in you, and you in Him, according to the grace of God and the Lord Jesus Christ" (2 Thessalonians 1:11–12 NASB).

Weakness doesn't disqualify us from serving God. Paul said the Lord told him: "'My grace is sufficient for you, for power is perfected in weakness.' Most gladly, therefore I will rather boast about my weakness, so that the power of Christ may dwell in me" (2 Corinthians 12:9 NASB). When teaching this lesson, Terry said, "Weakness is a badge of honor; in weakness we say we can't, but grace says we can."

Saint Augustine of Hippo says of grace: "Grace is that which delivers human beings from evil; and without which, they do absolutely nothing good, whether in thought, or in will and emotion, or in action. Grace not only makes known to people what they ought to do, but also enables them to perform with love the duty that they know." This sounds a lot like what my grandfather said about the Holy Spirit in his testimony in chapter 5.

Since the adversity of my last depression I have changed; I am more openly witnessing to others about Christ and looking for more opportunities. "For I am not ashamed of the gospel, for it is the power of God for salvation to everyone who believes, to the Jew first and also to the Greek" (Romans 1:16 NASB). "That He may grant you to be strengthened with power through His Spirit in your inner being" (Ephesians 3:16 NASB). "For God has not given us a spirit of timidity, but of power and love and discipline" (2 Timothy 1:11 NASB).

I have witnessed to and given my testimony to my new hairdresser who said she had problems with depression and anxiety and I recommended she memorize Philippians 4:6-7. I witnessed to a young man who was manager of our Hyundai service department who said he had anxieties from stressful work and gave him a copy of my first book about depression and a Gideon testament with helpful scripture for anxiety and other problems in the front and the plan of salvation on the last two pages. I talked with a fellow Linnaeus Gardner volunteer while we worked at the Tulsa Garden Center who was soured on Christianity by her experiences with Catholicism but didn't know about the gospel of Jesus Christ.

After hearing a song sung by our pastor—Ted Johnson—and Rob Haskins at one of our men's breakfasts at BCO, I decided to approach the panhandlers along the roadsides at the corners of intersections differently. I decided instead of dreading stopping by them with their signs that read "Hungry" and doing nothing but being anxious for the light to change to green I would do something positive. I pulled out several of my Gideon personal witnessing testaments (PWTs), testaments containing the New Testament, Psalms, and Proverbs, and placed a ten-dollar bill in each one and carried two in each of our vehicles. Now I'm glad to see the panhandlers and offer them a PWT with an explanation about the "Helps" in the front and "God's plan of salvation" on the last two pages. I get their name and tell them I will pray for them to have a better life through Jesus. You can listen to Don Francisco's message by Googling "Steeple Song."

Unable to fit this last bit of information into the text of this chapter and maintain a smooth flow of thought, I have saved the best for last by thanking my wife for all that she did during the eighteen months of my illness. She kept cooking for me despite my complaining about something every meal---even telling her more than once, "Don't ever fix this for me again." She drove me everywhere because I was fearful and anxious about everything including driving. She prayed for me many times, calming my anxieties and worry about minutia as well as my salvation. Along with my daughter, Angie, she arranged for me to see a new psychiatrist after a year of no improvement in my depression and anxiety. She remained with me 24/7 and ridded me of any access to guns when I was suicidal, which kept me from being admitted to a hospital for my third depression. She mowed the yard and planted annual spring flowers around the house for two seasons. She arranged for our membership at Planet Fitness and convinced me to begin regular exercise three days per week and start playing pickle ball two to three times per week. She never complained. She was such a strong woman of faith in the Lord when I was so weak. Thank you, Donna!

Summing up my adversity of this last depression, I would like to quote four verses from James.

> Consider it all joy, my brethren, when you encounter various trials, knowing that the testing of your faith produces endurance. And let endurance have its perfect result, so that you may be perfect and complete, lacking in nothing. But if any of you lacks wisdom, let him ask of God, who gives to all generously and without reproach, and it will be given to him. But he must ask in faith without any doubting, for the one who doubts is

like the surf of the sea, driven and tossed by the wind. (James 1:2–5 NASB)

God also accomplished the following in me: "Behold I have refined you, but not as silver; and I have tested you in the furnace of affliction" (Isaiah 48:10–11 NASB).

Two

MY FAMILY

THE PATH FOR BECOMING A CHRISTIAN

P aul tells us in Romans 3:23 that all men have sinned. In Romans 5:8 Paul tells us that God loves us and died for our sins. Jesus did this for me: "For the wages of sin is death, but the gift of God is eternal life in Christ Jesus our lord" (Romans 6:23 NIV). Paul seals the deal in Romans 10:9 (NIV): "That if you confess with your mouth, 'Jesus is Lord,' and believe in your heart that God raised him from the dead, you will be saved."

It would be many years before I fully understood that all men are born as "natural man" in sin as described in Galatians 5:19–21 (NIV). Paul said, "The acts of the sinful nature are obvious sexual immorality, impurity and debauchery; idolatry and witchcraft; hatred, discord, jealousy, fits of rage, selfish ambitions, dissensions, factions and envy; drunkenness, orgies, and the like. I warn you, as I did before, that those who live like this will not inherit the kingdom of God."

Jesus died on the cross for the sins that I was aware of at nine years old, and for many of these sins listed that I and all men inherit from birth. Jesus went on to say in Mark 7:20–23

(NIV): "For from within, out of men's hearts, come evil thoughts, sexual immorality, theft, murder, adultery, greed, malice, deceit, lewdness, envy, slander, arrogance and folly. All these evils come from inside and make a man 'unclean.'"

For several years I'd attended vacation Bible school and belonged to Royal Ambassadors. I knew lots of scripture, and it was the right time for becoming a Christian based on God's love for me. However, I was too young to appreciate all the guidance God would provide in my life in the future. I knew God loved me, but it would take many years of study to realize how much of a sacrifice He made for the forgiveness of my sins and how much Jesus suffered on the cross for me. God's work in my life has revealed to me the truth expressed in Romans 8:28 (NIV): "And we know that in all things God works for the good of those who love him, who have been called according to his purpose."

MY GRANDFATHER WAS A STRONG EARLY CHRISTIAN INFLUENCE

I can still remember my grandfather and Brother Dick Allison, our church pastor, reading the Bible and talking to me about God's plan for my salvation when I was nine years old. I accepted that plan and knew that Jesus Christ was my Lord and Savior. We were all in the front living room of my grandparents' house over next to the red brick fireplace with an oak mantel and bookcases around it. I'd spent many hours watching television, studying, and building model airplanes in that room. I was a happy child who spent a lot of time with my grandparents. But nothing matches the happiness and memory of that day when I welcomed Jesus into my life. Even as a nine-year-old, I knew what sin was in my life and was able to accept God's grace and his offer to forgive those sins.

My grandfather was a deacon at the small country church, Barren Run Baptist, where Brother Richard Allison was pastor.

Brother Allison was a seminary student at Southern Baptist Theological Seminary in Louisville, Kentucky, about sixty miles north of Hodgenville. We had many seminary students as pastors, and many of them rented the house next to my grandfather. My grandparents would often have the pastors and their wives over for lunch after church service on Sundays. My grandfather was active in the church and attended all Wednesday night and Sunday night services. Helping the pastor with my salvation on that Sunday after lunch was only one example of my grandfather watching over me that would continue throughout my life.

I was born on a hot July day in 1945 at my grandfather's brick house in a community called Tanner, about five miles south of Hodgenville, Kentucky, and as I like to remind myself, only four miles from Abraham Lincoln's humble birthplace. My parents lived there for two years with my dad's parents until 1947. My grandfather was a successful businessman and had built a new two-story brick house in Hodgenville and moved there in 1947. My grandfather owned a general store and farm implement business in Hodgenville. My parents moved into a nearby farmhouse that my grandfather had purchased with 190 acres of farmland in the 1930s, one mile south of Tanner. We all attended the small Baptist church located one mile west of Tanner.

When I was five years old, I didn't realize why I spent so much time at my grandparents' house in Hodgenville. It wasn't something I'd thought about as being unusual. I had more friends in the town of twenty-five hundred people than I did six miles out in the country where my home and church were located. My friends in town were the ones that I knew and played with on the street where my grandparents lived and later in the first-grade school activities. During the week, my dad took me to Hodgenville Elementary School on his way to work at my grandfather's store. When school was out each day, I walked four blocks to my grandparents' house or to a friend's house and stayed until my dad was on his way home. I participated in many church activities with my country friends, but I spent more time with friends in Hodgenville.

Many fun after-school activities were going on in town. When I was in the first, second, and third grades, I played cowboys and Indians with friends in the patch of honeysuckle vines along the railroad tracks down the street from my grandparents' house. I flew kites down by the railroad tracks over Jack Thompson's horse farm pasture. I spent many hours meticulously pinning down and gluing together balsa wood model airplanes in my grandparents' living room floor while watching television after school. I played with plastic building blocks, pick-up sticks, Chinese checkers, and an electric train. When I was in the fifth, sixth, and seventh grades, I played football, baseball, and basketball with friends after school on many days in the summer, fall, and spring.

My grandfather's store was a gathering place for my young friends and cousins whose parents came into town and shopped on Saturday nights. We'd play hide and seek and kick the can, hiding in the dark alleys and old buildings around the feed store and inside the feed store around the stacks of feed bags. Closing time at nine on Saturday nights always came too soon. After the store was closed, I'd stay with Grandpa while he oiled down the wooden floor. Then I'd walk down the street one block from the store with Grandma and Grandpa and spend the night.

On Sunday morning Grandpa and I would be in the car waiting for Grandma, ready for driving to Barren Run Church. On many of the six-mile trips back from church in the evenings, Grandpa and I would see who could spot the most rabbits. We'd often stop at the Dairy Queen in Hodgenville for ice cream during the hot summer months before going to their house. This was my weekly routine for almost a year when five and six years old and less frequently after that through the elementary school years.

MY MOTHER SAVED MY LIFE

One of the first events that I can remember about my mother, Zelma, was when she saved my life when I was choking on a piece of candy. I was about four years old and playing with my sister inside our house when I suddenly had a quarter-sized starlight piece of candy lodged in my throat. I couldn't breathe or talk. I was scared. Of course, my two-year-old sister didn't know what to do, so I ran outside to my mother, who was hanging clothes to dry on a clothesline in a grassy area across the driveway from the house. I tugged on her dress. When she saw me, I pointed to my throat, and she could see that I couldn't talk; she seemed to know immediately that I was choking. She turned me around and slapped me on my back and the candy popped out of my mouth. What an immediate relief. I had felt that I might die.

I could say that I was lucky, but for all these events to successfully come into play I now believe it had to be the providence of God that saved my life. Every time that I'm in a restaurant, and I see those after-dinner round flat white candies with short red spokes spaced around the edges I am still reminded of that episode with my mother.

My mom was a typical farm girl, born in 1925 with a twin sister named Thelma. Thelma has told me that Zelma was the one who got into more trouble with her parents. Anytime they wanted to go somewhere, Zelma would be the one asking permission from their parents to go.

Thelma thought it laughably funny when Zelma figured out the combination lock on her brother Marvin's bike and rode it on the road along the tobacco patch where Marvin was working.

When he spotted her, he began yelling, "What's she doing with my bike? How'd she get my lock off?" Thelma said that she had no idea how Mom got the combination to Marvin's lock.

Thelma has told me two stories about permanents that got her sister into some trouble when she was a teenager. Once Mom was in town with her family, and she snuck off to the beauty parlor for a permanent, something her mother would never consent to. But Mom had a rebellious streak, according to her twin sister, and was the more mischievous of the two.

The other time when a permanent was involved, Mom hid in the attic and gave herself a permanent with the carbide that was kept around the house to make light. Her dad bought five-gallon cans of carbide granules and poured them into a tank outside of the house and added water to produce a gas. The gas was piped into the house to lamp fixtures around the house, which could be turned on and lit to provide light as well as gas for cooking. Thelma said she had no idea how Zelma knew that carbide could be used for a permanent, and it was a wonder that her hair didn't fall out. Mom did make a mistake with the carbide and caused an explosion after the permanent that exposed where she was and what she was doing in the attic. I guess this made her dangerous as well as adventurous and rebellious.

Another example of her risk-taking was her barrel walking. She could walk on a fifty-gallon barrel across the yard and even jump a rope while rolling the barrel. She was good enough that she was invited to perform at the county fair, but her mother would never allow that.

Zelma was married to Wesley Thomas Hazle in 1944. W. T. lived at Tanner, a small community about six miles north of the farm of Zelma's parents. Zelma and W. T. had three children. We went to church Sunday mornings and evenings at Barren Run Baptist Church about two miles from our farmhouse and six miles from Hodgenville where Dad worked. We went to vacation Bible school each summer. She played piano at the church for many years, so we always attended all church services. Mom took my sister and me for piano lessons. I went to at least three different teachers for five years. She transported us children to all kinds of school, band, and sports activities.

Mom had homemakers' meetings and gave permanents to the

neighboring women at our house. I always hated that ammonia smell. Maybe her infatuation with permanents dated back to her younger years.

Mom fixed large lunches consisting of fried meats, mashed potatoes, corn, beans, other vegetables, rolls, biscuits and gravy, and deserts for the farmhands when they were putting up hay and cutting tobacco. She helped pull tobacco plants and set out tobacco. She helped put out some large gardens, and she canned vegetables and fruits and made jellies and preserves. Oh, and don't forget the delicious pies that she often made. She helped gather and wash eggs and candle and box eggs for sale from the long cage-layer chicken house on the farm. She milked a couple of cows we had and pasteurized the milk. Besides all these duties, she had to keep the house cleaned and all the clothes and linens washed.

MY MOTHER'S FIGHT WITH DEPRESSION

My mother's first bout with depression occurred in 1950, shortly after the birth of my brother Terry. She was hospitalized for almost a year and underwent electro-convulsive therapy (ECT). This depression could have been initiated by postpartum depression, which was not recognized in the early 1950s. Her hospitalization when I was five years old was the reason that my sister and I had stayed so much with my grandparents in Hodgenville. My baby brother, Terry, stayed with mom's sister, Rosie Mae, and her husband, James McCubbin.

My mother also had a family history of depression in her mother, grandmother, and three brothers. One brother, Marvin, was disabled most of his adult life with depression. Another brother, William Nathan, took his own life when he was fifty-four years old. Uncle William was a farmer with one of the cleanest, most productive farms in the county and a deacon in the church with no apparent reason to commit suicide except for an increased risk due to a family history of depression and suicide.

William Nathan's family history of depression was through his mother, Annie Catlett Hawkins. Mom and Marvin as siblings could also be considered as William Nathan's risk factors since Mom had previously received ECT, and Marvin had been diagnosed with depression earlier in his life.

Herbert was the one I always thought was normal. But his son Glenn revealed to me some problems Herbert had with anxiety when he was in his thirties, as described more in detail at the end of chapter 10. Herbert did not appear to have a problem with depression until his late seventies when he attempted suicide with car exhaust in his garage. However, his wife, Odell, found him before any damage could be done.

Annie Catlett Hawkins had problems with depression. She had spells of being disoriented and wandering around town lost on one occasion. She had spells of "memory loss" like being found at church and at a church association meeting wandering around in a disoriented state and having to be taken home. Once she became very lethargic, unable to do any of her normal activities. She could only lie on the couch and rest. Her strong religious beliefs and the inaccessibility to psychiatric care had probably restrained her from voluntarily obtaining professional help earlier in life. She rarely went to the doctor for anything according to Thelma. When the condition continued to worsen, she was taken to a psychiatrist when she was in her seventies in the early 1960s. She returned several times for ECT, which was still a standard treatment for severe depression in the early 1960s. She was also given some medications. The doctors said they could have helped her more had she been seen sooner.

Since her episode in the 1950s, my mother had managed to avoid another major depression until 1983. When I and my family returned to Kentucky for Christmas that year, we found Mom severely depressed. Due to a decline in the Kentucky farm economy and subsequent failure of Dad's implement business, he had declared bankruptcy. Their farm and house were to be auctioned in two weeks. Mom was physically sluggish with drawn facial features and dark circles under her eyes. She was withdrawn but easily angered. She could not take care of the house or prepare the family Christmas dinner that year. The situation reminded me of the news accounts I'd been seeing about farmers losing everything and some of them committing suicide. I was afraid that the same thing might happen to my mother.

I had become well educated about biological explanations for depression and the genetic tendencies for depression. I also knew how to get treatment for my mother. After all, I'd sought treatment for my depression in 1975 using imipramine (Tofranil) for two years, and after being diagnosed as bipolar II had done well on lithium since 1978.

While we were there for that Christmas vacation, I discussed seeing a psychiatrist with my mother. She had been reluctant about getting professional help. She swore that she'd never go through ECT again. Her first depression in 1950 had been a time when ECT was about the only accepted treatment for severe depression, and her treatments had lasted for almost a year. It was a more painful procedure in the 1950s than it would have been in 1984, but I couldn't blame her for being frightened of the possibility of going through that again. I tried convincing her that newer ways of treating depression without ECT were available and that no one could force her to have ECT. She trusted me, and the fact that I'd done well on lithium for five years gave her hope.

Within a week we were in the psychiatrist's office. I advised the psychiatrist of our family history and recommended prescribing lithium for her depression. His words were, "I've not heard of using lithium for depression, just for mania." It took me only a short time to convince him that since I'd done well on lithium, maybe we should expect her to do well also. I read later that lithium salts effective in the treatment of the manic phase of bipolar disorders reduce the cerebral levels of norepinephrine, an effect opposite to that observed with tricyclic antidepressants.[1] It's a wonder that lithium worked for both of our depressions.

During my first depression I had been treated with imipramine (Tofranil) for two years. After I had discontinued the imipramine (Tofranil) for one year while trying to make it without any medication, I was diagnosed as bipolar and switched to lithium carbonate. I am considered a bipolar type II because along with my depression my mania is mostly hypomania lasting at least four days. I don't have mania that lasts for a period of seven days or more, which would be the case for a Type 1. Lithium worked well for me for twenty-two years.

I believe the reason that my psychiatrist switched me to lithium was that imipramine (Tofranil), being a norepinephrine reuptake inhibitor, is known to potentially kick bipolar patients into their manic phase. A reuptake inhibitor holds the norepinephrine between two nerves longer, where it can increase nerve conductivity in the brain. Norepinephrine's characteristic as an excitatory transmitter gives it the potential to stimulate the manic phase of a bipolar patient. No one knows exactly how lithium works, but today lithium can be recommended as a treatment for bipolar patients either alone or in combination with an antidepressant. When used with an antidepressant, the lithium acts as a mood stabilizer lessening the risk for the antidepressant kicking a bipolar patient into a manic phase.

I suppose that my mother, although not yet diagnosed as bipolar, had a genetic makeup like mine, and the lithium worked well for her also. I consider the events in the psychiatrist's office that day as the providence of God for her also.

My education and personal experience helped improve her quality of life and maybe even saved her life. I felt that in some way I was returning the favor for saving my life when I'd been choking on the candy when I was four years old. Besides that, she was my sweet mother.

No doubt, the thought of losing the farm placed an additional prolonged stress on her. The lithium helped improve her nerve transmission and return the brain function closer to normal. The genetic tendency for a chemical imbalance was the most important component causing the depression. Without correcting the chemical imbalance, the stressful problems would probably have continued to overwhelm her. But the lithium helped, and she coped with the embarrassment of my parents' losing the farm and the financial hardship of bankruptcy.

Praise God that he had led me to college with my interest in agronomy. He had switched me to dentistry, where I had done research in pharmacology and had done much review of the medical literature in neurotransmitters and emotions. That had helped me understand my family's history of depression and how to get help for myself and for my mother's depression. It was also the period in medicine when new safe and effective medications for depression had been developed and accepted for use. This was true when she was using the older drug, lithium, instead of one of the newer antidepressants. I viewed that whole stretch of events as the providence of God for my mother and me.

When the house sold at auction that helped relieve some of Mom's stress. Donna and I bought the house and sixty-sixty acres on one side of the highway that split the farm. Mom and Dad could continue to live in the house, and we could continue our family traditions as we had done for many years. My sister and her husband bought the other 125 acres of the farm across the highway from the farmhouse.

I lost track of my mother's changes in psychotropic medications after she was on lithium for several years. She was diagnosed with Parkinson's disease by a general practitioner and prescribed Sinemet (carbidopa-levadopa) sometime in the 1980s. She was probably on Sinemet about ten years or longer. She never had a change in gait or salivary drooling associated with Parkinson's disease, only hand tremors. To determine if my mother truly had

43

Parkinson's disease, she was sent to the University of Kentucky Medical Center, where she was prescribed additional medications, which were not effective in reducing her tremors. The physicians concluded that she did not have Parkinson's disease and gave her a diagnosis of essential tremor.

My sister, Sharon, recognized an association with psychological changes when Mom was experiencing some infrequent episodes of urinary tract infections (UTIs). Then she would be withdrawn, less responsive, and have more difficulty taking her meds. Sharon was taking Mom to Rhonda Shircliff, an excellent advanced practice nurse (APRN) in Elizabethtown, Kentucky. Mom liked Rhonda, and Rhonda gave her special attention and sent her cards of encouragement.

Mom was stable psychologically while seeing Rhonda until a UTI episode led to admission to Jewish Hospital in Louisville with confusion and disorientation. According to her medical record, a physician tried to gradually discontinue her psychotropic meds to determine if they were causing her confusion. It was also discovered that Mom had not been taking all her medications as prescribed at home, and Sharon found many drugs stashed away in several locations in the small house where Mom was living. At the hospital, the physician first discontinued the gabapentin (Neurontin) and a few days later the antidepressant venlafaxine (Effexor). This put Mom into a catatonic state according to my sister who said Mom was in a fetal position and unresponsive when she went to visit her. Sharon was very upset because the physician had discontinued all of Mom's meds without consulting her. Eight days after admission, Mom was transferred to Frazier Rehab Institute, a geriatric psychiatric facility, for more evaluation and treatment. It took twenty-three days for Mom to recover enough to be discharged. Since Mom could no longer live alone safely, she was admitted to Sunrise Manor Nursing Home in Hodgenville.

Mom did well in the nursing home on venlafaxine (Effexor)

and gabapentin prescribed by Rhonda. She had been able to paint earlier in her life before her hand tremors made it impossible. She had one of her "old mill with a waterwheel" paintings in her room that people bragged on when they came into her room. She still could play the piano a little bit when she first went to the nursing home. She moved into the newly completed, beautiful Sunrise Manor nursing home in Hodgenville for the last two years of her life.

More frequent bouts of UTIs sometimes caused her to be withdrawn and unresponsive. This created difficulties with taking her meds and eating. She was hospitalized several times when stronger IV antibiotics and fluids were needed. Another very bothersome problem was her hand tremors, which made eating difficult. She often required assistance. She was mobile until the last year in the nursing home when she required a wheelchair.

Sharon was an invaluable caregiver for Mom, visiting almost every day, washing her clothes, helping her eat, taking her out to eat at restaurants when they were out shopping, and often eating at Sharon's home. She made countless trips with Mom to doctors' offices for routine checkups and minor illnesses and to the hospital emergency room, mostly for those bouts with UTIs. Sharon was always there making sure that her meds were managed well and given to her in Mom's preferred way of taking them. With the staff turnover and shift changes, it was a constant battle—whether to mix with applesauce or not, or whether to crush the pills or not. Sharon always had Mom's wardrobe filled with attractive, clean, neat, matching outfits. One of their favorite trips was seeing Rhonda, who had so much compassion for Mom. Sharon loved Mom and tried to make her as comfortable as she could be. Mom continued to live as a resident in the nursing home until she passed away in January 2015 from breast cancer at the age of eighty-nine.

MY HARD-WORKING FATHER

Wesley Thomas Hazle was his name. Everyone just called him "W. T.", and he was known as a hard worker. He got up early every day and finished whatever had to be done at the farm and got the tenant started before going to town to open the store at seven thirty. Sometimes when there was plowing and disking to be done, hay to be baled and put into the barn, tobacco to be planted and harvested, seed row crops to be sown, or corn, wheat, soybeans, and oats to be harvested he would remain at the farm. He would also remain there when animals required work such as cattle dehorning, calf and pig neutering, and sheep shearing. Dad had a farm tenant helping run the farm while he spent most of his time in the implement business selling farm machinery, repairing it, and selling parts. He could fix anything and would make trips to farms, sometimes fixing equipment and adjusting hay balers late in the day on his way home from work.

Dad liked sports. His favorite NFL teams were the Cleveland Browns and the Baltimore Colts. He watched football games on Sunday afternoons. He also listened to many University of Kentucky and University of Louisville basketball games when I was growing up.

Dad was also a ham radio station operator. He enjoyed playing with this all hours of the night in his bedroom. He had a photo developing lab in our basement. He was a member of the volunteer fire department in Hodgenville. I can remember him running to the fire station just one block from his store many times when the fire siren was going off in Hodgenville. He was an adventurous man.

My father quit attending Barren Run Baptist Church when I was five years old. I didn't know why; it just happened, and he never would say why. His mother said she thought it was something concerning a disagreement during the building of the new church. I missed my dad at church because I could always remember him singing bass in the choir. On a few occasions my mother and I would invite Dad to church in hopes of getting him to come back, but he never responded. The only time I can remember him going to church over the next thirty-three years was for my baptism. During those years I would always raise my hand for Dad when the pastor asked for those with special prayer requests. I prayed for him on many occasions, and I'm sure others were praying for him including my grandfather.

God eventually answered our prayers, but not the way I'd expected. The way God answered my prayer was very expensive for me. I'd thought that one day Dad would just start going back to church, and I'd know God had answered my prayer. It'd be that simple and be over. However, God answered my prayer in a way that tested my faith. It was one more experience that cost me financially and helped me trust God more.

Dad had moved his implement business three miles north in 1969. He built a large metal building with a shop, a parts room, a display room, and a very large room upstairs. For four years after the grain embargo in 1979 by President Jimmy Carter, the farm economy in Kentucky declined but had been predicted to improve.

My father asked to borrow some money from me to help his business, which he thought he could pay back when the economy improved. Donna and I loaned my father $20,000 to help him meet payroll and get through 1982. The money came from our college education savings account for our two daughters, who were then seven and eleven years old. Dad expressed confidence that the economy would improve and that he could pay back the principle with interest. But the farm economy in Kentucky didn't improve in 1983, and my dad took bankruptcy in 1984. We lost the $20,000. He lost his business and the farm where I grew up. This was a farm and house that my grandfather had purchased in the 1930s.

BUYING THE FARM AND SEEING
DAD RETURN TO CHURCH

When Donna and I bought the farm on January 4, 1984, that decision to bid on the house at the auction was more emotional than rational. My dad had rebuilt the two-story brick house in 1956 on the same spot where the old farmhouse had burned. The old white wood frame house had an outside front balcony on the second floor. It was the house where I'd played for ten years. I'd watched my dad proudly remodel the old house using all the spare time he could find between repairing and selling farm machinery, running a general store and farm implement business, and farming 190 acres. He had raised cattle, sheep, hogs, crops, and sold chicken eggs from a thousand chickens.

The next few years after my dad's bankruptcy presented some hardships for us that strengthened my faith in God and brought me into a closer relationship with my dad while we were living in Oklahoma. He did work on the farmhouse and buildings and maintained the sixty-six acres to help pay for his rent to the extent that he could as he had promised. My wife also had parents living near Hodgenville. Every six months we took our children, Wendy and Angie, to visit their grandparents in Kentucky.

A sentimental value of having had the farm in the family for more than fifty years influenced our decision to purchase the farm tract and house. I had memories of riding in Dad's Ercoupe airplane that he landed in the bluegrass field across the road from the farmhouse. I admired my dad for being able to fly. He'd flown over the Ozarks to Stillwater, Oklahoma, for a Flying Farmers convention. We flew over the farm and checked out the Herford cattle grazing on the fescue pastures. It's where I helped my dad plant crops, raise tobacco, and put up hay in the hot summers. We had many Thanksgiving and Christmas dinners at the farmhouse. Helping my parents have a house to live in after the bankruptcy and the sentimental value overrode any negative economic considerations. Besides, my dad had said he would be able to help by paying rent on the house. That would help us get through the financial burden, but he could only repay part of the money for rent. But I always remembered how my dad had helped pay for my dental school education. I still worried about how Donna and I would make it with the additional farm payments and how we would again save enough money for the girls' college education.

I began to realize that God might be using me in a physical way to help my dad return to church. I don't know what would have happened if I'd turned my back on him in a time of need. All I could remember were several scriptures reminding me to care for my parents. First Timothy 5:8 (NIV) reads: "If anyone does not provide for his relatives, and especially his immediate family, he has denied the faith and is worse than an unbeliever." Ephesians 6:1-3 (NIV) tells us: "Children, obey your parents in the Lord, for this is right. 'Honor your father and mother' (which is the first commandment with a promise) 'that it may go well with you and that you may enjoy long life on the earth.'"

I had prayed that my dad would return to church. God had answered my prayer in His own time after I'd carried out God's instructions in the Bible. It was a long process from the time my father quit attending church in 1950 until he started again in 1983. During that span of thirty-three years, I was saved, read the Bible, prayed, and remained in God's will before my prayers were answered. This is only one of many experiences that have demonstrated God's intervention in my life. It was rewarding to see him again singing in the choir and teaching a Sunday school class. This experience strengthened my faith in God and brought me closer in love with my mother and father.

I must admit that I didn't treat my dad with the forgiveness he deserved during his last ten years of life. I harbored some bitterness related to events concerning his inability to repay the previous $20,000 debt owed to us and events surrounding the purchase of the farm.

The day of the auction I was unable to be there because I had returned for work in Oklahoma. I arranged for Ronnie, my brother-in-law, to bid on the farm. I set an upper limit that I was willing to bid leaving him with a signed blank check. I'm not sure how dad and Ronnie worked it out to bid $10,000 more than my agreed limit, but that upset me. I had calculated the amount I could pay for the monthly mortgage payments considering some anticipated income from the farm crops and a reasonable rent from dad.

Dad was unable to get a job and pay our agreed rent, so I worked out an arrangement paying for his labor to care for the farm and house. He improved and maintained all the buildings and mowed the acreage placed in the Conservation Reserve Program (CRP). He managed the leasing of the tobacco crop with another nearby farmer which produced income for the farm. He returned some of the money to me for rent and I deducted his labor expenses for tax purposes on the farm business. That was a satisfactory arrangement and he kept his end of the bargain. That should have been enough to satisfy me, but I never forgave him for bidding more than I had agreed and for not paying back $20,000.

I regret telling him once that it would have been better if I had bought a small house for him and mom in Hodgenville instead of investing in a farm. I said this even though I enjoyed going to Kentucky twice a year with my wife and two daughters for vacation, family reunions, and Christmas in the large house where I grew up. I was glad the farm provided a place for mom to continue growing flowers, having a garden, and living in the same house in the country with a room to work on her paintings instead of a smaller house in town. Besides that, dad had sacrificed while helping pay for my dental education which was expensive. Recent dental graduates are now pegged with debts of $250,000 to $400,000 or more from the expenses of their education. I regret not having a discussion before his death thanking him for his help and offering forgiveness for my begrudging attitude about the farm.

At least when he was hospitalized during my last visit to Kentucky before his death, I was able to ask him an important question confirming his salvation. I asked, "Do you know the Lord Jesus as your personal savior?"

He said without hesitation, "Yes, I do." I was glad to hear that from him after having stayed out of church for thirty-three years. He had been active in the church for the last twenty years. I was hopeful that he hadn't done that just to please me.

It wasn't until after his death that I began to feel remorse for not being more loving to him—being reminded in scripture that God has commanded us many times to be forgiving of others. Ephesians 4:32 (NASB) reads: "Be kind to one another, tender-hearted, forgiving each other, just as God in Christ also has forgiven you." Jesus said when telling us how to pray: "And forgive us our debts, as we also have forgiven our debtors" (Matthew 6:12 NASB). "Whenever you stand praying, forgive, if you have anything against anyone, so that your Father who is in heaven will also forgive you your transgressions" (Mark 11:25 NASB).

No one should leave the unfinished business of forgiveness of another person before they depart from us, both for our sake and theirs. But I hope sometime in the future I will have an opportunity for reconciliation and be able to express my love and thankfulness to Dad. He had taught me everything I needed to know in life—even after his death.

Three

MY EDUCATION

MY EARLY EDUCATION

Looking back on my childhood, I consider myself blessed. My parents and grandparents were supportive of me in many ways. My mother took me to many church activities and piano lessons from the first through the fifth grades. She taught me right from wrong, with a belt sometimes, when I was playing with my brother and sister or friends around the house. My father took me to many little league baseball practices and games. When I started playing junior high basketball, he was there many times at practice and at every high school game watching his 110-pound son play the number six position on the team. He filmed many of the high school basketball and football games as well as developed the films for the school athletic department.

Both parents took an interest in enrolling me in the band when I was in the fifth grade. As much as I hated disappointing my mother after taking me to private piano lessons for five years, I was glad to see Mr. Gene Hoggard come to town and start band activities. Playing the piano with both hands was stressful for me, and playing a trumpet with one hand was much easier.

Dad took me to the new band director's house, and we picked out a trumpet when I was in the fifth grade. Those were exciting times. The smell of the valve oil still reminds me of getting my first trumpet. The brass was shiny as a mirror, and the contoured, smooth, red velvet liner inside the leather case protected its beauty. Mom and Dad tolerated the early sour notes and complimented me as I began to learn. I can remember practicing in their bedroom in the half of the house my dad had remodeled. The hardwood oak floors and plaster walls magnified the brassy sounds. It was loud, but they never complained. After several years, I had progressed well in the band, and they supported me with the purchase of a new Selmer trumpet in high school. I can vividly remember Mr. Hoggard presenting me with the new trumpet at one of our concert practices in the old Hodgenville Elementary School gymnasium. At $350 in 1960, it was an expensive purchase and a sacrifice for my parents.

THE BAND PRESENTED OPPORTUNITIES FOR MY DEVELOPMENT

I made many enjoyable band trips to state concert, ensemble, and marching competitions with my close friends. I spent two weeks each summer at band camp beginning in the seventh grade. There I developed discipline. Those were hot days on the marching fields, and long, lip-tiring concert band practices combined with a lot of rowdy times with other members of the LaRue County Band of Hawks. It seems a shame to condense all those eight years in band to just a few sentences.

The competitive and enjoyable camaraderie of the band was an important part of developing confidence and self-esteem. In the seventh grade, I made a memorable trip to the Lions Club parade in Chicago where I saw the movie *Psycho with my friend* W.C. Blanton. W. C. and I were so afraid after seeing it that we both slept in the same small YMCA room. A man down the hallway saw us enter the room together and yelled, "That's against the law." Being young and from a rural area we didn't know what he meant by that, but in today's culture I believe I have figured it out. Ha, we were too naive to know at the time.

I missed a trip to the Orange Bowl Parade because of conflicts with basketball games scheduled around Christmas. I played in the school dance band, called the Stardusters, for three years at high school proms and other events. I took pride in being a member with Mr. Hoggard being the lead saxophone player. We played a lot of Glenn Miller's big band music

I remember the proudest day of my band career was the day Mr. Hoggard presented me with the John Phillip Sousa Band Award as the outstanding senior band member. It was a Sunday afternoon during our spring concert when I played a solo in Hayden's "Trumpet Concerto" in the new LaRue County High School gymnasium. I was surprised to receive the award because I had always considered at least two of my classmates to be better musicians. They were Kelly Thompson and W. C. Blanton, who both toured Europe and played in the United States of America High School band. W. C. was also a Merit Scholar.

Mr. Hoggard helped me get a small scholarship at the University of Kentucky where I continued playing in the concert and marching band for two more years. My parents were always supportive of my development during these band activities. I can't measure the value of these band activities to my overall development but rank them as very important on a subjective level. They provided a valuable means for parental involvement. We had such an outstanding band director in Mr. Gene Hoggard and won many marching contests as well as many superior ratings at the annual state music festivals on the Western Kentucky University campus. These contributed to the development of a pride and confidence that no other part of my education offered. I consider that the providence of God—to have been from a rural area yet having been associated with such an outstanding music program. I thank God for sending Mr. Hoggard my way.

A SIX-WEEK TOUR OF EUROPE

Although my dad was not attending church and didn't offer much spiritual guidance during my elementary and high school years, he always behaved as a Christian father. My dad was supportive in many secular ways in my development. I remember his comment as we stopped for traffic on the square in Hodgenville on the way home late one afternoon when I asked him if he had $600 to pay for a trip to Europe for me. That day, I found out that I'd been selected as the only student from Kentucky to go with forty-nine other students on a 1962 six-week tour of eight countries in Europe sponsored by the National Association of Student Councils Tour for International Understanding. The trip was for the promotion of international relations. He said, "We don't have the money, but I can try to come up with it from somewhere." Dad bought me a 35 mm automatic camera for the trip. My grandfather took me to his favorite department store, Levi's, in Louisville to be fitted for a new suit for the trip.

What a deal; this was an event that added much more to my confidence. After returning from the summer trip, I gave several slide presentations that fall to civic groups. I was interviewed on the local radio station. One presentation was to students at the Kentucky state meeting of Student Councils in Danville, Kentucky, in the fall of my senior year. It was about this time that I began dating Donna Clayton, a sophomore student at LCHS who would become my wife five years later. It was an exciting time for me.

LCHS was a special school. It had been a consolidation of three smaller schools in 1959 when I was a freshman. We went to the state basketball tournament the first year of consolidation. The school offered physics, geometry I and II, trigonometry, algebra I and II, chemistry I and II, and biology, which made me better prepared than many of my freshman classmates at the University of Kentucky in 1963. I believe it was partly because LCHS was an outstanding school with a good school board and Mr. Everett G. Sanders as principal that I was accepted for the trip to Europe. I also had a unique Student Counselor adviser, Mr. Bill Nallia, who was also responsible for helping me get the European tour.

Four

⟨flourish⟩

GOING TO THE UNIVERSITY OF KENTUCKY

STARTING OUT IN THE COLLEGE OF AGRICULTURE

N o one in my immediate family or either of my parents' families had attended college, but there was never any question about me going to college. Most of my close high school friends were going. All through high school the curriculum I had taken was to prepare me for college. The high school counselor had helped me obtain a small academic scholarship. I began attending the University of Kentucky (UK) on a College of Agriculture (Ag) scholarship. During my first year, I was an aggressive Ag student majoring in agronomy. Having grown up on a farm, I was fascinated with crop production. I had never experienced the pain of hard labor on the farm, because Dad and a farm tenant always did most of the work. Living on a farm had been fun. I had helped assemble farm equipment at my family's business and had gone on many trips repairing farm equipment with my dad and grandfather.

Planting and harvesting crops had interested me, and I had

worked some doing that. I had enjoyed seeing tobacco, wheat, corn, soybeans, alfalfa, and clovers grow. Tobacco had especially interested me. It was a labor-intensive crop. Plant beds had to be seeded. Only about one-twelfth of an ounce of seed was required to set an acre of tobacco. Plants were pulled from the plant beds and wrapped in burlap bags. Plants were set one at a time by two persons riding on a tobacco setter pulled behind a small tractor. After the plants grew to about six feet tall, suckers had to be removed from each plant after topping the flower. Three or four suckers on each plant were removed by hand until MH-30 (malic hydrazide) was developed to chemically control suckers by stopping cell division. When ready for harvest, five stalks were cut and placed on each of many slender sticks driven into the ground in every other row. All these sticks were then loaded on a wagon, hauled, and hung in a tobacco barn. After it had "cured" while hanging in the barn in the fall, leaves were stripped from the stalk on cold damp days and hauled on a truck to the market.

I was always allowed adequate time to study and complete homework. Because of my good grades in high school, I was placed in the UK Honors Program. As a member of the Honors Program, I had the liberty of enrolling in graduate level classes of the College of Agriculture. I wanted to advance my education as fast as possible, because I had visions of doing research and improving crop production.

This was before I faced the reality that the United States was already producing more food than it needed in the 1960s. The government was paying farmers to store large amounts of excess grain in the Midwest and West-Central states. I decided that I wasn't needed to develop new and improved plants. I also had concluded that a career as a researcher would require living in a city working for a large seed company or university. I preferred studying something that would allow me to work near my hometown after college graduation. I can remember specifically praying several times asking for God's guidance while up in my small attic room on the third floor of FarmHouse Fraternity. I jokingly called it the upper room. The memory of my prayers offered in the small room on my knees by the bunk bed in the center of a room with desks on each side under the sloping ceiling walls is vivid.

SWITCHING TO THE COLLEGE OF DENTISTRY

God answered my prayer, but at the time I never saw it as a specific answer to my prayer. I did not know any dentist as a friend. I thought it had just been a coincidence that as a junior I had encouraged a friendly first-year dental student at the University of Kentucky College of Dentistry (UKCD) to join FarmHouse Fraternity. Harry Watts was connected to agriculture only through his father's occupation as a county agent in Fulton County, Kentucky. Harry was an amazing student and a good athlete. His uncle was a dentist in the nearby town of Versailles.

It was unusual that Harry was admitted into dental school after attending UK for one year. He had attended Murray State University for one year before that. Usually students start out in a predental curriculum and attend at least three years before applying to dental school. Harry joined FarmHouse, and we became good friends. After I expressed an interest in dentistry, he offered to show me around the dental school and introduce me to several professors. I doubt that Harry ever knew that he was considered an answer to my prayers, but I have since thanked him for his influence. This timing had to be part of God's plan for me—otherwise why would Harry have had only two years of undergraduate study. If he had three years, we would not have met when I was a junior considering a career change, which would have been poor timing for me!

It was also ironic that I had tried to resist the pressure to join FarmHouse during rush activities, a time when new members are recruited for membership in fraternities. It turns out that God led me into dentistry through a FarmHouse Fraternity brother. I've always thought this was the providence and concurrence of God that a dental student pledged FarmHouse and helped me get into dental school.

All my friends thought switching from agriculture to dentistry was a drastic switch. I'd just tell them that I was switching from doctoring plants to doctoring people, which was not that much different. I studied hard the next year because of what one of Harry's dental professors had said to me when Harry took me on the tour of the dental school. After noticing that I had a GPA of 3.75 he said, "Well, sonny, I see that you have some good grades here, but you still have to finish physics and organic chemistry. We want to make sure you didn't just get these good grades in basket weaving." I guess that was his take on the classes in the Ag college. He hadn't given me much credit for being in the UK Honors Program and the stiff competition from other students in those classes or that I had taken some graduate-level classes.

I took the Dental Aptitude Test and applied to the UKCD. I did well in physics and organic chemistry and was accepted in the UKCD after three years in the College of Agriculture. Proverbs 16:9 (NIV) reads: "In his heart a man plans his course, but the Lord determines his steps." Proverbs 20:24 (NIV) reads: "A man's steps are directed by the Lord. How then can anyone understand his own way?"

I'll never forget my mother's response while she was in the nursing home when I asked if Dad had ever complained that paying for me to go to dental school had been a hardship. She said his only comment was that he couldn't understand why I hadn't made up my mind to attend dental school sooner instead of wasting three years in agronomy. I wish I had known this before he died so that I could have explained that I was fortunate to have been admitted to dental school after only three years since I hadn't started out in a three-year predental curriculum. Many if not most in my dental school class had four-year degrees, and several had five years undergraduate coursework before admission.

GETTING INTO DENTAL SCHOOL WAS
THE PROVIDENCE OF GOD

As a matter of fact, after the professor's implication about the College of Agriculture, I consider getting into the UKCD after three years of undergraduate study another case of the providence of God in my life. That professor, Dr. Wesley O. Young turned out to be one of my favorite instructors at the UKCD.

Looking back, I believe God had prepared me for dentistry from the early vacation Bible school days at the small Barren Run Baptist Church where teachers and family bragged on my handcrafts. My belief that I was good with my hands in vacation Bible school handcrafts was one of the reasons I wrote on my dental school application that I thought I would be a good dentist. Since then I've wondered how the dentists on the selection committee viewed my handwritten statement about a vacation Bible school activity as proof of my good hands.

God had prepared me for dentistry by opening an entry-level position into college as an agronomy student. If someone had suggested going into dentistry before that, I might not have had the confidence to pursue it. God had answered my prayers for help in choosing a career in a better way than I could have imagined. At that time, dentistry seemed like a career end point, but the puzzle was far from being finished. Little did I suspect that God was preparing me for something else while studying dentistry.

Through all of this, He was teaching me how to be happy and content with what I was doing. As an agronomy student, I thought it was God's will for me to be a Christian agronomist, and I worked hard to become the best agronomist for whatever his plan was for me. As it turned out, it was just his way of leading me to the next step. I thought dentistry was the final step. I believed that I would go back to my hometown and be a Christian dentist, but I never made it back there either. I joined the United States Public Health Service (USPHS) as a commissioned officer after graduation from the UKCD in 1970 and remained for more than twenty-five years until retirement in 1995. Today, I realize that dentistry was the means by which God had prepared me for another important task.

LEARNING ABOUT NEUROTRANSMITTERS AND EMOTIONS

I have known since going to UK that it was by the providence of God that he got me into the College of Agriculture (Ag) at UK, so that he could get me into the UKCD, so he could allow me to do nerve research, so that I could learn about the brain, neurotransmitters, and happiness chemistry. My Honors Program project at the UKCD is what stimulated my self-study in neurotransmitters and emotions. Simply put, this is how I learned to handle depression and stay healthy, and God led me into positions to do that and help others in the process.

Studying the biological explanations for moods, energy levels, stress, violence, and making memories has become my avocation for forty-five years. It has saved my life and helped many of my friends and family live happier lives.

Dr. Donald Knapp, a thirty-eight-year-old pharmacist, dentist, and a pharmacologist was my mentor. In 1968, he had already formed a hypothesis about the effect of local anesthetic on nerves. He proposed that the lidocaine used by dentists to numb the jaw before working on the tooth or gums inactivates small protein plugs along the nerve axon. The effects of lidocaine on these small protein plugs prevents pain messages from being transmitted to the brain. Thus, without the nerve conducting a pain message, a dentist could drill and fill a tooth while using a local anesthetic without rendering the patient unconscious with a general anesthetic.

Dr. Knapp and I experimented with mice sciatic nerves, the section of nerve branching from the spinal column and extending to the calf muscle in the leg. It's the sensory and motor nerve that causes so much back and leg pain for people when it is pinched by the spine or by muscle spasms in the back or hips. Dr. Knapp and I used a sophisticated model using mice, tritiated leucine with an unstable hydrogen-3 atom that gave off radioactive emissions, and liquid scintillation counting of the radioactive emissions. Demerol was given in the thigh of the mouse on day one. The radioactive leucine (an amino acid) given on day three, one hour before sacrificing the mice, was incorporated into new proteins synthesized by the nerve to replace the inactivated protein plugs after exposure to the local anesthetic on day one. By counting the radioactive emissions, Dr. Knapp and I measured the amount of new protein plugs being made in the sciatic nerve axons three days after an injection of a small amount of meperidine (Demerol).[2]

Demerol is a narcotic with local anesthetic properties. After exposure to the local anesthetic, the nerve was hypothesized to make new proteins from amino acids to counteract and recover from the effect of the anesthetic. Adequate protein plugs are required to allow the sodium and potassium ion flux along the axon that creates the electrical impulse and carries a message from one nerve cell to another. In the case of a dental patient, this would be pain messages from the pain receptor nerve cells in the tooth to nerve cells in the brain that interpret the sensation as pain.

An equal amount of saline was injected into the other leg thigh for a control measurement. Of course, it also was exposed to the same amount of tritiated leucine, having been injected through the tail vein.

It was assumed that the saline injected leg was not affected because it was not anesthetized and could be used as a control leg for comparison to the leg given Demerol. The sciatic nerve tissue in the leg exposed to 2 percent Demerol had 1.5 times more new proteins measured than the saline-exposed leg. When 5 percent Demerol was used there was almost 2.0 times more new proteins in the Demerol anesthetized leg sciatic nerve than in the unanesthetized saline leg. It was hypothesized that some local feedback mechanism in the affected nerve had been activated to start increasing more protein synthesis after the protein plugs were inactivated by the local anesthetic.

Dr. Knapp hypothesized that the Demerol had activated the process of making more protein plugs to replace the protein plugs affected by the Demerol in order to continue nerve function of sending pain messages. The nerve adjusted to the numbing effects of the local anesthetic by making more protein plugs.

If the first dose of drug caused the nerve to increase production of the proteins being blocked by the drug, then a second dose of the drug three days later might have less effect or work for a shorter period. This phenomenon is known as drug tolerance. The drug effect would have been shorter because it was hypothesized that more protein plugs were available than normal for the nerve to continue function.

Dr. Knapp tested this hypothesis of tolerance using lidocaine— the local anesthetic normally used by dentists---by anesthetizing some lateral incisors on patients and testing the duration of return to stimulus with ice and again after an injection of lidocaine on day three. The time for return of the response to stimulus by ice was shortened on day three. The anesthesia didn't last as long. Apparently the nerve doesn't stop synthesis quite soon enough, and there is some overshoot of new proteins synthesized in the axon, explaining the tolerance effect and the shorter duration of the anesthetic. With more protein plugs to function in conducting the impulse, the anesthetic is not quite as effective for the same duration.

Obviously, synthesis of proteins by peripheral nerve should occur normally at a rate adequate for replenishing proteins lost by normal degradation and catabolism. However, this usual rate of synthesis can apparently be increased by the injection of an agent with local anesthetic action like Demerol.

This rate of synthesis can also be decreased by protein synthesis inhibitors. For example, Knapp, D. E., and Mejia, S.[3] reported that mice pretreated subcutaneously with 3.2 mg/kg of acetoxycyclohexamide (a protein synthesis inhibitor) incorporated only 28 percent as much tritiated leucine in the 10 percent TCA (trichloroacetic acid) precipitable protein in peripheral nerve as did saline pretreated controls.

Well that was part of my exciting exposure to research with peripheral nerve that stimulated my interest in the central nervous system (CNS) or brain. I couldn't help but see some of the new research about neurotransmitters and the brain when I was doing my review of the literature about peripheral nerve for my project thesis. Of particular interest to me were the articles about the new research involving the biology of those neurotransmitters that affected moods and affective disorders like depression. The tricyclic antidepressants were being researched for marketing, and much research was going on to find out how they really worked.

THE SERENDIPITOUS DISCOVERY OF AN ANTIDEPRESSANT

The really big difference in studying brain transmission and peripheral nerve transmission was the area of concentration of study. My study had concentrated on studying changes in the axons between nerve cells and nerve endings (see figure 1) called the sciatic nerve. Study of affective disorders in the CNS was concentrated on changes at the synapse. This is the space between the near contact of one nerve ending and another nerve ending or nerve cell. See figure 2, which shows the synapse with neurotransmitters being released from the nerve ending onto the receptors of a nerve cell. The release of neurotransmitters is stimulated by an electrical message that travels down the axon to the nerve ending. Quantity and quality of conductivity of nerve impulses across the synapse depend on the neurotransmitters in the synaptic space and receptors on the surfaces of the receptor nerve cells.

J. J. Schildkraut and S. S. Kety published one of the first discussions of chemical explanations for emotions that I read in their review of articles in a 1967 article published in *Science*.[4] They noted research that showed depression occurred in some patients on a blood pressure medicine called reserpine.

Axon

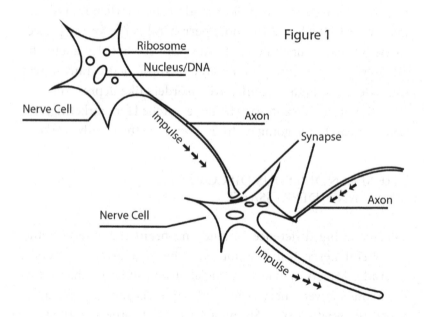

Figure 1

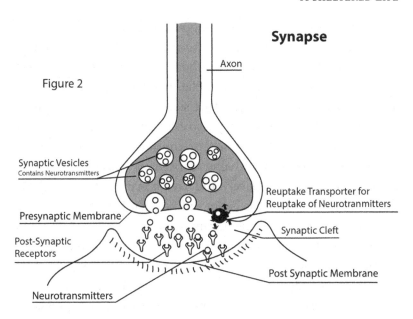

Figure 2

Synapse

Reserpine, used for the treatment of mania and excitement prior to the introduction of the phenothiazines, was also being used in general medicine for the treatment of hypertension. It had been reported to produce severe depression of mood in some patients using relatively large doses. Reserpine-induced sedation in animals was associated with decreased brain levels of norepinephrine, dopamine, and serotonin. They also noted how imipramine and two other tricyclic antidepressants inhibit the reuptake of norepinephrine in the brain, thus allowing it to remain in the synapse, explaining its antidepressant effect. Reuptake of the neurotransmitters back up into the nerve ending from where they were released is a normal process (see figure 2, Reuptake of Neurotransmitters). This also suggested that some depressions may be associated with a relative deficiency of norepinephrine and elations may be associated with an excess of such amines in the synapse.[4]

I'm not sure whether elations refer to hypomania or mania, but I assume there can be various degrees of elations. I have wondered sometimes if the condition of "happiness chemistry" could exist or be created by certain activities or drugs. I surely do believe this because I once tried to get a book published on the subject after seeing the statement that elations occur from an excess of norepinephrine. I also feel that such a chemical state can be created. Such happy states may also exist with varying degrees of excess serotonin and dopamine (also considered biogenic amines). These are feelings of well-being, confidence, positive thinking, creativity, higher energy levels, and having many options available for decision-making. This is not unlike what I suppose one gets from stimulants like amphetamines, but I cannot recommend recreational drugs as a source of happiness chemistry because of many obvious disadvantages such as addiction, crashes, depression, suicide, and others that I will not discuss here.

Another article describing the discovery of antidepressants notes how a drug, iproniazid, used for TB medication in 1953, resulted in some hospital patients having a gradual increase in social activity, "dancing with holes in their lungs" in a party mood, and wanting to leave the hospital early. It was referred to as a "psychic energizer" by Nathan Kline in 1957. Sometime in the mid-1950s the psychostimulant effect of isoniazid was referred to as "antidepressant."[5]

Imipramine had been used earlier in Europe as an antihistamine but was noted to improve patients' moods. It was first tested on schizophrenic patients but made them more agitated and was considered a failure. However, Roland Kuhn noted that three patients diagnosed with depressive psychosis showed marked improvement in "their general state." He wrote a letter to Geigy pharmaceutical company describing his observations. More research by the Swiss company J.R. Geigy culminated in the introduction of the first tricyclic antidepressant, imipramine, in 1957 as Tofranil on the Swiss market. It was marketed in the rest of Europe in 1958.[5] By 1967 with other tricyclic antidepressants it was found to be among the most clinically effective of the antidepressant drugs.

It was hypothesized that the effects of norepinephrine by imipramine resulted in part from the impairment of the inactivation of free norepinephrine in the synapse by cellular reuptake and was proposed to account for the antidepressant action of imipramine. This increased availability of norepinephrine made patients feel more energized and improved their moods, while the decreased brain levels of norepinephrine, dopamine, and serotonin with reserpine made patients less energized and more depressed.[4] As it turned out later in 1975, imipramine (Tofranil) was the antidepressant used to treat my first depression. For the researchers who discovered imipramine it was considered completely accidental or a "serendipitous" discovery. For me it was the providence and concurrence of God at just the right time.

The most widespread hypothesis of depression at the time imipramine was put on the market was that depression emerged from "intrapsychic conditions and conflicts leading to the conviction that chemical tools merely masked the true symptoms of depressive conditions."[6]

These humble beginnings in the 1950s and 1960s that provided the first biological explanations for emotions and treatments for affective disorders stimulated a massive amount of research that continues today with discoveries of newer chemical treatments for depression, obsessive-compulsive disorder, panic attack, bipolar disorder, aggression, and schizophrenia. This was the beginning of my science background that shaped my beliefs about neurotransmitters, emotions, and human behavior.

It was an exciting time to think that psychological illness might not all be from some earlier event in someone's life. In some cases, it proposed an alternative to psychological counseling by obtaining a chemical brain balance through medication. It was called a biogenic amine or catecholamine hypothesis of affective disorders.[4] However, even those developing this chemical approach to affective disorders might have been cautious because it was not possible either to confirm or to reject this hypothesis on the basis of currently available clinical data. Several years later the medical profession and the general population in America fully embraced the new concept of the chemical basis for emotions and the chemical treatment for mood disorders. Mental disorders have not fully been accepted as organically and medically based as much as heart attacks and diabetes. The stigma of mental disorders has not fully disappeared as expected.

ESKETAMINE, A NEW DRUG FOR DEPRESSION

This is where I would like to add a side article on the use of ketamine for depression. On March 5, 2019, I heard on the news that esketamine, a derivative of ketamine, was approved by the FDA for use as a depression drug. This is the first drug for depression that can relieve depression in hours instead of weeks as has been required by all other antidepressants for the last thirty years. Esketamine can benefit five million treatment-resistant patients of the sixteen million in the United States with major depression.

For as many as ten years, doctors had been legally prescribing generic ketamine, a drug approved by the FDA as an anesthetic, for off-label medical uses like depression. Some doctors were using intravenous infusion costing more than $500 per treatment for depression; another, Dr. Demetri Papolos, was prescribing an intranasal form of ketamine for children and adolescents having a disorder that included symptoms of depression.

Johnson and Johnson (J&J) developed the nasal-spray drug called Spravato with the assistance of Janssen Neuroscience, a unit of J&J. J&J needed a good new drug after all the suits against them resulting from the alleged cancer-causing effects of talcum powder. J&J is being very cautious and is not allowing Spravato to be dispensed directly to a patient for home use, because "like ketamine in high doses, both drugs can cause sedation and out-of-body experiences. And ketamine, often called Special K in its illicit form, has become a popular party drug." However, ketamine mixed with opioids is much more likely to produce deaths from overdose than opioids alone. Esketamine is only administered in a very low dose—unlikely to produce side effects such as hallucinations—by approved and certified treatment centers where patients can be observed. The FDA is requiring a warning label that reads, "Patients are at risk for sedation and difficulty with attention, judgment and thinking (dissociation), abuse and misuse, and suicidal thoughts and behaviors after administration of the drug." (Google, "esketamine FDA approval 2019" and select "Ketamine-Derived Drug Spravato for Major Depression Gets FDA Approval: Shots-Health News") The dissociation risk was one of the main reasons many thought the drug might not receive FDA approval. "It is the first truly new depression drug since Prozac hit the market in 1988." It works by a different mechanism than I have just described for antidepressants.

One limitation for the drug for many might be the costs. J&J said the wholesale cost of each treatment with esketamine will range from $590 to $885, depending on the dose. This means that twice-weekly treatments during the first month will cost centers that offer the drug at least $4,720 to $6,785. Subsequent weekly treatments will cost about half as much. This does not include administrative and observation costs by the treatment centers administering the drug. It is truly a miracle drug for the 20 percent of treatment-resistant patients with depression and bipolar disorder.

GOD'S ULTIMATE PLAN FOR ME

Dentistry is my profession. I went into dentistry to help people. It has been exciting and rewarding, and I worked hard at being the best dentist that I could. In my senior year, I was awarded the Academy of General Dentistry's award for the best general dentist in my graduating class at the UKCD in 1970. I graduated fifth "with distinction" in my class while participating in an Honors Program research project. I dedicated myself to my job as a clinician and administrator of dental programs in the USPHS. I give the taxpayers more than their money's worth as a government employee because of my Christian work ethic. There were many opportunities when I could just as easily have slacked off and taken the easy way with less effort and stress. In the end the hard work benefited my development.

Dentistry provided me with the income and position for furthering my education about biological explanations for behavior. The interest in chemical explanations for moods and happiness that I had obtained through reviewing the literature for my honors program project in dental school turned out to be my passion and avocation.

My USPHS commissioned officer retirement as a captain (0-6) in 1995 has provided a substantial income on which to live comfortably and spend time working on my avocation. God continued favoring Donna and me with good health and adequate part-time employment. Donna retired from physical therapy practice in 2013. I still did some part-time consulting for Delta Dental Plan of Oklahoma until 2017 at the age of seventy-one. I believe God's purpose in clearing the way financially was to allow me time for writing. God gave me a story to tell that will hopefully lead others to depend on the Lord and teach them a little about the science of depression. Writing about this story, although with a few down times, has been an enjoyable and rewarding avocation.

Five

A SPECIAL RELATIONSHIP WITH MY GRANDFATHER

OUR RELATIONSHIP BEGAN EARLY

God had also favored me through the presence of my grandfather until his death in 1980. I maintained a close bond with my grandfather (everyone called him Albert or "A. L.") throughout his life. After attending Stratton Business School in Louisville, Kentucky, he returned home and told his family they were spelling their last name like a girl's name. Around 1930 he had the spelling of his and his eight siblings last names changed to Hazle. His father's name was changed to T. B. Hazle.

When I was in the first grade, my sister and I stayed at his house while our mother was hospitalized for depression most of that year. When my parents' house burned in 1956, my grandfather picked me up from school one afternoon when I was in the sixth grade at Hodgenville Elementary School. We arrived at my home just in time to see one side of the house cave in. All I can remember is how orange the flames were that filled the house with the roof already collapsed. Being six miles from town there had been no water supply because no rural water supply was available at that time. What water the fire trucks could carry didn't help much to slow the fire of the all-wood forty-five-year-old frame house that A. L. bought in the 1930s with 195 acres. My parents had started living in this house in 1947.

Although we had lost all our worldly possessions, we could thank God the fire had not happened at night while we were sleeping. The fire was suspected to have started in the attic next to the room where I usually slept—maybe an electrical short. There would have been no smoke detectors to alert us in 1956. God had sheltered me and my family from potential harm again. After the fire, we all moved to Grandpa's house in Hodgenville, which he had built in 1947. And we all lived there for a year while Dad finished building a new two-story brick house on the same site as the old house in 1957 without the help of contractors.

My grandfather set a good example by reading the Bible, praying, and attending church regularly. Grandpa Hazle helped me lead my first Wednesday night prayer service when I was fourteen years old using the scripture in 1 Corinthians chapter 13 about love. He helped me study that scripture and prepare for the service, for which I was very thankful.

There were many hunting trips with my grandfather. While rabbit hunting with beagles he taught me how to wait for the beagles to run the rabbit in a circle and look for the rabbit ahead of them hopping slowly through the brush out thirty yards in front of us. He would teach me to look for the signs of where rabbits had stayed in overnight sleeping spots cupped out in clumps of grass and how to spot them in the morning after a snow. There was a knack to finding a rabbit crouched in a field of heavy grass covered with snow. I learned to look for signs that rabbits were in an area by looking for the fresh little balls of scat and urine. He taught me how to distinguish fresh from old tracks and the direction of travel in the snow.

My grandfather taught me all the tricks of squirrel hunting.

He'd drive out from town and pick me up early in the morning at the farm. I'd have my .22 rifle or 410-gauge shotgun. We'd go out before sunrise on some August mornings when the dew was heavy. At daybreak, we'd listen for the noise of water splashing from tall oak and hickory trees as the squirrels made their way to feed in the tall Kentucky forest. He showed me how to spot squirrels shaking the stalks in a cornfield across the road from the woods. We'd find hickory trees that had piles of fresh hickory nut shavings on the ground indicating recent activity and a good place to be located at sunrise waiting for the squirrels to arrive.

Once I watched my grandfather retrieve a wounded squirrel that ran into a tree hole about five feet from the ground. My grandfather stripped a limber tree branch about four feet long and inserted it into the hole as far down the tree trunk as it would go and began to twist it. He pulled the squirrel out by its tail wrapped around the stick. Then he had to finish killing the squirrel. I was amazed that he did this on the first try. I later had the opportunity of doing the same thing while out hunting with a friend. He was amazed and very impressed. So was I that it had worked so well on the first try!

After our squirrel hunts, we'd visit with the landowner. Grandpa would thank them for allowing us to hunt and sometimes go into their house or sit on the front porch for a visit. Mr. McCandlis was one of the elderly farmers we visited several times in the Oak Hill community south of Tanner, near Maxine, another location where my grandfather had owned a store earlier in his life. The McCandlis two-roomed, unpainted frame house with a tin roof was down a dirt road at the edge of the woods where we hunted. The musty-smelling house had two screen doors and was shaded by tall oak trees. The small wooden porch with rocking chairs was always a comfortable place to discuss some Bible scripture and other topics while drinking well water from an aluminum cup. Grandpa took time to visit with people even though he was a busy, successful businessman. Other people he would stop and visit sometime when I was with him were his African American friends in the "Georgetown" section of Hodgenville. He discussed many general topics with them, but usually got around to discussing some scripture before we left.

When we returned to his house with the squirrels, we always went to the drain in the basement. Here he demonstrated making a cut through the hide just underneath the tail, stepping on the tail, and pulling on the hind legs to skin the squirrel. We'd make the right cuts through the meat for the separation of the shoulders, back, and legs. We'd also save the liver, heart and head for grandma to prepare with the other meat breaded in heavy flour and slow fried in Crisco in a covered skillet on the stove.

Of course, Grandma made mashed potatoes, biscuits, and gravy to go with the squirrel for lunch. Grandpa taught me how to get the brain out of a fried squirrel's head in one marble-sized piece. Eating this was a practice that I later discovered in my forties was dangerous. It's been reported that the human version of mad cow disease can be carried in nerve tissue of squirrels and has since been blamed for some deaths in Kentucky where eating squirrel brains is common. Maybe God was watching over me again, but I don't believe that mad cow disease was common in my younger days. At least it was never mentioned then.

After Donna and I were married, we'd come home from college for a visit on weekends. Grandpa would always take us to his grocery store and help us stock up on groceries before returning to UK. By the time we had moved to Galveston, Texas, he'd been diagnosed with Parkinson's disease. I'd been the first to notice his thumb with a steady tremor called a "pill rolling tremor" when we were talking in his general store one day and suggested that he be checked for Parkinson's. He'd call Galveston each week in 1970 to ask how we were doing. I believe that this continued contact was another way that God was watching over me and keeping me close to Him.

When we'd return for visits about every six months, he'd

always ask us to spend a night with him. Grandma would fix a good fried chicken dinner the same way she fixed the squirrel, with mashed potatoes, biscuits, and gravy. Sometimes we'd listen to Kentucky basketball games. As he got older, he'd cry each time we said goodbye before I left him as I returned to my USPHS stations in Texas, North Dakota, and Oklahoma. Some of that emotion probably was due to his Parkinson's, but I knew that he was thinking as I was. That thought was that we might not see each other alive again. I supposed that was why the tears were in his eyes. Donna and I were attending the 1980 American Dental Association Convention in Kansas City when I was notified that he had died. I'm sorry I wasn't there with him. I knew he was in the hospital, but not for something serious to cause his death. He had devoted much of his time and money for me during his lifetime.

WHY MY GRANDFATHER SHELTERED ME

I believe that God sent my grandfather to provide Christian memories in a way that no other person could have done. Before my grandfather died, he recorded a tape for me—given to me after his death. The tape is a cherished possession. It's ironic that the tape player that I'd given him was used for presenting me a tape of such spiritual significance. The tape recorder had been given to him for a Christmas present under the guise of having him tape University of Kentucky basketball games and mail them to me in Oklahoma. He always mentioned listening to the games, but I couldn't tune in the radio broadcast of the games while living seven hundred miles away. I thought my request would encourage an activity that would help keep his brain active and keep us connected. He enjoyed listening to Kaywood Ledford announce Kentucky basketball games.

My grandfather faithfully sent me a recording each week, but shamefully I never listened to every tape. That was before I became the avid UK fan that I am today. Today I wouldn't miss listening to any games, but instead I can watch every UK basketball and football game on my TV or computer. My main objective was in providing a means for my grandfather to keep stimulated and for us to have something in common. In fact, God used this as a means for assuring that I would hear my grandfather's testimony after his death. Through my gift to him he had returned an even greater gift to me. Before he died, he had recorded his story of salvation and rededication of his life for serving God.

On his fifty-seventh wedding anniversary he recorded how he began his business and life's vocation as owner of a general country store. He described how he met and married my grandmother and how much he loved her. He described God's blessings of being brought up in a Christian home.

He also described an unusual event that took place in his life when he was six years old. He said, "I was awakened about two thirty a.m. by hearing my mother's voice in a room by herself talking to God. The door between the rooms was closed, and I couldn't understand anything she said. I knew it was my mother's voice, and I found out later that she was in fellowship with God." This prayer had left an impression on my grandfather's mind, and he said, "Forty-one years later God used this prayer and made himself known to me."

On the tape he described how he had become a member of Barren Run Baptist Church in 1915 at age fourteen. He said he had received little training in church during his first thirty years as a church member. Church was held once every third Sunday of the month. Even though he was a church member, he was not "a member of the family of God." He had set goals and reached them—to have a successful business and a nice house—but something had been missing. He said that he "knew nothing about the power of God, couldn't make a commitment, and his soul was troubled."

My grandfather was forty-seven years old when he experienced these events. He said, "God worked with me for three nights, allowed me to make a commitment, and became Lord in my life." It was an unusual event my grandfather described next. He had a vision of his mother standing behind his wife who was cooking in the kitchen. Then, he remembered it couldn't be his mother; she had passed away five years earlier. He thought he was going to get to say something to her, and about that time he woke up. He said God put before him the prayer that had come from the heart of a godly mother forty-one years earlier. He said that he had failed to give God any credit for the despair of his soul during the dream. He thought his despair was due to the love for his mother and being disturbed by her prayer. The next night was similar. He heard the prayer of his mother again and said it was more disturbing on the second night. He continued, "although there was no dream. The third night was the same as one and two, but my soul was more troubled." He wondered, "Why would any mother pray a prayer like this for her son?" To his amazement, God answered his question by saying, "This prayer is just beginning to bring forth fruit."

My grandfather continued: "You too may be able to pray a prayer, and it will bring forth fruit. I've never heard the open voice of God but this one time, but many times during the past thirty-two years he has spoken to me through the silent voice of the Holy Spirit."

He quoted James 1:12: "Blessed is the man that endureth temptation; for when he is tried, he shall receive the crown of life, which the Lord hath promised to them that love him." He continued, "I didn't know how to appreciate the Word of God. For more than thirty-three years my home, family, and business had first place in my life. I was a church member but didn't know about the power of God and the Holy Spirit." He then quoted scripture from I John 2:15–17: "Love not the world, neither the things that are in the world. If any man loves the world, the love of the Father is not in him. For all that is in the world, the lust of the flesh, and the lust of the eyes, and the pride of life, is not of the Father, but is of the world. And the world passeth away, and the lust of it; but he that doeth the will of God abideth forever." My grandfather said, "I didn't know about the love, peace, and hope that lives in the hearts and minds of Christians. I didn't know that God has given us the Holy Word and Holy Spirit to direct our living—to tell us the things we should do and should not do."

This event that my grandfather recorded for me seems to qualify as a miracle in his life. He was not only a rational, successful businessman who knew how to make money from buying and selling, but also a man having a true relationship with God. Yes, I have had prayers bear fruit, and some fruit has been delayed in coming. Some of my most memorable prayers were for my father to come back to church, which took thirty-three years to be answered. Other memorable prayers were asking God to help me find his will for me when I decided to change to something besides agronomy. Grandfather's precious testimony is one-of-a-kind. I'm just now understanding all that he said.

By now you're probably wondering what all this has to do with my Christian memories and God sheltering me. Basically, I believe that God passed on a vision of His will for me through my grandfather. God watches over me, one of his Gentile children, just as He did his Hebrew children as described in the Old Testament. They were God's chosen people, but I was chosen also. Through Jesus, I received the blessings promised to Abraham and his descendants—that is, to be blessed and protected by God as found in Genesis 12:2–3 (NIV). "I will make you into a great nation and I will bless you; I will make your name great, and you will be a blessing. I will bless those who bless you, and whoever curses you I will curse; and all peoples on earth will be blessed through you." "For I am not ashamed of the gospel, for it is the power of God for salvation to everyone who believes, to the Jew first and also to the Greek" (Romans 1:16 NASB).

God used my grandfather not only for assuring that I became a Christian but for making the Christian memories in my life that would keep me close to Him. These memories have encouraged the installation of the attributes of Jesus in my life. My grandfather took up where my father left off. My grandfather's rededication of his life to serve the Lord in 1948 came at a good time for me, just three years after my birth—his first grandchild. And some people say miracles don't happen these days. By definition, a miracle is an "extraordinary event manifesting divine intervention in human affairs." In short, it's something that can only be done by God. My salvation is a miracle, but the timing of my grandfather's rededication is also a miracle for me. He sheltered me for the rest of his life.

EXAMPLES OF GOD SHELTERING BIBLICAL MEN FOR THEIR DEVELOPMENT TO SERVE HIM

The Bible describes how God used the strong faith of Hannah and Elkanah for passing on God's vision for their son, Samuel. It was remarkable that Hannah had a child after many years of suffering through the stigma of infertility. When God did answer her prayer and remember her with a son, she paid much attention to his development and "the boy Samuel grew up in the presence of the Lord" (1 Samuel 2:21 NIV). Through Samuel, God anointed Saul as king of Israel (1 Samuel 15:1 (NIV).

David followed Saul as king of Israel, and Christ descended from the lineage of David.

God had to provide for that vision to be passed on through many generations as described in 1 Samuel. The godly influence of Hannah and Elkanah on their son Samuel in his early years remained with him after Hannah "lent him to the Lord." He was taken to live in the temple with Eli, the priest. Eli lacked the parenting skills of Hanna and Elkanah, and Eli's sons were described in 1 Samuel 2:12 (NIV) as "wicked men who had no regard for the Lord." Samuel's early training by Hannah allowed him to maintain his devotion to God and remain strong despite the negative influence of Eli's family.

This demonstrates what is supported through science today—that early development in the first few years of life establishes behavior that remains with us throughout life. Changing that behavior is difficult. In Samuel's case, the early exposure to his mother's influence was beneficial. Samuel became useful to God as a prophet, a judge, and even a city manager (*Shaping the Next Generation,* by David and Elaine Atchison, 1998, LifeWay Press).

A similar story exists about Moses. In Exodus 1:22 (NIV) the Egyptian Pharaoh ordered his people: "Every boy that is born you must throw into the river, but let every girl live." The movie *The Prince of Egypt* tells the story of what miraculous events happened to Moses. From the moment of his birth, God protected Moses. His parents provided baby Moses with a water-resistant basket that floated him safely in the Nile River where he was discovered by the Pharaoh's daughter. The adoption of Moses by Pharaoh's daughter provided him with the best education available, something his biological parents could not have done. God protected Moses so he could use Moses to deliver his people from the bondage of the Egyptians. God had a plan for Moses. God has a plan for each of us.

I'm not a Moses or a Samuel, but God had a plan for me as a believer in Jesus Christ. God used my grandfather in fulfilling that plan just as he has used others to watch over his children in fulfilling his plan for them. Samuel and Moses happen to have their lives recorded in the Bible, but they are no more special than anyone else who accepts Jesus as his or her savior. This is the message of the Bible. God promises these blessings to those who accept his Son, Jesus. It's the message of his love for us. It is difficult to comprehend, and none of that was obvious to me at the time it was happening. Now I'm sure of His involvement. God has a plan for each Christian believer.

God knows us from the time of conception and wants each of us to be a believer, but the choice is ours. Romans 10:9–10 (NIV) says, "That if you confess with your mouth, 'Jesus is Lord,' and believe in your heart that God raised him from the dead, you will be saved. For it is with your heart that you believe and are justified, and it is with your mouth that you confess and are saved." Activities coming from the heart are sincere—sometimes evil—without question or hesitation they can be our first nature. Without accepting Christ and practicing Christian principles, some men remain as natural from birth with evil in their hearts. If as Christians we repeat Christian principles often enough, our decisions and actions become our second nature without hesitation. That's what we strive for—not constantly questioning ourselves whether our actions are right in God's eyes but just doing the right thing automatically. These are second nature responses. They are our first impulses without thoughts affecting our actions.

God gives us the freedom of denying Jesus as our savior. The absence of positive action on our part is considered a denial of God. We must make the decision—confess with our mouths and believe in our hearts that Jesus died for our sins and arose from the dead. My grandfather helped put me in position to assure that for me. He took up where my dad left off when he quit going to church. It wasn't that my dad was a sinful man. Quite the contrary, he lived a Christian life but never contributed to my spiritual development as my grandfather did. My grandfather played the same role for me as Eli and the Pharaoh's daughter did for Samuel and Moses.

MY INFIRMITIES AND
SEEING A PSYCHIATRIST

G od has watched over me, but my life has not been all roses
and happiness. It was a crisp October day in 1975. The
Indian summer weather in Oklahoma was invigorating. I was
a thirty-year-old dentist, home from work early that afternoon
because of mental exhaustion. There was no particular reason
for the depression. I did suspect some bipolar disorder tendencies
since I had made some aggressive, grandiose dental program plans
for my service unit dental program during the winter and early
spring but because of my dysthymia had difficulties accomplishing
those plans during the summer. I had been assigned to start doing
Quality of Dental Care Reviews for other dental clinics in the
Oklahoma City area Indian Health Service (IHS) but dreaded
beginning those reviews. I'd wake up at four o'clock in the
morning unable to sleep, dreading the coming day. At the area
dental meeting that summer I had feared others would detect my
lack of confidence and question my competence.

That year my bout with dysthymia, something a little less
than clinical depression, which had occurred each summer

since 1971, had progressed to a depression by mid-September. Things that were once stimulating and fun were no longer that way—a condition called anhedonia. I wanted to withdraw from interacting with people for fear that they would detect my feeling of incompetence. Work and decision-making had become much more stressful, and I dreaded it. Negative thinking was the norm for me. I was lethargic and fearful of attempting anything new. I had insomnia, and I was having suicide thoughts.

DSM-IV CRITERIA FOR MAJOR DEPRESSIVE DISORDER

The following are the DSM-IV Criteria for Major Depressive Disorder (MDD) that I met:

- Depressed mood or a loss of interest or pleasure in daily activities for more than two weeks
- Mood represents a change from the person's baseline
- Impaired function: social, occupational, educational
- Specific symptoms, at least five of these nine, present nearly every day:

    1. Depressed mood or irritable most of the day, nearly every day, as indicated by either subjective report (e.g., feels sad or empty) or observation made by others (e.g., appears tearful)
    2. Decreased interest or pleasure in most activities most of each day
    3. Significant weight change (5 percent) or change in appetite
    4. Change in sleep: Insomnia or hypersomnia (excessive sleeping)
    5. Change in activity: Psychomotor agitation or retardation

6. Fatigue or loss of energy
7. Guilt/worthlessness: Feelings of worthlessness or excessive or inappropriate guilt
8. Concentration: diminished ability to think or concentrate, or more indecisiveness
9. Suicidality: Thoughts of death or suicide, or has suicide plan

DSM – V proposed (not yet adopted) anxiety symptoms that may indicate depression: irrational worry, preoccupation with unpleasant worries, trouble relaxing, feeling that something awful might happen.

Screen for conditions that may mimic or coexist with major depressive disorder:

- Substance abuse causing depressed mood (e.g., drugs, alcohol, medications)
- Medical illness causing depressed mood
- Other psychiatric disorders: mania, hypomania, bipolar, schizoaffective, schizophrenia, etc.
- Bereavement unless symptoms persist for > two months or show marked functional impairment, morbid preoccupation with worthlessness, suicidal ideation, psychotic symptoms, or psychomotor retardation.[7]

THE DEPRESSIVE EXPERIENCE WAS INEVITABLE—IT WAS IN MY GENES

The fact that I had this repeated cycle for five years of winter and early spring excitement with energy for dental program planning and writing a book, followed by a dysthymia in late spring and early summer each year made me believe that situational stresses were not causing my depression in 1975. I suspected that my family history of depression and maybe bipolar disorder might be a primary genetic etiology. There did not seem to be any major stressful events in my life or any other psychological explanations for the annual mood swings occurring at the same time each year.

I thought about the possibility of mercury exposure causing depression. Depression is one of the early signs of mercury toxicity. Many people know of the stories about the "mad hatters" in Europe who went crazy because they were exposed to mercury while making felt hats. But our dental clinic was supposed to be safe. We had periodic mercury vapor level tests and had never had any bad reports since I'd come to the W. W. Hastings Indian Hospital in Tahlequah, Oklahoma, in 1973.

Sometime later I did a demonstration for some dental assistants that made me skeptical of those mercury vapor level test results. I held my arm next to one of the old gray mixing capsules that we loaded with mercury and alloy tablets each time we made the silver putty-like mix for filling a back tooth. When it finished mixing in the amalgamator, the hair on my arm was covered with hundreds of tiny droplets of mercury. I wondered why the vapor from that had never shown up in any tests. By the time I discovered this we had recently begun using the new, safer, manufactured capsules that didn't leak. Since the problem had been corrected, I never reported the demonstration.

By October I'd lost confidence in my ability to do dentistry. I had left work early one afternoon. Standing in front of the picture window of our small living room, I looked out at the slender pecan trees, dropping their leaves on the bluegrass lawn. The dead leaves reminded me that everything had to die sooner or later. I cradled my younger daughter Angie in my arms. As I looked at her, my smile turned to a frown and a few tears came splashing down on her face. Angie was only one month old and of course could not know why her daddy was crying.

I was crying because I thought I might be going on a trip from which I'd never return. I didn't want to leave her, but the pain of staying was becoming more than what I thought might be the pain of leaving. I was contemplating suicide. The only visions I had that day were about which way to kill myself.

Lethargy had returned to me each year after the age of twenty-six years. I could sense the gradual impending return of the dysthymia each year. I'd find myself without energy for work, hobbies, sex, or play and wishing I hadn't made so many commitments earlier in the year. The fear of not making it back to normal was ominous, with the consequences to my career and family always on my mind.

At work, the most insignificant decisions had become stressful. I worried about my career as I considered whether to stay in the USPHS or go into private practice. The sleepless nights had become more frequent. Many nights I'd find myself awaking in a cold sweat, dreading the coming events of the day. Finding a means of escaping was on my mind. I thought maybe I could just drop out and become a janitor. That would surely solve the stress of decision-making. But the thought of explaining that plan to friends and family brought on more stress. The stress I was feeling that October day had become unbearable, thus the overwhelming thoughts of suicide. But God had prepared a way out of this infirmity.

I'd read personal accounts of how lithium and tricyclic antidepressants had improved some people's moods. By July 1975, I'd asked one physician for medication, but he preferred waiting a while longer. To him I'd appeared in control well enough to keep trying on my own in part possibly because of the detrimental effect of being diagnosed and treated for depression could have on my career in the USPHS. He had requested either a urine or blood mercury level test, of which the results came back within normal limits.

However, three months later I feared that the loss of my ability for thinking rationally might result in suicide before I could receive chemical help. I had been considering how my mother's brother had committed suicide at the age of fifty-four. I wondered how he had been a successful farmer and a deacon in our small church and yet lost enough control over his actions to have committed suicide.

It was about this time that I had learned of my mother's ECT in 1950 when she was twenty-five years old. Another brother of my mother had some mental problems and had not responded well to treatment. There were still social, professional, and possible career consequences to seeing a psychiatrist in 1975, but I'd made up my mind that medication could work. It was probably my last hope, and I was fearful of losing my control over resisting a suicide attempt. As I sat crying in that same physician's office in October, my distress was more evident than on my previous visit three months earlier, and he made a referral to a psychiatrist at a hospital about seventy miles away.

I can still remember the paradox of that bright, sunny, October day in 1975. My wife was driving me through the painted foliage of the Cookson hills on the way to the psychiatrist's office in Fort Smith, Arkansas. We stopped at Church's Fried Chicken in Fort Smith, and I placed an order as if nothing was wrong, but there I was sick enough to commit suicide. Donna was so understanding, accepting, loving, and helpful that day. It was no stress at all for me going to see the psychiatrist.

The psychiatrist recommended admitting me to the hospital because of my suicidal thoughts. I agreed with the physician's recommendation and spent the next ten days in the hospital where I was started on the tricyclic antidepressant medication, imipramine (Tofranil). It was the same one that I was already familiar with, having read about its discovery in the late 1950s, when I was doing my Honors Program thesis at UKCD in 1969. I spent two weeks in the hospital for my protection and for giving the drug a chance of having an effect. It usually takes three to four weeks for the tricyclic antidepressants to work.

At the time it seemed like a major disruption in my work, but getting well was more important. I missed three weeks of work. Some periods of anxiety upon returning to work and some "blue" days occurred but no depression. It was great to be back at work, and I told others that I felt like "super-dentist." I had a positive attitude, and it was so great not to have the suicide thoughts cluttering my mind.

Discussing my sudden absence from work with other hospital staff and friends was not as difficult as I had feared. I thought the depression had been mostly genetic because of what had happened each summer for the last four years and my family history. I had confidence in the drug, and it had worked well. God had provided an effective drug, which had only recently---relative to the existence of depression for thousands of years---become available and had good scientific research to support it. Through all the experience of my first depression, God sheltered me and protected me from suicide, one of the most common sequela of depression.

MY FIRST AND LAST ATTEMPT AT
GOING WITHOUT MEDICATION

I used the tricyclic antidepressant for two years and then quit taking any medicine for a year. I was determined at least to give it a try at making it on my own without medication. I discontinued the imipramine (Tofranil) in the fall of 1977. I tried transcendental meditation, vitamins, vinegar and honey, exercise, psycho-cybernetics, positive thinking, psychological self-help suggestions, and relaxation techniques. No matter how hard I tried to stay positive, the dysthymia was creeping back by the end of spring, an ominous warning of an impending depression by summertime.

I wasted no time having my psychiatrist put me on medication that summer of 1978. I believe maybe he chose lithium the second time because he may have known that imipramine (Tofranil) increases the norepinephrine in the brain synapses, and for a bipolar patient, that can possibly result in an increase in the manic phase. In 1990 Prozac was added by my internist in hopes of decreasing the lithium dosage, which was causing hand tremors—something a dentist doesn't need.

Seven

A VERY SUCCESSFUL PERIOD IN MY USPHS CAREER

The period from 1978 until my retirement in 1995 was an exceptionally productive time for me in the USPHS. In addition to performing the duties of my position description as chief of a large IHS Service Unit Dental Program I completed clinical quality assurance evaluations for seventy-five dental clinics in the IHS Oklahoma City area from 1975 to 1990. I was chairman of the committee appointed to update and revise the IHS Dental Program Quality Assurance document, which was distributed to 250 IHS and tribal clinics.

While chief, Claremore Service Unit Dental Program at the Claremore Indian Hospital (CIH), my staff and I promoted school-based oral health education programs and screening for three thousand third- and sixth-graders each February for Children's Dental Health Month from 1988 to 1995. Oral health education was for the prevention of periodontal disease, dental decay, oral cancer, and tobacco use. Dental sealants were provided at some schools for first- and sixth-graders to protect them from getting cavities in the grooves of their first and second permanent molars.

Fluoridation efforts were successful over a twelve-year period for 150,000 people in the Claremore Service Unit including eighteen thousand people in Claremore. An alcohol, tobacco, and other drug (ATOD) screening and referral program was developed at CIH for the dental program. The program won first place in the 1994 IHS dental program prevention awards. This program, which I presented as a table clinic, won first place at the 1995 Oklahoma Dental Association (ODA) meeting. A first-place award was also received at the 1996 annual ODA meeting for a table clinic presentation on "Non-Surgical Treatment of Periodontal Disease," and a third table clinic placed second in 1997.

The "Non-Surgical Treatment of Periodontal Disease" research project was a new approach using antibiotics after dental prophylaxis as a treatment instead of the traditional surgical approach. Dr. Tom Rams, a periodontist from the University of Pennsylvania, was overseeing the research project at the CIH beginning in 1993. I was coinvestigator and coordinator for the IHS periodontal research project, which was never completed because of my retirement in 1995.

I was chairman of the Oklahoma Public Health Association (OPHA) Oral Health Section for 1994–95. I was awarded the Preventive Dentistry and Public Health Award by the OPHA Oral Health Section in 1994 for exceptional contributions toward maintaining the dental health of the people of Oklahoma. As a result of involvement in several preventive programs I was invited to present "Dentistry's Role in Primary Care" to a work group for the Institute of Medicine at Newport Beach, California in 1995. This included screening and referral of diabetic patients, taking blood pressures for dental patients, and ATOD screening and referral. I was involved in clinical research and presenting at national and state meetings. I gave nine dental presentations at the annual USPHS Professional Association meetings.

I was also awarded fellowship in the American College of Dentists in 1994, to which only 3.5 percent of dentists in the

United States are inducted. I am a member of the American Dental Association and the Oklahoma Dental Association. I was a preceptor for the Oklahoma University College of Dentistry for fifteen years and for Baylor College of Dentistry for a fewer number of years.

Fifteen PHS awards, including Outstanding Service and Meritorious Service Awards, were received.

All these accomplishments were in addition to working as a clinician and managing a busy fourteen-chair expanded duties dental clinic with five dentists, a contract oral surgeon, and sixteen dental auxiliaries. Of course, accreditation by the Joint Commission of Accreditation for Hospital Organizations had to be maintained for the CIH Dental Services. There was also an area dental lab with four employees at CIH, which required some time for management.

Thanks to Dr. Byron Jasper and Dr. Robert Best, my two deputy chiefs while I was chief of the Claremore Service Dental Program for seventeen years, for assuming management of the program's five field dental clinics. The tribes gradually took over operation of all five dental clinics by the time I retired.

Praise God for allowing me to have a successful USPHS career while there was a high probability that I was living with the genes for depression and did have one major depression while on active duty in the USPHS. The diagnosis and treatment for one major depression in 1975 did not prevent me from being promoted to captain in a timely manner.

97

MANIA AFTER TWENTY-
TWO YEARS OF PEACE

P raise God for twenty-two years without depression. By the
end of 1999 my depression had been in remission since 1978,
and I was still productive and enjoying life. But about this time
my tremors became more bothersome when performing clinical
dental procedures. I was still working in clinical dentistry part
time as an associate in private practice with Dr. Steve Deem and
at the Claremore Indian Hospital. The decision was made to
discontinue the lithium and remain on the Prozac (fluoxetine)
in order to decrease the tremors. In retrospect, that probably was
a dangerous move for a bipolar patient. Dr. Ron Feive explains
why in his book *Prozac*, published in 1994[8]. Without a mood
stabilizer such as lithium, Tegretol (carbamazepine), or Depakote
(valproate), patients on Prozac (fluoxetine), a selective serotonin
reuptake inhibitor (SSRI), may develop high levels of serotonin
causing an overbalance of excitement thus kicking a bipolar
patient into the manic state.

DARRELL HAZLE

THE MANIA FROM TAKING PROZAC
WITHOUT A MOOD STABILIZER

Although I had read Dr. Fieve's book I had not remembered his suggestion that a manic condition could be created with the discontinuance of lithium while still on Prozac (fluoxetine). I might have reconsidered the decision of buying forty acres and starting a duck farm at the end of 1999 had I remembered that.

For two years I thought I had been doing well on Prozac (fluoxetine), and after switching to Paxil (paroxetine) due to insomnia in November 2001. Because Paxil (paroxetine) is an SSRI like Prozac (fluoxetine) it too can kick a bipolar patient into a manic phase without a mood stabilizer due to the possibility of increased serotonin levels. I was also still taking some topiramate and timolol for my essential tremor. I thought I was doing well, but the change to slightly more mania, a hypomania, had been so subtle that neither I nor my primary care physician had diagnosed it. I suppose he was not aware of the necessity for a mood stabilizer. My physician had switched me from Prozac (fluoxetine) to Paxil (paroxetine) because of my complaint about insomnia, which was the most common side effect of Prozac.

I rather enjoyed having all the extra energy and often worked from sunrise to sunset on the farm. Many days in those summers the temperature was above one hundred degrees. My wife couldn't believe it. I guess that was one thing that God hadn't protected me from—my pride and overconfidence. It also cost me thousands of dollars.

I BOUGHT FORTY ACRES AND
STARTED DUCK FARMING

I was more positive about the success of the venture than I should have been, and the idea was not so far out that anyone could tell me for sure that it absolutely wouldn't work. I'd always considered myself as having an experimental spirit. I enjoyed doing and succeeding at projects that others hadn't done—quite the opposite of when I was depressed.

In September 1999 I purchased forty acres for $72,000 suitable for what I thought was the development of a shallow-water project for wildlife conservation and duck hunting. Well, it was not the most ideal site for a wetlands project because it didn't have any flat bottomland. It was prairie with some moderately sloping land with two ponds. But the land was only one mile from Oologah Lake to the west and half a mile to the south. I had hunted Oologah Lake for twenty years and knew that ducks liked visiting surrounding ponds during duck season. Some local farmers said that ducks darkened the skies coming off the lake in the fall. I was assisted by the US Fish and Wildlife Service. They provided incentive money and technical advice in developing a shallow-water project that would include sixteen acres of surface water, but there were additional expenses.

My goal was having a place to hunt ducks when I was a little old man—too old for breaking ice and hunting on the lake. I had never seen very many older men out hunting ducks on the lake. I thought there must have been good reasons for that. I loved duck hunting but no longer looked forward to breaking ice in a boat in the cold Oologah Lake water. News reports of some hunters dying of hypothermia while duck hunting in Oklahoma were common every few years. By developing the land for duck hunting, I looked forward to having a safer place to hunt.

That idea was doable, and had I stopped there, I would have been okay. Instead, I added duck farming to my original goal. I decided to establish a resident population of ducks while also producing enough ducks for sale for a profit. I would sell ducks and lease hunting rights to other hunters for a profit until I got older and could not hunt on the lake. I ignored my friends' advice when they suggested difficulties in accomplishing this.

They said varmints would kill the ducks, so I built flight pens with six-foot fences and electric wires. One pen was fifty feet by one hundred feet and covered with netting. This pen had three thirty-foot utility poles with cables supporting the netting. There was a forty-foot by sixty-foot pen around the two small tank ponds, and half of it was covered by netting. I placed chicken wire and electric wiring around a large pond to keep out varmints where I had placed nesting bins. I developed nesting habitats inside the penned areas by building fifty nesting bins out of plastic nursery plant containers. I prepared five large floating tires with two or three nesting bins each and anchored them in the ponds as floating nesting spots. Friends said the small ponds inside the smaller fenced pen would fill with litter. They did, and I developed a cleaning system to circulate clean water from an adjacent pond to remove the waste litter. That never worked very well.

I laid twenty-five hundred feet of PVC water line using a ditch witch and a backhoe to bring clean rural water to the ducks for drinking. I did this in 105-degree summer weather and came close to heat stroke more than once. I was at the farm when it was fifteen degrees with six inches of snow trying to keep them supplied with water. I had a generator to circulate water in one pond and keep an open spot for drinking water for the free-flying ducks when the pond froze. My friends said the ducks wouldn't stay around. But an old duck farmer said that ducks were a "slave to feed" and would stay if they had feed. I countered this problem by planting three acres of maize along the largest pond. I planted 150 Chinese sawtooth oak and cypress trees around the pond edges for food and cover. All these extra expenses added up to $20,000 the first year.

I bought three dozen free-flying wild mallard ducks from the duck farmer in Arkansas. When asked about incubating and brooding chicks, I responded that I'd let the hens do that job. Others asked if there was a market for ducks. I said yes, people would buy them to eat and establish their own resident flocks. There were also the dog trainers who used about 250 ducks at each of their retriever test events as well as for training the dogs. But, despite existing optimism, there were some simple reasons for the failure of that venture.

I GAVE UP ON THE DUCK FARM

The hawks, owls, and land varmints still caught many ducks, and the feeding areas were overrun by mice. The bobcats, opossums, skunks, coons, stray dogs, and raptors seemed to spread the word that Doc's Duck Farm was a free smorgasbord. My farm experienced the worst three-year drought since the dust bowl in Oklahoma. Some ponds went dry, and I had no water to circulate and clean the smaller fenced ponds where the ducks raised. The penned ducks on dry land had only raised one-third of what I'd expected. Most of the free-flying ducks wouldn't go to the maize fields to feed in the fall. They were spoiled by the feed that was available in one pen that was not completely covered with a net. They learned to fly back into the pen for easy meals of wheat and chicken-layer feed.

The flocks of migrating blackbirds ate most of the maize anyway. When ducks did go to the fields, several were killed and eaten by hawks. The ducks still drank the littered water instead of the clean rural water that was available. The market for my ducks never materialized. In short, the venture was not cost effective, and I could not make a profit. The "ducks that blackened the sky" mentioned by farmers turned out to be cormorants that flew over my farm in large flocks each morning in the fall. After about three hundred trips to the duck farm and back for three years, and spending an additional $20,000, I gave up.

I began selling off all remaining 450 ducks in November 2002 except for those one hundred free-flying ducks on my farm. These ducks soon ate all the natural vegetation in the farm ponds, and I had to feed wheat and chicken feed to keep them around. That was too expensive. More than once when I was sweating in 105-degree weather and freezing in icy weather, I'd think the ducks were laughing at me for working so hard. I guess it was just retribution for my having killed so many of their kind in the past thirty years. I now believe that this failed venture was proof of my hypomanic phase, and I had to turn my efforts toward getting well.

Another discouraging event happened at the farm in early December 2002. I arrived at my gate early one morning to see my lock on the chain around the gate and corner post had been cut. Tire tracks were in the light snow that had fallen overnight. I looked across the field, and my 1980 Chevy Blazer was missing. I called the sheriff's office and reported the robbery. Within a few days my truck was found on a dead-end section line road down by the lake. The wheels had been removed, and it was sitting on cinder blocks. The windows were broken out and the steering column busted to get at the starting mechanism. All my tools and equipment, valued at $600, were gone. What a mess and a total loss.

The next day my friend who also had some items stolen from his property in the same area, called me and said his items were found at a location about ten miles from my farm; he suggested that I should come and look for my stolen items. The owner of that location was a person living in Foil, Oklahoma who had previously been arrested twice for making meth and stealing a pickup motor from the local school. My friend was picking up some of his things.

I was working at the Claremore Indian Hospital dental clinic that day, and by the time I got off work, the sheriff had left, and I was unable go on the property to search the place for any of my stolen items. However, my friend picked up the wheel rims for my old Blazer with all the tires missing. It was my conclusion that the meth maker and his friends had been high on meth when they broke into my place and destroyed my Blazer---probably after they realized the transmission had some slippage. I figured maybe they had planned to install the motor they had stolen in my Blazer but had changed their plan when they discovered the faulty transmission. All I received from my insurance was the fee for towing the Blazer to a salvage yard for parts.

Nine

❦

MY SECOND DEPRESSION AND DISCUSSION OF ATOD ABUSE

THE INSOMNIA AND SUICIDE THOUGHTS RETURNED

The troublesome insomnia that I'd experienced the previous year was returning by October 2002. I began losing my self-esteem and again had thoughts of not being able to continue working as a dentist. I turned to God and reading the Bible.

I read His word in 2 Corinthians where Paul boasts of his suffering for the glory of God. Chapter 12 verses 7–10 (NIV) read:

> To keep me from becoming conceited because of these surpassingly great revelations, there was given to me a thorn in my flesh, a messenger of Satan, to torment me. Three times I pleaded with the Lord to take it away from me. But he said to me, 'My grace is sufficient for you, for my power is made perfect in weakness.' Therefore, I will boast

all the more gladly about my weakness, so that
Christ's power may rest in me. That is why, for
Christ's sake, I delight in weaknesses, in insults,
in hardships, in persecutions, in difficulties. For
when I am weak then I am strong.

God gave me depression instead of a "thorn in my flesh." I read
about Paul's sufferings in chapter 11. Paul withstood flogging,
stoning, robberies, hunger, thirst, drowning, imprisonment,
insomnia, and going without shelter. His perils made me feel as
if I was a crying, spoiled baby for what little physical pain that
I had suffered. It was the mental anguish that caused me great
pain. But I knew that God would not give me more troubles than
I could handle.

We had decided to sell the family farm property in Kentucky
since my parents could no longer take care of it. The house
needed numerous repairs and replacements. We listed it with a
real estate agent, but no offers had been received. I worried about
this. Working part time at the Claremore Indian Hospital dental
clinic was stressful because of the relentless heavy workload.
These worries along with the failing duck farm would have
seemed manageable had I been well, but I was not. The feelings of
inadequacy that had started in October had evolved into suicidal
thoughts.

In November 2002 it had been exactly one year since my
primary care physician and I decided that switching from Prozac
(fluoxetine) to Paxil (paroxetine) would help the insomnia that I'd
had in November 2001. Insomnia was listed as the most common
side effect of Prozac. The switch did help some. However, I'd
started waking up early again at 3:30 a.m. and had plenty of
energy. My wife commented several times during the last half of
that year that she wished she had the energy that I had for doing
so many things. Maybe I should have realized that I was probably

being hypomanic because of not taking a mood stabilizer with the Paxil.

I began having doubts about publishing a book that I'd been sending to agents. I lay awake and worried about anything that popped into my head. I worried about selling the farm in Kentucky. I worried about selling the duck farm. I had turned from hypomanic to being depressed again. It wasn't the stress of working at the hospital and worrying that caused me to be depressed. It was just time for another depression because of those bipolar depression genes I had inherited.

Worrying was a symptom of depression, which had also occurred with my other depression in 1975. The depression was part of my bipolar cycle following the hypomania for the last two years.

I agreed with Rebecca Woolis, MFT, who wrote in her book *When Someone You Love Has a Mental Illness* that "Stress does not cause mental illness. However, it appears to increase the seriousness of the symptoms in people who are prone to the disorders." She suggested that "stress can be one factor in determining when the symptoms get better or worse." She had already noted that most professionals believe that heredity is the most important factor in determining who is likely to develop major affective disorders and that their primary cause is physiological.[9]

After a miserable Thanksgiving occupied with suicide thoughts, I was about ready to give up. Finally, the suicide thoughts motivated me to see a psychiatrist the first week of December 2002. As my psychiatrist told me, I needed help for my mental pain just as if I was having a heart attack, because it could kill me. I knew I was at a dangerous point when the suicide thoughts began coming. He started me on Zyprexa (olanzapine).

Within four days of seeing my psychiatrist I was feeling more positive about living, and my suicide thoughts had vanished. The Zyprexa that he had prescribed had been on the market for two years. He was encouraged about its success after I told him that my mother had greatly improved after starting on it about six weeks earlier. Problems had turned into challenges for her instead of hopeless situations.

PROFESSIONAL HELP FOR SUICIDE THOUGHTS

The rate of suicide is about twelve times higher among people with mental illness than among the population at large. About 10 percent of people with major mental illnesses ultimately kill themselves.[9] If a relative or someone you love is considering suicide, the following information by Rebecca Woolis in her book[9] will be helpful in prioritizing the urgency in obtaining professional help.

Someone's likelihood of suicide is usually expressed in terms of the following categories (listed in order of increasing seriousness).

- Ideation: thoughts or feelings about killing oneself, without any immediate plan or intention of acting on them.
- Gestures: self-destructive acts that a person connects with suicidal thoughts or feelings (taking ten aspirins, self-inflicted injuries). These are often seen as an effort to communicate to which a response should be made.
- Attempts: a wide range of actions in terms of lethality.

Warning signs of suicide include:

- Movement into or out of a depression if the person:

  1. exhibits feelings of extreme worthlessness or expresses concerns about having committed an unpardonable sin,
  2. expresses utter hopelessness about the future and shows a lack of desire to make any future plans,

3. hears voices instructing him or her to hurt or kill himself or herself,
4. exhibits a sudden change in mood from severe depression to inexplicable brightness or serenity,
5. gets his or her affairs in order—for example a will or systematically contacts old friends and relatives,
6. discusses a concrete, specific suicidal plan.

- Talking about having supernatural powers or being indestructible.
- Previous suicidal gestures or attempts or extreme impulsivity, combined with any of the above.[9]

Most suicides are preventable, according to the American Foundation for Suicide Prevention. Karen Cassiday, PhD, 2016 president of the Anxiety and Depression Association of America (ADAA) says the following about suicide. "Sadly, many who are at risk for attempting suicide never receive the treatment they need because of stigma, lack of access to care, or lack of knowledge about their symptoms."[10]

"Both depression and anxiety carry a high risk of suicide," says Mark Pollack, MD, ADAA past president and Grainger professor and chairman, Department of Psychiatry at Rush University Medical Center. "More than 90 percent of those who die by suicide have a diagnosable illness such as clinical depression, and often in combination with anxiety or substance use disorders and other treatable mental disorders."

The stimulants (cocaine, meth, nicotine, and amphetamines), depressants (alcohol and barbiturates), antianxiety drugs (Valium, Xanax, Ativan and Klonopin), and opioids (prescription pain killers, Oxycodone, Hydrocodone, Oxycontin, Fentonyl and heroin), and the rebounds when recovering from these drugs in combination with depression disturbs your normal neurotransmitter chemistry badly. This results in the chances of suicide being greatly increased. The increased risk of suicide when mixing drug and alcohol abuse with depression or even when one only has a family history of depression cannot be overemphasized.

Although the initial effects of stimulant drugs may be to increase a feeling of well-being, pleasure, and euphoria, they often produce the opposite effect of depression during the recovery from the drug effects referred to as a "crash." The crash compounds the illness of depression and interferes with any treatment medications. The illness of depression is dangerous enough without mixing it with drugs.

Of course, the main problem with opioids is death from unintentional overdose by causing respiratory depression. But an unknown number of these may be suicides. You can save a life by administering NARCAN during an opioid crisis. For instructions on the access and use of the nasal spray, Google "NARCAN" and select "NARCAN (naloxone)–Nasal Spray 4 mg."[11] You can screen yourself for depression on the ADAA website, adaa.org. Go to adaa. org and select "Understanding the Facts." Find the "Depression" heading and below this select "Symptoms," then scroll down to "Screen yourself or a family member for depression" and select this. Take the test, print the page and share it with your health care professional.

Suicide affects all groups, including children. It was the tenth-leading cause of death in the United States in 2016 with nearly forty-five thousand deaths. In 2017, according to the most recent statistics from the Centers for Disease Control and Prevention, forty-seven thousand deaths occurred from suicides in all ages. More people died from suicide than automobile accidents. The suicide rate was fourteen people in every one hundred thousand, up 33 percent from 10.5 per one hundred thousand in 1999. In 2017 it was the second-leading cause of death for persons between the ages of ten and thirty-four and the fourth-leading cause of death for middle-aged Americans.

To talk to a skilled, trained counselor at a crisis center in your area at any time, call 1-800-273-TALK (8255), the National Suicide Prevention Lifeline. Proposed to be changed to 988. (http://www. suicidepreventionlifeline.org/).[12]

ZYPREXA THE MIRACLE DRUG FOR MY MOTHER AND MYSELF

After several years on lithium between 1984 and 2002, my mother was started on Zoloft (sertraline). Mother had always been more depressed during the winter months even when taking Zoloft, a selective serotonin reuptake inhibitor (SSRI). She subsequently developed tremors, which at least partly were attributed to her being diagnosed with Parkinson's disease. In 2002 she was taking Premax and Sinemet (carbidopa-levadopa) for Parkinson's, and Zoloft (sertraline) for depression.

When she became depressed again in the fall of 2002, her psychiatrist started her on Zyprexa (olanzapine). Within ten days there was an amazing difference in her mood. I could hear it in her expressions over the phone. She became more active and regained interest in painting. She reported that she went out walking for exercise using an umbrella when it was drizzling rain. However, she kept saying that she never felt the manic, overly energetic feelings that she had experienced in the springtime when coming out of depression.

I was relieved and encouraged when my psychiatrist suggested Zyprexa (olanzapine) for me. I called my mother as soon as I came out of the psychiatrist's office and told her, "Thanks for staying alive." I was so glad that she had taken Zyprexa and had success with it and that I had a chance to try it.

The first morning after taking Zyprexa and a sleeping pill, Restoril (tempazepam), I was zonked. It was a blah day. However, by the fourth day I was out running errands and taking care of business as usual.

The suicide thoughts had passed. I wanted to listen to Christmas music. The Mannheim Steamroller Christmas music had been my favorite since early 1990. It was again stimulating and exciting. Before the Zyprexa I wouldn't listen to it. None of my old memories of musical tunes did anything to help improve my mood. After Zyprexa, the music brought back good memories of Christmas. On a warm winter day, the smell of decaying vegetation was a good smell because it reminded me of the fun of duck hunting, which I had also lost interest in that fall.

These things brought me to the conclusion that recalling good memories was only possible when good brain chemistry existed. Zyprexa had done that.

ZYPREXA QUIT WORKING AFTER THREE MONTHS

All this good feeling was before the Zyprexa quit working after three months. It worked almost as a miracle drug for my mother and me, but the effectiveness of the drug had ended abruptly for both of us. It had only lasted three months for each of us. Because of our similar genetic makeup, we had reacted the same way to Zyprexa just as we had both responded well to lithium because we were both bipolar with a similar genetic makeup.

For six weeks after the Zyprexa (olanzapine) quit working, all I could do was lie in bed or on the couch all day and worry or think about suicide. I feared that I wouldn't be able to make payments on the duck farm and house mortgage if I couldn't work. This worry was probably unfounded because I still had my USPHS retirement income, but it still felt very real in my mind.

Nevertheless, I read Psalms to see what David was thinking when he was depressed. In some verses he expressed morbid separation from God as in Psalms 22:1-2 and 13:1-2. Some scriptures praised God as in Psalms 23, 27, 30, 34. Peter advises in 1 Peter 5:6 (NIV): "Humble yourselves, therefore, under God's mighty hand, that he may lift you up in due time. Cast all your anxiety on him because he cares for you."

My psychiatrist increased the Paxil and Zyprexa (olanzapine) and added lithium over the next two months. I was no longer suicidal. It took another five months of experimenting and finally adding 200 mg of Lamictal (lamotrigine) before my energy returned. It was now into August 2003, and I was barely making it but never really feeling back to normal. Throughout the winter months my condition deteriorated, and by March I was again depressed and suicidal.

I agreed on an admission to a treatment facility called Brookhaven in Tulsa on March 23, 2004. The goal was to put me in a safe place while receiving some counseling and finding a more effective combination of psychotropic medications. At the time of my admission I was taking Xanax XR (alprazolam), Ambien (zolpidem), Zyprexa (olanzapine), Lamictal (lamotrigine), and Paxil CR (paroxetine). I was discharged on April 2, 2004, taking Ambien, Zyprexa, Xanax XR, and Wellbutrin XL 300 mg (bupropion).

Except for the eighteen months of depression 2017–18, I have done well on these meds that I was discharged on minus the Ambien, which was discontinued about a year later. The Wellbutrin XL had been increased to 600 mg. However, when I started seeing a different psychiatrist in 2013, the Wellbutrin XL was reduced to 350 mg due to risk for seizure with high dosages of Wellbutrin XL (bupropion).The fact that I had remained well for fourteen years reminds me of God's promise in 1 Peter 5:10–11 (NIV): "And the God of all grace, who called you to his eternal glory in Christ, after you have suffered a little while, will himself restore you and make you strong, firm, and steadfast. To him be the power for ever and ever. Amen." Praise God for watching over me and providing good research, good medicine, and good doctors.

Through all my episodes of illness I had managed to continue working in the clinic part time with intermittent breaks. I had started doing some clinical record documentation reviews for Delta Dental Plan of Oklahoma in 2000. These were required by the IHS for some patients that the IHS dentists referred to contract dentists, usually specialists, in private practice.

The life I have through Jesus is a miracle. God has given me a good life even when I was having periods of depression, which were challenging, learning experiences. Since my last episode February 2017 to August 1, 2018, I have not had a bad day but a normal life without further depression.

I have been maintained on Wellbutrin XL (bupropion) and Zyprexa (olanzapine) and Xanax XR (alprazolam). Now I am also taking the following vitamins and supplements daily: Centrum Silver Men 50+, vitamin D3, coenzyme Q10 100 mg, vitamin B_{12} 1,000 mg plus folic acid 400 mcg chewables, vitamin B_6 150 mg, flaxseed oil 1,000 mg, choline/inositol 500 mg/500 mg, Biotin 500 mcg, Alginol[R] (Seanol[R] Brown Algae) 400mg, and PerfectAmino[R] (eight essential amino acids) 3,000mg. The first six of these were recommended by Dr. Christner; the last four I have added. I am not aware of any good randomized controlled double-blind studies that indicate they are safe and effective, but I assume they are safe because I have had no adverse side effects. Because I have not had a bad day since August 1, 2018, I continue to take them. I am not aware of any harm caused by taking these other than the expense. With only testimonies to support them, their effectiveness is considered anecdotal, and until two years ago I never believed in taking supplements because of my science background.

I have eliminated a few others that I was taking, because I observed no negative effects when I stopped taking them. Others I have continued taking because I thought I had noticed a difference---such as fatigue, worry, or negative thinking---when I quit taking them. But maybe that was just coincidental with some other negative events that would have happened anyway.

I keep looking for negative effects when I quit taking one for a few weeks—even repeating this process with those I have tried quitting at least once before. I'm a one-specimen experiment, which is highly unreliable and inconclusive. I wish there were better statistical data available about their effectiveness.

In the next chapter, Guidance and Protection, I will describe some interesting experiences with family members and others who have sheltered me for a happy and successful life. Also, I will share some other events that I consider the providence of God. But first I would like to discuss helpful information that I have learned about some drugs related to depression and other health problems.

DISCUSSION OF ALCOHOL, TOBACCO AND OTHER DRUG (ATOD) ABUSE—ALCOHOL, VIOLENCE, DEPENDENCE, AND CREATIVITY

After recently reading a research article, "Neurobiology of Aggression and Violence,"[13] I am sure of a hypothesis I had developed in the 1990s about alcohol and violence. It is not the violence during alcohol intoxication that I am referring to, but the violence that occurs from the rebound effect several hours after extensive drinking has stopped. Another article, "Alcohol, Sleep, and Why You Might Re-think that Nightcap,"[14] reinforces this idea.

There are several points to remember from these articles, the first of which is that aggression originates in the amygdala, a structure in the limbic system of the brain. Anything that activates the amygdala increases aggression, and anything that inhibits the activity of the amygdala decreases aggression. GABA (gamma aminobutyric acid) is the chief inhibitory neurotransmitter sending messages through the brain and is involved in regulating communication between brain cells. The role of GABA is to inhibit or reduce the activity of messages between neurons or nerve cells. GABA can be thought of as the stop sign or red light for messages

117

from one nerve cell to another. GABA inhibits the aggression of the amygdala.

Glutamate is the chief excitatory neurotransmitter and excites the brain and enhances transmission between nerve cells. Remember that the glutamate is the go sign for messages. Alcohol inhibits glutamate, which sedates the brain and results in decreased anxiety. Glutamate and GABA neurons comprise 90 percent of all brain cells. Alcohol also mimics GABA at GABA receptors, which decreases anxiety and also results in an excess production of GABA, which is recycled into excitatory glutamate in glial cells adjacent to GABA neurons[14] (see figure 3, this chapter). This increase in glutamate after a night of drinking results in a rebound with increased stress, anxiety, and aggression when sobering up.

After consulting some emergency room physicians to confirm that much domestic violence occurs on Sunday afternoon or evening, I developed a hypothesis that more violence occurs when sobering up after extensive drinking.

The supposed scenario went like this. After working five days, many men start drinking Friday at p.m. and maybe continue the next day. Men with ADHD (attention deficit/hyperactivity disorder), borderline personality disorder, PTSD, antisocial disorder, psychosis, or substance abuse are at more risk for committing abuse and violent behavior when they begin to sober up after extensive drinking.[13] This would most likely occur on Sunday as they sobered up preparing for work on Monday, but could occur sooner in the weekend if they sobered up on Saturday.

Aggression and violence occur when anger-producing events affecting the amygdala are not sufficiently restrained by the failing effectiveness of inhibitory GABA and increased excitatory glutamate.[13] Alcohol affects many neurotransmitter systems, thereby making it difficult to fully understand all the ramifications of drinking alcohol. This same aggressive state could apply to road rage.

Many people who abuse alcohol also smoke. Smoking and

nicotine vaping release more norepinephrine from the adrenal glands and in the brain causing more excitation of certain brain neuronal circuits, resulting in a feeling of well-being, and possibly stimulating the amygdala. Nicotine also releases more dopamine in the brain. Dopamine is the feel-good rewarding neurotransmitter that makes people want to continue smoking or vaping nicotine.

Alcohol sedates and reduces anxiety. Continued exposure to alcohol over time desensitizes GABA receptors, meaning that the available GABA does not work as well for slowing messages and calming anxiety or subduing aggression from an aroused amygdala. This desensitization may cause people to feel increased stress and anxiety when they become sober, which may make them want to drink and smoke more frequently. Tolerance to alcohol is built over time with repeated sequential drinking episodes and can lead to alcohol dependence and addictiion.[15]

The flip side of overconsumption of alcohol is drinking in moderation. Creativity can result from drinking only one to two glasses of wine at 6:00 p.m., causing one to wake up from 2:00 a.m. to 4:00 a.m. wide awake with creative ideas. I was reminded in 2014 by Bonnie Bruerd, an IHS hygienist consultant, that I had told her about this phenomenon in the 1980s; she said that she remembered what I had told her every time she woke up at 3:00 a.m. after drinking two glasses of wine the evening before. Back then this was just an idea I had because of my awareness of the rebound effect of alcohol on GABA; however, I never knew the details or had the scientific conclusiveness provided by these two articles referenced in this subtitle until 2019.[13, 14] This rebound is to a lesser extent than that required for abuse and violence because of the smaller amount of alcohol consumed.

It is ill-advised to even drink smaller amounts of alcohol on a regular basis for several days consecutively. I don't know how many consecutive days are required, but I suspect it's different for different people. One reason for this recommendation is the increased risk for tolerance and addiction to alcohol—also because of the insomnia it might produce.

Figure 3, this chapter, taken and modified from "Alcohol, Sleep and Why you Might Re-Think that Nightcap"[14] demonstrates how excess GABA is metabolized and recycled as excitatory glutamate neurotransmitters. It's in glutamate-releasing brain regions like the reticular activating system (RAS), which partially modulates sleep/wake and arousal and awakens a person later in the night. It may be the increase in excitatory glutamate that is responsible for the creative ideas in the brain.

An average person metabolizes 0.25 ounce of alcohol each hour. If a person drinks ten ounces of wine (about two glasses) containing twelve percent alcohol, this amounts to 1.20 ounces of alcohol. That means it would take an average person about five hours to metabolize the alcohol. "So, keep the drinks small and keep it early—an evening cap."[14]

I mentioned a similar event resulting in creativity when I forgot to take my Xanax in chapter 1 in the subtitle "The Creative Urge." Xanax is a benzodiazepine that works similarly to alcohol. The Xanax substitutes for GABA at the GABA receptors—relieving anxiety, increasing GABA production, desensitizing GABA receptors, and causing an increase in glutamate.

I repeat what I said there: "The only sure way to prevent alcohol abuse and addiction is total abstinence. If you don't drink, don't start. Multiple factors are involved—including genetics—that predispose a person to alcohol dependence. Not many people consider their risks for addiction to alcohol the first time they use it; addiction just happens with frequent consumption of even small amounts over time. If you do drink alcohol, God commands us not to drink to excess or drunkenness. Our laws require us not to be drunk while driving.

When you drink alcohol (ethanol or ethyl alcohol), the liver converts it to acetaldehyde. If you are Native American, beware that you may have alcohol dehydrogenase (ADH) deficiency, a deficiency of the enzyme that controls the metabolism of ethanol; or you may be an individual who has inherited a genetic tendency that makes this enzyme less active or inactive. This may extend your metabolism time or even make you alcohol intolerant. What little you do drink stays in your bloodstream longer. If you drink over several hours without metabolizing alcohol at the average rate of 0.25 ounce of alcohol per hour, the cumulative inebriation could be much greater than someone with average metabolism who drank the same number of drinks.

The extent of this occurrence is more related to a higher degree of Native American blood quantum than it is tribal membership. You may be a tribal member—possibly with a much lower blood quantum—and not be significantly affected by this phenomenon.

Figure 3 Source: Wikimedia Commons, modified and translated in English. Graphics by Carlos Angon.

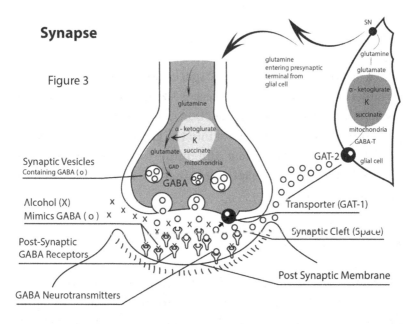

Directory of Terms

GABA (Gamma-aminobutyric acid) Inhibitory NT

GAT-1 (GABA transporter-1 removes GABA from the synaptic cleft)

GAD (Glutamate dehydrogenase) enzyme

GAT-2 (GABA transporter- 2 transports GABA into the glial cell)

Glutamate (Glutamic acid) Excitatory NT

K (Krebs cycle)

α-ketoglurate (α-ketoglutarate) enzyme

Mitochondria (organelle for biochemical processes)

succinate (intermediate in metabolism in the Krebs cycle)

NT (neurotransmitter)

glutamine (amino acid used in synthesis of proteins such as glutamate)

ALCOHOL (X) CAUSES AND EXCESS OF GABA

When alcohol enters the synaptic space and substitutes for GABA, it results in excess of GABA by desensitizing GABA receptors and stimulating the increased production of GABA.[16]

The excess GABA (o) flows into the glial cell, which converts GABA into glutamine. The glutamine flows out of the glial cell back into the presynaptic terminal where it is converted to glutamate (figure 3).

MAINTAINING BALANCE

Any excess of glutamate is supposed to be automatically converted to GABA. **This is the way it maintains balance; anytime glutamate levels start to build up too high, then it is converted**

to GABA to calm things down. Google "conversion of glutamate to GABA."

How about that for an awesome complex process created by God to maintain balance! Yet, to think humans can upset this balance by abusing alcohol and other drugs. It must be displeasing to God.

Don't disappoint God; God can break you free from the alcoholism in your life. Remember his promise: "No temptation has overtaken you but such as is common to man; and God is faithful, who will not allow you to be tempted beyond what you are able, but with the temptation will provide you with the way of escape also, so that you will be able to endure it" (1 Corinthians 10:13 NASB). Also, "Trust in the Lord with all your heart and do not lean on your own understanding" (Proverbs 3:5 NASB).

NICOTINE THE MOST ABUSED DRUG IN AMERICA

Until 2019 vaping nicotine was seemingly harmless as it was a recommended method of tapering off nicotine as an aid to quit smoking tobacco. Vaping has become widely used for much more than just an aid for reducing tobacco use in America; nicotine has become an addiction, called "the most abused drug in America," by millions under eighteen years old who would never have started using tobacco. The CDC reported on September 12, 2019, that a federal survey shows 27.5 percent of high school students have used an e-cigarette in the past thirty days—over five million students. The FDA regulates electronic nicotine delivery systems (ENDS) as a tobacco product, which requires retailers to only sell these products to customers age twenty-one and older. Several cities and states had increased the legal age to purchase ENDS to age twenty-one before the federal government did in 2020. Google "FDA youth restrictions for nicotine vaping."

It will not surprise me if the FDA accumulates more data

on the long-term health risks for adults and restricts the use of ENDS more in the future. I say this because of my review of the literature about nicotine when doing alcohol, tobacco, and other drug (ATOD) use prevention more than twenty-five years ago. In 2019 there have been hundreds acutely affected by a severe lung illness from using ENDS—sometimes with other chemicals—resulting in hospitalization of more than one thousand people. There had been prolonged irreversible lung damage in many with the death of more than forty people by November 2019, and the numbers were increasing each month.

On October 16, 2019, a Michigan teenager, age seventeen, underwent a double-lung transplant as a direct result of vaping. One causative factor found in nearly every marijuana vaping product, Vitamin E acetate, has been identified. It was being added as a thickening agent to dilute the cannabis oil.

I believe plenty of evidence shows that nicotine is absorbed through the oral mucosa and lungs into the bloodstream, which stimulates the adrenal glands to release cortisol, adrenalin, and norepinephrine (NE) into the bloodstream. Blood also carries the nicotine to the brain, where it immediately results in the release of dopamine (D) and norepinephrine (NE) in synaptic spaces affecting the brain creating a feeling of well-being and anxiety relief. These neurotransmitters are responsible for the pleasure response—a feeling of well-being, confidence, and elations. Dopamine is the feel-good neurotransmitter thought to be responsible for causing a user to want to do it again. Increased NE creates feelings of elation. This feeling of well-being causes addiction and is providing a lifelong funneling of money into the vaping industry for young and old people alike. Withdrawal from nicotine eliminates the artificial increase in the good feelings. Withdrawal from nicotine causes irritability, anxiety, and mood-related symptoms including depression and insomnia.

"Whether you're smoking traditional cigarettes or e-cigarettes, you're still being exposed to nicotine, which can have harmful effects on your immune system. Nicotine increases cortisol levels, while reducing B cell antibody formation and T cells' response to antigens," explains Dr. Spangler June 10, 2015.

Cortisol is a protein synthesis inhibitor. This has adverse effects on the immune system cells' ability to fight viral and bacterial infections. Many cancer treatment chemicals are immune suppressant drugs because they are also protein synthesis inhibitors. Protein synthesis inhibition by cancer treatment chemicals could contribute to cognitive impairment from chemotherapy, called chemo brain or chemo brain fog, by inhibiting the synthesis of neurotransmitters in the brain.

It is widely accepted that tobacco use affects the gingival sulcus lining around the teeth by suppressing the white blood cells that fight bacteria on the teeth resulting in more periodontal disease. This destruction causes gingival recession, exposed roots, increased root sensitivity, bone loss, and loss of teeth.

Chronic use of ENDS with its increased cortisol and increases in the adrenalin and NE simulates a chronic low-grade stress response in the body. Surely everyone knows that chronic stress is an unhealthy condition causing many ills of its own.

Vaping is a relatively new phenomenon, and not enough time has passed to see the effects of nicotine alone on the immune system and in vascular diseases. A recent study of 160,000 people indicated that people who smoke cigarettes and vape have two times more the risk of stroke than those who only smoke cigarettes. Without conclusive research at the cellular level and with animals, it may take many years for conclusive epidemiological studies to prove the association of vaping nicotine with these health risks.

Nicotine, which increases NE in the brain acting similarly as antidepressants, is hypothesized as being used by many—more in the northern states and Alaska—to self-medicate for seasonal affective disorder (SAD). SAD is a depression caused by decreased sunlight in winter months. It's ironic that nicotine would be used for SAD, because withdrawal from nicotine can also cause depression, which promotes continued use of tobacco and nicotine vaping.

Bupropion (Wellbutrin) is the only drug approved by the FDA for SAD; it increases NE and D release at the presynaptic membrane (see figure 2, Chapter 4). Bupropion is usually started in the fall ahead of the shorter winter months because it may take three to four weeks to work.

Nicotine and bupropion only help people feel better temporarily, but the Lord is the only way for true everlasting peace. Jesus said in John 14:27 (NASB), "Peace I leave with you; My peace I give to you; not as the world gives do I give to you. Do not let your heart be troubled, nor let it be fearful."

Bupropion is also an antagonist at nicotinic receptors, meaning it inhibits the stimulation of nerve cells by nicotine—thus decreasing the reward system of nicotine. These actions are more mildly stimulating than nicotine.

This reminds me of a telephone conversation I had in the early 1990s with Dr. Robert Mecklenberg, retired admiral and previous director of the IHS Dental Program. After retirement he was providing national continuing dental education presentations to train private dentists in the use of tobacco cessation programs for their patients. The main pharmacologic aid available then was the nicotine patch and nicotine gum used to wean patients off tobacco. When I asked how he was going to manage the depression some people experienced when finally withdrawing from nicotine, he said, "I never heard of depression after quitting tobacco."

I said, "Withdrawal from nicotine results in a relative decrease in the NE and D and can cause depression and make them want to continue using tobacco." I suggested prescribing an antidepressant, which increases NE and D temporarily while the brain readjusts to withdrawal. But maybe he thought having a dentist prescribe an antidepressant would have been a radical idea. I don't believe he ever incorporated the idea in his presentations. It was a unique idea for tobacco cessation programs. A Wellbutrin (bupropion) was remarketed in 1989 and about 1995 began to be used as a tobacco cessation agent—now the only antidepressant approved by the FDA for tobacco cessation. Zyban (bupropion) was later marketed for smoking cessation.

A new drug, CHANTIX[R], increases NE as bupropion does, and it also blocks nicotine receptors. It was marketed specifically for tobacco cessation and began to be widely promoted on TV. Remember the cute "It's tough to quit cold turkey. CHANTIX[R] can help you quit slow turkey" advertisements in 2019. Go to URL www.mayoclinic.org/diseases-conditions/nicotine-dependence/ diagnosis-treatment/drc-20351590.

It is also known that smoking increases the risk of dying from heart and blood vessel (cardiovascular) disease, including heart attack and stroke. It is my opinion that this results from the effects of nicotine circulating in the vascular system as much as it possibly does from other chemicals in tobacco smoke that contact the lung tissue—another reason for concern about vaping nicotine.

Lung tissue is by far the main tissue directly affected by smoking, causing lung cancer and chronic obstructive pulmonary disease (CPOD). Lung cancer attributed to smokeless tobacco use is uncommon. Smokeless tobacco has been promoted as a safe substitute for smoking because it doesn't cause lung cancer; however, it causes oral cancer as well as being associated with an increased risk for heart disease and strokes. The increase risk for breast cancer in women who smoke is possibly also related to the effects of nicotine on the immune system and not the smoke, which does not contact breast tissue directly like it does lung tissue.

"Tobacco use causes a multitude of serious health problems, besides increased risks for heart disease and strokes, which are cancer, lung diseases, diabetes, and COPD, which includes emphysema and chronic bronchitis. Smoking also increases risk for tuberculosis, certain eye diseases, and problems of the immune system, including rheumatoid arthritis." Google "tobacco use and health problems."

As a student at the UKCD in 1966 I had seen many pathology slides of patients with large cancerous lesions in their mouths; myself and all my classmates wondered why patients would ignore something that gross for so long. I thought it was just because this was the way things were in the 1960s, but by the 1990s, thirty years later, things had still not changed. People continue to ignore warning signs and symptoms of oral cancer.

I was amazed in the 1990s when I saw an elderly female patient in my chair with an ulcerated growth under the tongue the size of a grape just behind the lower front teeth. This patient had no good reason for ignoring it for so long. Bilateral palpable lymph nodes were in her neck, an ominous sign that the cancer had spread from the local site.

Another patient had a large brown crusted lesion on the lower lip that had been there for more than six months, and I was told by the patient that it was a fever blister. The patient failed several appointments for a biopsy of the lesion and ignored warnings of consequential death for several months until there were also swollen cervical lymph nodes—a sign of metastasis to other parts of the body.

Both these lesions were probably squamous cell carcinomas usually associated with tobacco use or in the case of the lip lesion possibly also excessive exposure to sunlight without sunscreen protection. The problem of ignoring warning signs of oral cancer still exists today, maybe because of a lack of awareness of warning symptoms or other reasons that I do not understand.

It's estimated that forty thousand people in the United States. received a diagnosis of oral cancer in 2014. According to the American Cancer Society, men face twice the risk of developing oral cancer as women, and men over fifty face the greatest risk.

An example of an exception to this statistic about oral cancer being more common for men over fifty is the nineteen-year-old high school athlete from Ada, Oklahoma, who died of oral cancer from using smokeless tobacco. You can find a video of the tragic story of Sean Marsee, the outstanding track star from Ada, Oklahoma, who died of oral cancer at the age of nineteen in 1984 by Googling "Sean Marsee story video." Sean had won twenty-eight track medals in the 400-meter relay while running the anchor leg for Talihina High School. He was diagnosed at the age of eighteen after showing his mother an ugly sore on his tongue. He had started using smokeless tobacco when he was twelve years old. He thought it was harmless because high-profile sports stars were using and marketing smokeless tobacco. Other boys on the track team were dipping, and the coach knew but didn't seem to care. For another presentation by a young oral cancer survivor, Google "WHAT presents 'experience with tobacco' YouTube."

The most common risk factors for oral cancer are tobacco use, excessive alcohol use, excessive exposure to sunlight, and human papilloma virus (HPV). Using both alcohol and tobacco together increases the risk even more because of a synergistic effect.

The most common symptoms of oral cancer include:

- Swellings/thickenings, lumps or bumps, rough spots/crusts/or eroded areas on the lips, gums, or other areas inside the mouth
- The development of velvety white, red, or speckled (white and red patches in the mouth)
- Unexplained bleeding in the mouth
- Unexplained numbness, loss of feeling, or pain/tenderness in any area of the face, mouth, or neck
- Persistent sores on the face, neck, or mouth that bleed easily and/or do not heal within two weeks
- A soreness or feeling that something is caught in the back of the throat
- Difficulty chewing or swallowing, speaking, or moving the jaw or tongue

- Hoarseness, chronic sore throat, or change in voice
- Ear pain
- A change in the way your teeth or dentures fit together
- Dramatic weight loss

Go to www.webmd.com/oral-health/guide/oral-cancer#1.

Every dentist, regardless of specialty, should be doing an oral cancer screening exam and documenting it in your record at least once each year. You should hear them say, "The soft tissue is within normal limits (WNL)," or receive a comment about their findings. If they are not doing this, you should ask them why not. If they are doing it, you should thank them for being conscientious and concerned about your overall health and not just about your teeth. They should also be taking and documenting your blood pressure and updating your medical history and medications at each visit.

I emphasize oral cancer screening because not all dentists are performing this screening on all patients as they should. "Researchers at Brigham and Women's Hospital in Boston looked at a nationally representative sampling of civilian, noninstitutionalized individuals in the United State from 2011 to 2016 who had seen a dentist in the previous two years. Patients age thirty and over self-reported if they had received an intraoral or extraoral exam with screening. Of these individuals, 37.6 percent reported receiving an intraoral exam and cancer screening, while 31.3 percent reported receiving an extraoral exam and screening.[17]

To reduce the risk for oral cancer, use sunscreen on your lips with a SPF of at least 45 and when there is frequent continuous exposure to the sun, wear a wide-brimmed hat. Don't consume alcohol frequently or excessively. Don't smoke or chew tobacco products. Young boys and girls can be vaccinated for HPV preferably before puberty. Get regular dental checkups with oral cancer screening.

My patient who didn't seem to want treatment was a most

unusual patient. The case reminds me of someone who fails to respond after receiving the gospel of Jesus Christ and the plan of salvation. Both situations can be a matter of life or death—one concerns eternal life.

As Christians we are commanded by God to be good disciples for Christ and witness to unbelievers. "Go therefore and make disciples of all the nations, baptizing them in the name of the Father and the Son and the Holy spirit, teaching them to observe all that I commanded you; and lo, I am with you always, even to the end of the age" (Matthew 28:19–20 NASB). Witnessing is an obligation because of God's demonstrated love for us, but it is the responsibility of the person hearing the gospel to accept the grace of Jesus Christ as their Lord and Savior. The person witnessing cannot save the person hearing the gospel of Jesus Christ. Only they can do that by answering God's call when He knocks at their door. Revelation 3:20–22 (NASB) reads: "'Behold, I stand at the door and knock; if anyone hears my voice and opens the door, I will come in to him and will dine with him, and he with Me. He who overcomes, I will grant to Him to sit down with Me on My throne, as I also overcame and sat down with My Father on His throne. He who has an ear, let him hear what the Spirit says to the churches.'"

Every US state has a telephone tobacco quit line. For options in your state, call 800-Quit-Now (800-784-8669). By Googling "Nicotine Anonymous" you can find many references to a twelve-step program more spiritually oriented for quitting nicotine as with Alcoholics Anonymous. Although I recognize the value of spiritual emphasis in this program, I also believe it may require pharmacologic assistance in a significant number of individuals.

BENZODIAZEPINES (BENZOS) AND
UNEXPECTED PROBLEMS

A problem with benzodiazepines (benzos) is emerging as possibly the next prescription drug crisis. The problems with these antianxiety drugs like Ativan, Klonopin, Xanax, Valium, Librium, and hundreds of others, whose use began with Valium in the early 1960s, are now pandemic worldwide with Japan having the most prescribed per capita. Originally thought not to be addictive, Valium was promoted as being safe and effective in the United States because it did not cause death from respiratory depression as seen with higher doses of opioids. It was prescribed for millions of anxious housewives and stressed men. That opinion about it not being addictive changed after several years of experience.

Valium became the most prescribed drug in the whole world and the most profitable drug prescribed in the United States. From 1996 until 2013 usage went from eight million to fourteen million people in the United States. Benzos like Valium, Ativan, Klonopin, Xanax, and others were prescribed for simple things like sleep and ordinary daily stress as well as for anxiety for longer than the recommended two to six weeks—many for years at a time. Drug overdose deaths involving benzos by opioid involvement rose from 1,135 in 1999 to 11,537 in 2017. They were involved in about 30 percent of prescription drug overdose deaths in 2013, second only to opioids, which were involved in 70 percent of overdose deaths according to the Centers for Disease Control and Prevention (CDC). Risk for overdose death from benzos is generally low to moderate but higher when used with alcohol and other drugs like opioids. Google "the next US drug epidemic as of 2019."

When people try to quit abruptly without tapering over the recommended four-week period, depending on the dosage and duration, severe problems can result. Withdrawal can result in tremors, increased anxiety, insomnia, difficulty walking, sensations of vibrating on their insides, electrical tingling, and numbness in limbs, tinnitus (ringing in the ears), muscle pain in the jaws and back of the neck, disabilities from work, depression, and suicides. It is thought as many as one in five hundred have suicidal actions.

Withdrawal from benzos is considered more difficult than withdrawal from heroin. People have expressed withdrawal as "pure torture," left with the only option of continuing the benzos. Doctors don't seem to know how to help some patients withdraw when recommended tapering methods fail, so internet networks have developed with individuals recommending unproven regimens for quitting. Some have tried tapering as little as one hundredth of their dose daily with four injections per day. But this may take as long as 1.5 years, and the math in calculating dosages is complicated; these are not researched, proven recommended standard withdrawal methods. Not all patients have difficulty withdrawing, but some of those who do can wind up with permanent brain damage. For a reliable quitting protocol and a discussion of benzodiazepines go to "benzo.org.ukashton/manual."

Benzos work to reduce the activity of nerves in the brain and spinal cord by enhancing the effect of the inhibitory neurotransmitter GABA in the amygdala, like alcohol. In short, they slow down the body's central nervous system (CNS) thereby reducing the anxiety. When combined with other meds, benzos can slow the brain's function creating surges in dopamine, a neurotransmitter affecting movement, pleasure, and addiction. Abrupt discontinuance of the benzos results in a rebound effect with severe withdrawal symptoms for many people while the body attempts to readjust to a more normal state.

The takeaway about benzos is not to take them longer than the recommended several weeks.

I have attempted to the best of my ability to increase your understanding of the science related to depression, addiction to drugs, and violence following alcohol intoxication. I've made recommendations for obtaining help for these problems. God makes this instruction available for us because of some very smart people he put on this earth to help us.

But don't be misled because I haven't used as much scripture in these subtitles about ATOD. Don't neglect to ask for help with these problems from Jesus and the Holy Spirit. The Holy Spirit speaks to you through scripture to tell you right from wrong and how to behave.

If you're not a church attendee associated with the body of Christ, find a gospel-teaching church to associate with other Christians. Experience the hope and joy in your heart of serving Jesus Christ and others. If you're already a Christian, don't be wise in your own eyes; pray asking God's help and read the Bible often. He will give you peace. Prescribed drugs can make you feel better, but only God can give you real peace that is everlasting. Read John 14:27 again! "These things I have spoken to you, so that in Me you may have peace. In the world you have tribulation, but take courage; I have overcome the world" (John 16:33 NASB).

If you have an alcohol or substance abuse problem, call 1-800-662-HELP (4357) or go to the Substance Abuse and Mental Health Services Administration (SAMHSA) website at www.findtreatment.samhsa.gov.

PSILOCYBIN AND TREATMENT FOR ALCOHOL AND NICOTINE ADDICTION

The following has not been proven by randomized, double-blind trials using high numbers of patients; however, some studies for using psilocybin (PC), a hallucinogen derived from mushrooms, for treatment of alcoholism began as early as the 1960s with LSD.[18] But studies were ended in the early 1970s by President Nixon. All federal funding was cut off, and PC was classified as a Class III drug primarily because of the negative associations from recreational use of psychedelics (LSD) by the hippy culture. However, "psilocybin is characterized by low physiological toxicity and low abuse liability, as demonstrated by marginal levels of nonhuman drug self-administration."[19]

Several lines of evidence suggest that these classic (5-HT2A) agonist hallucinogens have clinically relevant effects in alcohol and drug addictions. Recent studies have demonstrated that the self-reported "mystical" dimensions of the PC experience (feelings of unity, sacredness, ultimate reality, transcendence of time and space, deeply felt positive mood and ineffability) significantly predict the lasting personal significance of the experience and personality change in normal volunteers receiving PC.

Ten individuals were selected from seventy volunteers with DSM-V diagnosed alcohol dependence to participate in a "Psilocybin-assisted treatment for alcohol dependence: A proof-of-concept study." Abstinence did not increase significantly in the first four weeks of treatment with motivational enhancement therapy (psychosocial- talking intervention focused on changing drinking behavior) without receiving oral PC, but increased significantly following oral administration of PC. Gains were largely maintained at follow-up to thirty-six weeks. No significant treatment-related adverse events happened. Also noted were significant improvements relative to baseline in craving, self-efficacy, and motivation. This article also has many good references from previous studies on this subject.[18]

In another study published in *Neurotherapeutics*, 2017,[19] for addiction, small open-label pilot studies have shown promising success for both tobacco/nicotine and alcohol addiction. The results of one study of treatment-resistant tobacco/nicotine-dependent smokers is noted here.

Fifteen screened participants were given oral doses of PC, 0.29 mg/kg on their target quit date and sometimes a second or third dose of 0.43 mg/kg was administered two and eight weeks respectively after the target quit date depending on the psychedelic response from the initial dose of PC. At six-month follow-up, twelve of the fifteen participants (80 percent) were abstinent from smoking based on biological verification with breath carbon monoxide and urine cotinine results. At a 2.5-year follow-up after their target quit date, nine of fifteen (60 percent) were biologically verified as abstinent.[19] That is an excellent quit rate for any smoking-cessation program.

For mood and anxiety disorders, three controlled trials have suggested that PC may decrease symptoms of depression and anxiety in the context of cancer-related psychiatric distress for at least six months following a single acute administration.[19]

Modest drug-related adverse effects at the time of administering psilocybin were readily managed. There can be some "bad trips." Funding in the United States has yet to support therapeutic psilocybin research, although such support will be important to thoroughly investigate efficacy, safety, and therapeutic mechanisms. Self-administration of psilocybin without professional assistance evaluation, dosing, and monitoring is not recommended.

I recently noted ongoing research studying the safety and effectiveness of psilocybin use at John Hopkins University; Google "john hopkins university psilocybin study."

GUIDANCE AND PROTECTION

MY UNCLE RED'S HELP IN MY LIFE

I will start with my dad's brother, Uncle Red (Charles R. Hazle), just because he is another person who has played such a significant role in my life. Everyone called him "Red," probably because of his red hair. The first memory of Uncle Red is when he gave me an electric American Flyer model train for Christmas when I was five years old. The engine and coal car were very detailed cast metal with white rimmed wheels. It had a small smokestack that puffed white rings of smoke when a drop of special liquid was put into the stack. It was smaller than the Lionel model trains but I thought more detailed and more realistic looking. I kept the train at grandpa and grandma Hazle's house and played with it in the living room and the basement. I built all kinds of obstacles for it to run over and through. My friends and I had lots of fun playing with the train.

Red was drafted into the army in April 1952. He has told me about carrying a BAR (Browning automatic rifle), which weighed more than he did. He had a South Korean boy who carried his ammo. Once he was trapped too close to the enemy line and had to lie in a truck track in the snow all day hiding out of sight from the enemy until dark when he returned to his squad. The minus-forty-degree temperature caused frostbite to his legs. Later in life he had severe discoloration and swelling below his knees from the frostbite, and this affected his mobility. Phyllis, his wife, and I kept encouraging him to go to the Veterans Administration (VA) for several years before he finally went for help. I think he felt getting help from the VA was more like welfare instead of an earned entitlement. They did help him a lot with his legs and other health problems. He found out that frostbite was the most common ailment from the Korean War.

Only two men out of eighteen in his BAR troop returned home from the war. Red was required to stay in the service for only twenty months instead of the usual twenty-four because of his hazardous duty. God was surely watching over him.

When he returned home, he bought a new green 1953 Chevrolet. By that time, with an adjacent building and land becoming available, my grandfather was ready to expand and split the general store, feed store, and implement business between Red and my dad. Red took the feed store, and Dad took the implement business.

Red had told me when I started in the first grade that he would give me fifty cents for every A. I had earned some money before he went into the army, but it was in this new feed store that I can remember going with my report card from school to collect the money. He also told me that if I ever got a whipping at school that he would give me another one when I got home. I never collected for one of those. It was in his new green Chevy that Red took me with his date, Phyllis Wagoner, to see *The Glenn Miller Story* starring Jimmy Stewart, at the Horse Cave drive-in theater south of Phyllis's home.

Red worked hard to succeed at his business of supplying mixed feed to farmers and bagged feed at the store. He had hardware, equipment parts, insecticides, garden seeds, and various other items for sale. He sold flowers, garden plants, and seeds when they were in season. He also sold small engine equipment items like chain saws and weed trimmers and maintained an active repair business for these items. No one had a stronger work ethic than Red all through his life. He especially exemplified this later in life when in his late sixties and seventies he got up at four o'clock in the morning three or four days a week and made a one-hundred-mile round-trip to Louisville, purchasing fresh produce to sell in his store.

When I went to the University of Kentucky, I wasn't allowed to have a car on campus my first year. I had to catch rides for the ninety-mile trip home to Hodgenville to visit family and Donna Clayton, my steady girlfriend, who was still in high school. This worked well, and there was rarely a time that I couldn't find someone to ride with. When the second year came, and I was living off campus in FarmHouse Fraternity, guess who bought me a car? It was Uncle Red. He took me to Hardin Motors in Elizabethtown and bought a 1960 blue hardtop V-8 Chevy. That was in 1964, so it was a nice car. Of course, this was good for my independence at UK and getting around Lexington. I was already thinking about the next year; if Donna went to Georgetown College as planned, I could drive the twenty-five miles to visit her.

It was the next summer that I started working some for Red driving his Hi-Boy sprayer to spray tobacco with insecticide and MH-30. The MH-30 was a sucker control chemical that saved farmers from hand-removing suckers from between the top several leaves and the stalk of each plant after the bloom was removed. The plants were about six feet tall when they were topped and ready to be sprayed. The Hi-Boy was a tall tricycle sprayer with large wheels on each side and one in the front that allows the driver to sit up high and steer. It had booms that opened out and sprayed three rows on each side in addition to the two rows on each side of the seventy-five-gallon tank in the middle.

One spraying job I did was in a part of the county that was very hilly. At that farm I had one patch of tobacco to spray on top of a hill, and then one patch about half a mile down a hill. I was a little concerned about the lower patch because I had noticed the sprayer motor missing sometimes going up even small hills. The other concern was the brake on the front wheel. It worked well moving forward but not as well rolling backward. After finishing the patch on top of the hill, I went down a narrow gravel road that dropped off down a steep hill on one side and had a six-foot ditch on the bank side.

After spraying the bottom patch, I started back up the hill. It wasn't bad until near the top where the grade was a little steeper. The motor sputtered and then died. The sprayer began rolling backward, picking up speed. I had already decided that I would rather crash into the deep ditch than down the steep hillside. I was trying to stay away from the steep drop-off side of the road and get back over to the ditch without going perpendicular into it. By the time I went into the ditch I had picked up enough speed that the abrupt stop of hitting the bottom threw me backward off the seat and onto the boom. I felt a sharp pain in my side and back. It was a fairly good landing for the sprayer except for a bent boom on one side. I didn't feel as if I had any broken bones, just a sore back and side. I was relieved that I had not gone down the steep hillside. I had the farmer bring his tractor and pull me out of the ditch. When I got back to Red's store, I explained how the brake had not worked and asked him if he could improve the motor to prevent stalling out. I didn't believe he could do much about the brake on the front wheel.

There was one more incident that didn't hurt me physically but tore up the sprayer and hurt my pride. The incident happened because of my poor, inattentive driving, and demonstrates something about Red's character. I was out in the Nolin section of LaRue County where several long straight stretches of gravel road were followed by ninety-degree turns. I spotted the most beautiful, fully filled out, golden-leafed tobacco patch that I had sprayed with MH-30 a couple of weeks earlier. It was all the same height. I mean it was perfect. I kept admiring this patch as I was going into one of those sharp turns. Before I knew it, I was in trouble; I was going a little too fast into the curb and was too close to the ditch. When I looked in my rearview mirror the sprayer reminded me of an elephant turned upside down, with the tank its belly, and the wheels its legs sticking straight up. My first thought was what will Red say about this? It was all my fault for being distracted and not paying attention. I was wondering how much damage had been done to the booms and how to upright it. What a mess!

Well, when we were all back at the store, and the mess was straightened out, Red never chewed me out or got angry with me as I had expected. Maybe he knew that I was embarrassed enough about the incident that he didn't need to say more. It was a stupid lack of attention that could have been avoided. I shouldn't have expected Red to be angry because I can't remember Red ever losing his temper with anyone. I can remember him speaking to employees with sternness but not anger—and red-headed people are supposed to have a temper. If Red ever had a temper, he had learned to control it well. Red was that way with employees and even with the mayor of Hodgenville that harassed him for more than a year about fixing up his large old stable barn across the street from the feed store. Red had been mayor himself some years before, and he seemed to take the harassment as sort of a game between him and the mayor. Red eventually fixed up the old stable barn a few years later.

Red loved UK basketball and football. He had managed to get on the list for six season tickets for UK basketball and football games. Of course, this required annual donations to UK for maintaining his status as a season ticket holder. I know Red has donated more money to UK than I ever have as an alumnus—about $100,000---just to be able to purchase tickets every year. Local UK fans were always coming into Red's store and asking if he had any extra tickets to the games. He used to take me to watch the annual Notre Dame and UK game at Louisville when Digger Phelps was coaching Notre Dame. These were not considered home games, thus not part of the season tickets, and I don't know how he got those. UK basketball games were always sold out at Rupp Arena, and tickets were hard to get and very expensive. For many years UK had the highest average attendance at basketball games in the NCAA—more than twenty-three thousand. When Donna and I were living in Texas, North Dakota, and Oklahoma, and came home for Christmas, Red always had UK basketball tickets for us.

When Red got older and couldn't attend the games, he was allowed a one-time pass of the season tickets on to two of his children, Chuck and Kathy. They continued to help me with tickets around Christmas time when I was in Kentucky. When not going to the games I would always go to Red's house and watch UK play basketball or football on TV. Sometimes Red would pull out his Hodgenville High School basketball pictures for me to see. He told me that a recruiter from the University of North Carolina (UNC) once came down to the dressing room after a game and asked him to play basketball at UNC.

I'd have to say my Uncle Red and Grandpa Hazle were "cut from the same cloth." In his later years, every time I'd say goodbye to Red before returning to Oklahoma, he'd get teary-eyed. I knew that he was thinking the same thing that Grandpa Hazle was thinking when that used to happen to him. They knew it might be the last time we could see each other alive. One morning I woke up thinking about all the things Red had done for me, and I began to get teary-eyed. I got up and wrote him a letter thanking him for everything that I could think of. Red told me and Phyllis one day that he wanted me to have a part in his funeral. I said I would be glad to.

Red and Grandpa are alike in another way. Together they sent me weekly spending money through the years I attended UK until I was married in 1967. Even when I worked part time in research for one of the College of Agriculture professors for a year and a half, they still sent money. This allowed me to spend more time studying and doing well every year at UK. I asked Red about the money one time, and all he said was, "Oh, it wasn't much, just some money from the cigarette vending machine in the store." Another gift that Uncle Red gave to Donna and me was a paid vacation at a hotel on Miami Beach for several days. He had been awarded this by one of his suppliers for outstanding sales. He also gave us tickets to the Kentucky Derby one year. If Red and Grandpa Hazle weren't sent by the providence of God to help me throughout my lifetime, I don't know what else to call it.

I'm not sure why Red favored me so much, but the things Red did for me tell you a lot about how Red related with so many people. First, Red was a Christian. Red was a proud but grateful man. He loved God and told me more than once how thankful he was to have returned home from the war. He said he sometimes would look around church at his family of children and grandchildren and think of all the men in his group that had not been able to return home and have families—that was sixteen out of the eighteen in his troop. That had to have been the providence of God for Red. Red respected all persons regardless of their socioeconomic status or race. I watched him treat all people without prejudice when they came into his store. Red loved people. Red was faithful to and protected his wife and family so they could have a good life. There will never be another Uncle Red.

THE POWER AND BLESSING OF A CHRISTIAN WIFE

I could not leave out the most important person in my life since I left my family and married Donna Sue Clayton fifty-three years ago. Finding and living with a Christian woman has been another blessing that God provided to shelter me.

It was my grandfather who took me to a new go-cart track near Hodgenville. When I first arrived at the track, I saw this girl with long, silky, light brown hair blowing in the wind. She was sliding gracefully around the curves and gunning the go-cart on the straightaways. At fourteen years old, I was attracted to this thirteen-year-old girl, the daughter of the track's owner. When she was in the eighth grade all those classes were moved to the new LaRue County High School (LCHS). I saw her off and on in the hallway that year, and the next year we were in band and student council together. But it wasn't until I was seventeen that I asked her for a date.

The summer of 1962 I went to Europe for six weeks. When school started that fall, I noticed Donna even more, because she marched in front of me in the LCHS marching band. She was rank leader for the clarinets, and I marched directly behind her as rank leader for trumpets. It was that fall semester of my senior year that I finally asked her for a date one evening after a band trip. That night, her mom let us double-date with her sister and one of my classmates, W.C. Blanton. On our first date we went to see a Three Stooges movie in Hodgenville and have been together ever since.

Donna was from a Christian family and was active in the Girls Auxiliary, a counterpart to the Royal Ambassadors in the Baptist church. We dated more that school year and went to the prom together my senior year. I spent many summer evenings at her house after working at farm jobs during the day. I liked her parents, and our families were compatible. We dated heavily that summer, to drive-in theaters, hayrides, picnics, and church functions.

In the fall of 1963, I attended the University of Kentucky (UK) ninety miles away in Lexington. Staying together seemed difficult because of our separation. We both lacked experience at dating others. We were going steady, which meant that Donna wore my high school ring and didn't date anyone else. There was some pressure from friends and adults to break up and date others because we were young. Going steady was fashionable in the early 1960s. We did try a period of dating others for a short time—I believe just so we could say we did it. I didn't really want to be with anyone else.

We dated for two more years while she was in high school and wrote each other often. I came home as often as I could. She graduated in 1965 and enrolled in Georgetown College twenty-five miles from UK for her first year. I made many trips to Georgetown in the 1960 Chevy that Uncle Red had bought me. Then Donna transferred to UK to take the required courses for her physical therapy major. We were married August 18, 1967. I was a second-year dental student, and Donna was just beginning her third year of college. We had a lot of help from our families. My dad paid for my tuition, and Donna's parents paid for her tuition that first year of marriage. My grandfather would load up our car with groceries from his general store each weekend we were home, and Red would send some spending money from the cigarette vending machine. The second year Donna was awarded a VA student loan, which covered her tuition and our housing and gave us a little extra spending money. The loan would be forgiven if she worked for a hospital that did rehabilitation after she graduated. I had a student loan and scholarship money to help with my tuition, and we both worked full-time during the summers. We survived until Donna graduated and began working in 1969.

THE TRANSFER TO GALVESTON,
TEXAS, IN THE USPHS

After I graduated in 1970, we moved to Galveston, Texas. I was a commissioned officer in the USPHS in a general dental practice residency. Donna worked for the University of Texas Medical Branch in Galveston. Our time in Galveston was more like a vacation, with both of us out of school and making spending money. We enjoyed the coastal activities, the good seafood, gulf party fishing trips on the *Texan*, the beach, and traveling to Mexico. It was late one afternoon when we returned from a deep-sea fishing trip that we saw people boarding up their windows and leaving town. A hurricane was headed straight for Galveston. Being in the USPHS, I had to remain on the island. We escaped when the hurricane turned northeast during the night. God had protected us again.

THE TRANSFER TO FORT YATES,
NORTH DAKOTA IN 1971

Still a commissioned officer in the USPHS, I joined the IHS division of the Department of Health Education and Welfare after my general practice residency in Galveston. On July 1, 1971, we transferred to Fort Yates, North Dakota, a town that was made an island in Lake Oahe by the damming of the Missouri River at Pierre, South Dakota; it was connected to the mainland by a causeway. In Fort Yates it began snowing around Halloween and the 150-mile-long lake that surrounded us didn't thaw until May.

In September of our first year there I almost missed taking Donna to the hospital in Bismarck in time for the birth of our first child. It was about 1:30 p.m. on a Saturday. I had been dove hunting that morning and was getting back into my car after lunch for more hunting that afternoon. It started sprinkling rain on my windshield, so I went back inside. When I came back into the house Donna remarked that water had begun running down her leg. She began to feel strange and went to lie down. It was about two weeks before her due date, and she had just seen her obstetrician earlier that week. Nevertheless, we decided to call the doctor and were told to leave for the hospital soon. I drove seventy-five miles to the hospital in Bismarck, and a healthy Wendy Julann was born by eight o'clock that evening. Had I gone dove hunting I might not have returned home till about 6:00 p.m. Thank God for the rain on my windshield that day. God is always in control. Job 37:5–6 (NIV) reads: "God's voice thunders in marvelous ways; He says to the snow, 'Fall on the earth,' and to the rain shower, 'Be a mighty downpour.'"

I enjoyed working in the two-chair dental clinic in Fort Yates, spending most of my time doing pediatric dentistry and seeing adult patients with urgent needs. One dental assistant, Doris Jacobsen, was experienced and outstanding to work with. The other younger one was somewhat of a management problem for me at times, but we survived and got the job done together.

School programs required oral hygiene and preventive dentistry program planning. We had area dental meetings to attend in the summer of 1971 and 1972 in Aberdeen, South Dakota. It was by this time in the summer that I was experiencing some dysthymia and had uneasy feelings about my confidence. The second year was worse than the first. The first meeting in 1971 was soon after my transfer from Galveston. I was still beaming with confidence from my residency and had not yet had any problems in my new assignment.

I enjoyed my work at the Indian Hospital in Fort Yates and became good friends with the two pharmacists, Mike Brown and Jim May, and one Native American young man. We enjoyed hunting and fishing several times each week around Fort Yates. Donna also became good friends with many of the other commissioned officers' wives and enjoyed most everything about North Dakota except the severe cold and my being gone hunting so much. She did become very ill in early 1972 and had to undergo surgery in Bismark related to complications of Crohn's disease, which wasn't even diagnosed at that time. Mainly due to being tired of the cold weather and to advance my career in the USPHS, I put in for a transfer and in February 1973 was assigned as chief of a large IHS Service Unit Dental Program at the W. W. Hastings Indian Hospital in Tahlequah, Oklahoma.

DONNA'S THREE MAJOR SURGERIES

Donna had three major surgeries between 1972 and 1974. The first was mentioned previously and happened while we were in North Dakota. After our transfer to Tahlequah and several more bouts with severe pain and dehydration, she was diagnosed with Crohn's disease. Despite medications and close supervision by her gastroenterologist, Donna suffered a perforated colon in early 1973. We had to rush back to Tulsa from Kentucky because of her severe abdominal pain. She was taken directly to St. Francis Hospital where they did surgery for a bowel abscess that resulted in having most of her large intestine removed. The surgery also resulted in a temporary colostomy, which was reversed six months later.

She recovered well, and our second daughter, Angela Christine, was born at Muskogee General Hospital on September 12, 1975. Also during that period I was fighting depression and was admitted for treatment in mid-October 1975. Through all her medical problems, childbirth, and my depression, Donna never complained. Her faith in God grew stronger. Her prayers for healing were answered in a miraculous manner. She has not had any symptoms of Crohn's disease since the last surgery in 1974 and is still very physically active playing tennis and pickleball.

She has always been a model Christian wife and very active in every church we have attended. She has supported me during my depressions. She has been the ideal Christian mother of our children and grandchildren. During every move of my USPHS career she has always said, "I'll go where you want to go." Several experiences have indicated to me that God has been watching over Donna. Her prayers for healing have been answered. She demonstrates the "purity and reverence" as described by Peter in 1 Peter 3:2 (NIV): "Wives in the same way be submissive to your husbands so that, if any of them do not believe the word, they may be won over without talk by the behavior of their wives, when they see the purity and reverence of their lives."

God put me in contact with a virtuous woman as described in Proverbs 31:10–12 (NIV): "A wife of noble character who can find? She is worth far more than rubies. Her husband has full confidence in her and lacks nothing of value. She brings him good, not harm, all the days of her life." "Enjoy life with the woman you love all the days of your fleeting life which He has given to you under the sun; for this is your reward in life and your toil in which you have labored under the sun" (Ecclesiastes 9:9 NASB).

POOR PLANNING FOR A RIVER FLOAT TRIP

In all of Psalm 91 we are told of God's protective care for us in several ways if we call on his name. Here is one example in Psalm 91:9–10: "If you make the Most High your dwelling—even the Lord, who is my refuge—then no harm will befall you, no disaster will come near your tent." There have been several times in my life when God has protected Donna and me from harm. Some to me seem possible only through the providence of God because the timing resulted in an intersecting of events that would have had very low odds of occurring by chance. This is one of those events.

During the summer of 1973, when Donna's sister and husband were visiting us in Tahlequah from St. Louis, we planned a float trip down the Illinois River using my fourteen-foot flat-bottom boat. We left one car at Echota landing along state Highway 10 and drove up the river about three miles. We put in at 1:00 p.m. expecting to be back down to Echota at about 5:00 p.m. where we would load up and drive back upriver to pick up the other car.

We were having fun floating down the river, and about six I'd begun to wonder where Echota landing was. There hadn't been many people along the banks for a while, nor were there any other canoe floaters except for one exhausted man and his young daughter on a fiberglass paddleboard. He asked if he could ride in our boat because he was so tired. We agreed, and a couple of us got out to float on his paddleboard, which looked like a surfboard.

The man told us he was supposed to meet his wife at the Highway 51 bridge, which was another two to three miles down the river from Echota landing. We asked some people standing on the bank how far it was to Echota, and they told us that Echota landing was twelve miles down the river. They said it was about six miles to walk out to Highway 10 from where we were. They also told us about a steep mudbank at a sharp turn in the river that came close to a gravel road on the east side of the river. What neither we nor the worn-out man had known about was the large horseshoe loop in the river between our points of departure and destinations. I had never heard stories about it, and I hadn't looked at a map.

It would be dark soon, and thunderheads and lightning were moving towards us. Donna had been having severe pains in her side for a couple of hours, which we assumed were related to her Crohn's disease. The thunderheads and lightening appeared to be getting closer as the sun was setting, and the sky was turning darker.

We came to a sharp bend and saw a mudbank that we thought was the bank the people had told us about. The stranger and I grabbed some roots sticking out of the mud and climbed up the fifteen-foot bank. We topped the bank and began walking across the weedy bottomland.

My new friend began yelling, "There goes my truck! There's my wife."

We both took off yelling and running as fast as we could in hopes of catching the truck before it went out of sight. His wife glanced our way, and the truck stopped. We walked the rest of the way to the truck and began to discuss our stories with her. She'd been waiting at the Highway 51 bridge and mentioned to someone that her husband was overdue for arrival at the bridge. They had told her about the large horseshoe loop in the river. They also told her about the small gravel road that went on the east side of the river and passed near the bend in the river. We had arrived at the bend at the same time.

We pulled the boat out of the river and loaded the boat and surfboard on top of the camper and strapped them down just before the rain started. We all rode back to our car in a thunderstorm, staying safe and dry inside his camper. We were all thankful.

The fact that we had been told about the mudbank near a gravel road by the only people that we had seen after we entered the horseshoe bend surely was a God thing. That our new friend's wife had also been told about the gravel road coming within two hundred yards of the river bend on the east side was fortunate. That she had driven up the road and intercepted us at the very same time that we climbed up the riverbank was another piece of the puzzle that God made fit. That we had picked up the stranger and his daughter was a God thing for all of us. I think all these events had to be the providence of God. I always thought that my wife was better at having her prayers answered than I was, and she was probably praying hard that evening.

A NEAR MISS WITH A LOG IN THE VERDIGRIS RIVER

This December duck hunting trip was in the late 1990s. My friends Lorn Rohr, Bob Newlon, and I were going down a foggy Verdigris river below the Highway 60 bridge about an hour before sunrise in my semi-v sixteen-foot aluminum boat. I had the throttle on my 25 hp Johnson wide open. We had the spotlight turned off because we could see the river better in the moonlight—we thought.

We were approaching the big ninety-degree right turn in the river. I was thinking that I was close enough to the left bank where the channel of the river was and clear of the shallow water to the right side when Lorn yelled out, "Log!" I quickly steered the boat to the left, but just as it started in that direction there was a loud thump and the front of the boat shifted to the left abruptly. I knew that it felt like a glancing blow to the bow. We stopped to check things out. There was no water leaking in the boat, but a pointed stub had made an indent three inches long by one-half inch deep in the aluminum bow. We went back to see what we had hit. The large mud-lodged log had some broken off limbs three feet long and four inches in diameter with one coming to a point that protruded about twelve inches high out toward the river channel. That could have been a real disaster if the boat had been to the right about two feet more. Had we hit the log we might have been thrown out of the boat into the cold water. Maybe God was watching over us that morning.

TERRY WHITFIELD AND SOME SECRET WHITE BASS

In 1979 I became good friends with one of my patients, Terry Whitfield, with whom I hunted and fished many times for seventeen years. Terry was from Vinita, Oklahoma, and wanted to do some early spring white bass fishing. Terry said he knew where to catch some on Big Cabin Creek, but we would have to take a boat to get to the spot. He said the landowners on each side of the creek would not allow fishing or trespassing on their land, but we could still fish in a boat. There was a bridge up the river near this fishing spot where we put our boat into the water. This was a cool day in March, and snow flurries had been predicted for that day.

We did get my fourteen-foot Lonestar boat with a 9.5 hp motor in the water without much trouble, from the bank below the bridge. The creek was up four feet that day. As we headed downstream, I spotted a logjam blocking the creek except for a twelve-foot-wide slot on the right side. But a problem was the one-foot-diameter dead tree trunk upright in the middle of the slot. I had to make a quick decision. Did I go to the bank side of the trunk that was covered with protruding tree roots that could hang on the boat, or to the left side where we might possibly get sucked into the logjam by the current? I thought that I could avoid the logjam if I went straight through fast enough, so I chose that side.

I was wrong. I tried to run through the slot, but the current was so strong that it sucked the boat sideways into the logjam. The next thing I knew the side of the boat away from the logjam was sucked under the water, and the left gunnel was at about water level with the bottom of the boat pressed against the logjam. I was standing in chest-deep water on the right gunnel of the boat. I thought of the motor covered with water, so I removed it and walked it about thirty feet over to the bank. Terry was grabbing the tackle boxes and all items that floated his way and throwing them on the bank side above the roots. The current sent everything toward the opening where Terry was standing.

The next problem was how to get the boat out of there. I had built extra foam flotation in the boat and knew that if we could push it into the slot below the log it would probably float. The problem was that we couldn't budge the boat because the water pressure from the current was pushing it against the logjam. We tried with a large limb and rope, using a tree on the bank, making a lever arm to pull the boat forward. We still couldn't move it. We had probably been struggling for thirty minutes when a couple of young men from Vinita came walking down the bank on the logjam side and offered to help. With the lever and three of us pushing, we were able to move the boat into the slot where it could float through the slot. We pulled it up on a gravel bar and drained all the water out and then pulled it up a low bank.

I got the truck and pulled it into the field, loaded the boat on the trailer, and placed the motor back on the boat. We did have some snow flurries that day, and I looked at Terry all cold and wet. What a coincidence that he had on the T-shirt that I had bought him the preceding summer when I was on a consulting trip to Pensacola, Florida, for the Poarch Creek Tribe. It read, "Even the worst day fishing is better than the best day working." I just had to ask him if he still believed that. He gave me that big grin and a little grunt and shook his head. That was Terry Whitfield's signature response.

Thank God for watching over us. Had we fallen out of the boat on the other side and been sucked under the water against the logjam, we could have drowned.

A NEAR ROLL-OVER IN MY SUBURBAN

The duck farm I owned in early 2000 was located on forty acres twenty-six miles north of Claremore. The US Fish and Wildlife Department had assisted me in building some ponds with adjacent shallow-water berms and water control structures to manage the sixteen acres of surface water on the farm. I initially had planned to develop the area for duck hunting, but I decided to expand that plan and also raise ducks for sale.

I had been raising ducks inside a fence around two twenty-by-forty-foot ponds adjacent to each other. The litter accumulating in the ponds was becoming a problem even with circulating fresh water from an adjacent large pond. I was in the process of purchasing materials for a larger fifty-by-one hundred-foot pen on dry land. Angie, my youngest daughter at twenty-five, had asked if she could go with me to see the duck farm sometime. I told her when I would be going, and she agreed to meet me at my house on that day.

A friend had loaned me his four-wheel tandem trailer, and I went around town picking up five six-inch-by-eight-foot posts, about fifty T-posts, and fifteen bags of Quikrete mix. I instructed the last loaders not to put the heavy bags of Quikrete mix near the back of the trailer to reduce the weight in that area as much as possible. I strapped everything down, picked up Angie, and took off to the duck farm.

We got to the north side of Claremore just past the Baker Hughes Company where the speed limit increased to 65 mph, and we began to pick up speed. Somewhere around 55 mph the trailer began to sway, and I took my foot off the gas pedal. The trailer was already beginning to make wider sways to the left and right. I could see it going into the left lane beside me. I cut the Suburban in that direction. Then it went back to the right. I was turning to the right, but this time the trailer pulled the Suburban sideways. From there it went back to the left, and I cut that direction, and it pulled the Suburban sideways again. It felt almost perpendicular to the road, and we were sliding sideways down the highway. The trailer went back to the right but not as much. We were finally slowing down enough that I thought I could apply the brakes. When the trailer was back behind me, I braked. There was a jolt of the Suburban and skidding of trailer tires. In my mirrors I saw one bag of Quikrete mix thrown onto the pavement behind me by the sudden whiplash of the trailer, and then another flying into the ditch on the right side as the trailer whipped back around for the last time. I pulled off the road and picked up the bag of Quikrete mix in the highway. Surprisingly it was not split open very much, but the one in the ditch was ripped open and about half empty.

Through all this, no cars had been near us in the two northbound lanes of route 66 highway. Praise God for that. I was also thinking how thankful I was that I had just changed the shocks on the Suburban within the last two months. After I had repositioned some of the bags of Quikrete mix, I checked the tie-down straps.

I had decided that if I didn't exceed 45 mph maybe we could still make it to the duck farm. As Angie and I got into the Suburban and were buckling our seat belts she turned to me and said, "Dad, do you think God was watching over us today?" I said, "I know God was watching over us today. I think we almost rolled over."

A few years earlier I'd been involved in a similar situation when pulling Lindel's camper trailer while on a hunting trip to Norton, Kansas. It was a little scary when his camper started to sway while a semitrailer truck was passing us on the left side, and we were going under an overpass. I only had the right lane and shoulder for space to maneuver. The degree of sway had not nearly approached the degree that it had when Angie was with me and we were taking up two lanes plus the whole shoulder; but this had given me some experience handling a swaying trailer. Thank you, Lord.

ANOTHER FAVORITE UNCLE

My uncle Herbert Hawkins was someone I regrettably failed to give much credit for a life well lived in my first book. Uncle Herbert was one of three brothers of my mother. He was born in 1917, eight years before my mother. Herbert's father wanted him and his other sons to stay at home and help on the farm. Glenn, Herbert's son, told me how his dad's father, Wilburn, used to whip Herbert and Marvin attempting to "break them." When Herbert was sixteen years old, Wilburn whipped him with a pear-tree sprout and kicked him. Herbert told Glenn that Wilburn had told Logan, his brother, that he could never break Marvin. Marvin, the younger brother, was more independent and owned a motorcycle when he was younger.

Herbert was drafted into the army when he was twenty-four

years old in 1941. After basic training, Herbert was shipped to Karachi in western India, which he said took three months to get there. Because he was familiar with using a farm tractor, Herbert was given a job loading cargo planes that flew over the Hump at the eastern end of the Himalayan Mountains to resupply the Chinese war effort of Chiang Kai-shek and the units of the US Army Air Forces (AAF) based in China. Glenn said Herbert was discharged from the army in 1945 after three and a half years, but six months of that was going and coming by ship.

After Herbert returned from the army, he took farm training classes provided by the government for veterans. He then continued to help his father on the farm. He married Odell Chelf in 1946. They lived with Herbert's father and mother for a while before moving to a house on the farm of his older brother, William Nathan, about eight miles away. While there he worked with William Nathan and continued to help his father. After the birth of his first son, Jerry, he bought an eighty-acre farm and house one-half mile south of where he had grown up. Here Herbert and Odell had two more boys, Joel Henry and Glenn.

Herbert was a Christian man and active in the Bacon Creek Baptist Church near his home. He was a deacon and later the church treasurer. He was well respected in the community for his farm production and clean farming practices; he helped neighbors when they needed help farming. For years he continued to help farm 245 acres his father owned. They raised pigs, cattle, grain crops, tobacco, and alfalfa. Alfalfa later became their main cash crop in the 1960s. They sold alfalfa to buyers in Kentucky, Tennessee, Alabama, Florida, and North Carolina. Herbert was also well known for his productive gardens and beautiful flowers that he and Odell grew at his father's place after his parents' death when he took over the 245-acre farm.

Herbert was always the one I thought never had any problems with depression. He joked around with me. He once said, "Come on down and visit, and we'll open a keg—of nails." But I never knew until I talked with Glenn in 2019, who said Herbert was prescribed Valium by Dr. Bradbury for thirty years beginning in the late 1950s. Glenn said Herbert told his family it was for arthritis, but Glenn thought they were told that because Herbert didn't want them to know it was for anxiety. Glenn said it was very difficult for his dad to get off the Valium, but he did it by cutting the pills in half. In the 1980s Herbert was treated for depression with Sinequan, a tricyclic antidepressant, which Glenn said Herbert told him that it just numbed him and left him in a daze with no emotions. He tried lithium for a short time because that was working well for my mother and me at that time, but it didn't work for Herbert. In 1997 his condition deteriorated. It was in 1998 at the age of eighty-one that he attempted suicide using car exhaust in his closed garage, but Odell had missed him, went to check on him, and found him before any damage was done.

After that he received electro convulsive therapy (ECT) and Wellbutrin. He received several treatments that Glenn said caused some memory loss, which improved after one month. He later received two more ECT treatments, and Glenn said his dad had more memory loss from which he never fully recovered. When I would visit Herbert after that he was never as jovial; he was less talkative, and his face was expressionless. His decrease in facial expressions could have been partially due to his Parkinson's disease.

In 2007 Herbert was diagnosed with Parkinson's disease (PD), but he was never prescribed Sinemet. Glenn said he was prescribed gabapentin for PD by Dr. Godfrey. Herbert had several risk factors for PD among which were living on a farm, being around farm animals, and drinking well water, which are considered potential triggers for anyone with a predisposed heredity risk for PD. Herbert also used two pesticides, paraquat for killing weeds and rotenone for killing fish, that are the two most concerning in the studies of thirty-one pesticides associated with PD. (Google "the relationship between pesticides and Parkinson's" by the 2019

APDA) I can remember Herbert talking several times about using rotenone to clean out the fish in his ponds so he could restock them. Glen said Herbert used Paraquat on his fields when he started using no-till farming practices many years before his death. He also used it to kill weeds in his fence rows. He was probably heavily exposed to Paraquat for several years. Herbert was having much trouble swallowing from the effects of PD a few years before his death in 2011. But he certainly had a life well lived.

Eleven

⚬

THE GIDEONS AND BECOMING A CHRISTIAN

You can learn about the Gideons and their ministry from their website, www.Gideons.org. This website also directs in how to become a Christian. By scrolling down to the bottom of the web page and clicking on "Resources," then selecting "Become a Christian," and "Know Jesus as Your Savior" you will find verses describing the plan of salvation and encouragement to get involved with a local Bible-teaching church. I was called to join the Gideons in 2000.

The Gideons International and the Auxiliary of the Gideons International have a passion of seeing the lost come to the saving grace of our Lord Jesus Christ. That is their mission.

They do this by:

- Personal witnessing
- Distributing God's word at schools, nursing homes, hospitals, prisons, state and county fairs, and more.
- Attending weekly prayer breakfasts where they pray for local pastors and other Gideon and Auxiliary members locally and around the globe.

At local camp meetings and at the annual state and international conventions they learn more about what is happening in the ministry in their state and around the world. They hear about and quite possibly will participate in someone giving their life to Jesus Christ. The Gideons is a flexible ministry where a person can spend only about two hours a month at the camp meeting, or add thirty minutes a week or so at the prayer breakfast, or a little more time doing Bible distributions, church speaking, or some other Gideon or Auxiliary activity.

The Gideons International membership consists of business and professional men, except clergymen, who:

- Believe in the Bible as the inspired Word of God
- Believe in the Lord Jesus Christ as the eternal Son of God
- Have received Him as their personal Savior
- Endeavor to follow Him in their daily lives
- Are members in good standing of an evangelical or protestant church, congregation, or assembly
- Believe in the biblical standard of marriage between one man and woman

Gideons also distribute God's word to:

- Military
- Hotels/motels
- Lawyers
- Men's addiction recovery facilities
- International countries
- And more!

Gideons also speak at churches to share about the ministry activities, manage the Gideon Card program, and raise money for the purchase of Bibles. Gideons serve as an extension of missionary ministry of a church, often going where churches cannot or prefer not to go. Gideon Camps are in over two hundred countries.

Gideons are supported by the Auxiliary membership, who have the same biblical beliefs as their Gideon husbands.

The Auxiliary also distribute God's word to:

- Doctor offices and staff
- Dentist offices and staff
- Veterinary clinics and staff
- Graduating nurses
- Domestic violence shelters
- Pregnancy centers and more

The need for God's word is very great, especially as some are turning to other religions or cults. The persecution of Christians is increasing as demonstrated by the numerous public beheadings of Christians by Islamic state terrorists. President Putin signed laws that took effect July 20, 2016, in Russia prohibiting the sharing of faith in homes, online, or anywhere but recognized church buildings. Special permits must be obtained to distribute literature and materials outside places of worship. The laws place broad limitations on missionary work, including preaching, teaching, and engaging in any activity to recruit people into a religious group. This means "believers will find themselves in exile and subjected to reprisals because of their faith."

Since 1908 Gideons have distributed and placed 2.5 billion scriptures (Bibles and testaments). It took only fourteen years to distribute and place the last one billion. Worldwide about 80 percent of the distributions are to youth.

The plan of salvation is in the back pages of most Gideon New Testaments, which also include Psalms and Proverbs. You may also find help about knowing Jesus from a Christian friend or ministers of many Christian evangelical churches.

BECOMING A FRIEND OF GIDEONS

If you do not wish to become a Gideon or are unable to qualify for membership you can still share in this ministry and share God's Word as a Friend of Gideons: www.gideons.org/friends or call 615.564.5000.

Two options exist to serve in this ministry and receive exclusive benefits and privileges for the year in appreciation for registering as a Friend of Gideons[20].

As a prayer partner:

- e News

  Receive current testimonies and the latest results of scripture distributions Gideons are regularly conducting around the world.

- Gideon Prayer Calendar

  This annual calendar highlights the key prayer needs of our association, from around the globe, with daily focus on specific countries and ministry leadership. It also includes an easy-to-follow daily Bible reading calendar to strengthen your devotional life.

- Invitation to events

    Gideons in your area will keep you informed of specific local events that you can attend.

As a financial partner:

(Also includes all the above benefits as a prayer partner.)

- New Testaments

    The New Testaments are designed with a special Helps section as well as the Plan of Salvation, making it easier for you to witness, as the Lord leads. You will have the option to receive up to twelve New Testaments and will have access to purchase additional copies.

- The Gideon Magazine

    You will receive this full-color publication three times a year. The magazine includes inspiring testimonies, recent scripture distribution stories, and much more.

- *Secret to an Open Door*, by Dave Morel

    In this book, you will find the secret that made the apostle Paul one of the greatest evangelists of all time—a secret that makes personal evangelism easier than most of us ever imagined.

Twelve

MAKING MUSIC MEMORIES

THE BENEFITS OF EDUCATION AND LEARNING

O riginally, I had planned a part 2 for this book called "How to Have Happiness Chemistry," with 105 scientific references. My older daughter, Wendy, who has a Master of Public Health (MPH) degree, suggested that it was too scientific and should be for a different audience. I agreed and decided to at least leave you with a way to stimulate your brain through making music memories—something I have practiced for fifty years.

Learning through education adds more options in your brain from sensory input. The response of your brain to education is the creation of more nerve connections, more neurons, more pathways, and more neurotransmitters in your brain. This results in the creation of more ideas and options from future sensory input from watching, listening, smelling, tasting, and feeling everything in your environment. This provides more options for future decision-making and a way of having an edge over depression through stimulation. The sequela of depression in many cases is suicide. In my estimation and experience, this is a matter of being out of options. Anything you can do to have more creativity and options in your brain will be to your benefit.

Gilbert Highet has conveyed the pleasures of learning in his book *The Immortal Profession*[21] and through his teaching at Columbia University. He sees learning as a natural, inborn, and essential pleasure of humans. He suggests that learning should be fun and occurs not only through books but through travel, arts appreciation and participation, music, and learning crafts. He equates the pleasure of learning with true happiness, which continues to expand throughout life provided one continues to learn. In my opinion, the amount that one can continue to learn is limited by what one has learned in the past.

Learning when one is young not only helps to secure a better job and economic security, it forms a broad foundation for your "bank" of happiness chemistry.

STIMULATION THROUGH MUSIC MEMORIES

People usually have no problem finding means for stimulation in America unless they are depressed. Opportunities are abundant. I don't need to list all the sports participation and observation, music participation and appreciation, vacations, family activities, eating for enjoyment, socializing and partying with friends, and on and on. Some may say, yeah, but these are limited by income. That is true, but no matter what one's income, there are usually popular means of participating in some stimulating activities. It might not be taking a vacation to a tropical island or touring a foreign country, but many local activities and participating on the internet are available.

Working on books is exciting and stimulating for me. I'm anxious to find new information in the literature in Pub Med searches over the internet that supports what I have to say. Sometimes I can hardly wait to read the next abstract in my searches. The new information is often surprising and rewarding. It is always stimulating new ideas, and the internet makes it so much easier and less expensive than it once was.

One of my favorite pastimes for stimulation has been making memories with specific songs and being able to replay those songs many years later and recall the same exciting emotions as I had originally experienced while listening to the music. It is a trait of mine to listen to songs and ignore the lyrics and hear only the music. That may also be the reason that I prefer mostly instrumentals. I may like a beat, rhythm, instrument, tune, or all of those for the event I am experiencing.

A TV show described a man who was using older music for Alzheimer's patients in a nursing home to help stimulate old memories and note their increased responses to the music. These memories were incidental to events in their lives concurrent at the times that the music was popular. Imagine what their response and benefit could have been if they had purposely tried to make memories of the events for specific songs by repetition of those songs earlier in their lives? How well our brains function in the later years of life seems to be out of our control to the extent that 50 percent of people over age eighty-five develop Alzheimer's. This is a disease that "slowly and relentlessly destroys not only memories but all the cognitive process by which people define themselves," according to Catherine Arnst in a review of *The Forgetting Alzheimer's: Portrait of an Epidemic* by David Shenk (*Business Week*, Nov. 26, 2001, p. 21).

I try to match ahead of time if I'm going on a vacation, hunting trip, or tennis tournaments with my grandsons some music that I think goes well with the experience. The secret is to pick "virgin music" for the playlist. By this I mean music that you have not listened to before and had a chance of already having made memories associated with the songs. The second thing is to have a way to listen to the song or playlist repeatedly while you are actively doing whatever you normally do during the event or period of which you want to make the memory. Be prepared to get some complaints from your partner for having the earphones in your ears, or just use one ear and keep the other one open for your partner.

I had noticed that I had incidentally accumulated over the years many memories of past events or periods of time in my life without purposeful effort. These are songs that I associated with high school and college activities and dating my future wife for five years in the 1960s. Also, there are many songs by B.J. Thomas and Bobby Goldsboro that I listened to over the radio while working in the dental clinic in Fort Yates North Dakota in 1971 and 1972. Most people have these "oldies but goodies" songs in their memories, and companies make money compiling collections of groups of these popular songs for people to purchase. With a little effort you can make your own "oldies" playlists for certain memorable periods in your life. I have some playlists for "High School," "UK 1," "UK 2," "Galveston & Fort Yates," and "Tahlequah."

Not all my accidental memories of songs are positive. I can remember several songs associated with working in the dental clinic at Fort Yates, North Dakota, during the winters of 1971 and 1972. My dental assistant had the radio on every day playing tunes that were popular at that time as we worked. When I hear Bobby Goldsboro's "Honey," "And I Love You So," and "Danny Is A Mirror to Me," I'm anything but energized. I still like the songs, but I'm am reminded of standing in front of the window in the dental clinic and feeling sad. I can still picture the snow-covered, icy Lake Oahe on cloudy days. Hunting and fishing seasons were over until the month of May when the ice thawed. It meant staying inside for several months except for some occasional ice fishing and weekly card games at friends' homes. Only the memories of a few songs give me these sad, lonely feelings. Most are upbeat and stimulating like B.J. Thomas' "Raindrops Keep Falling on

My Head," "I Just Can't Help Believing," "Hooked on a Feeling," "Close to You," and Elton John's "Your Song."

My first experiment at making purposeful memories with music was during two duck hunting seasons in the early 1980s. During these two seasons I played only three cassette tapes going and coming from duck hunting. These tapes were "The Gambler," by Kenny Rogers, Crystal Gayle greatest hits, and volume 2 of the Judds' greatest hits. Now if I want to recall those duck-hunting emotions, I get out my duck call, put my feet in ice water and put on Crystal Gayle. Just joking about the ice water.

One experience that I am reminded of is driving along a lake road on a cold morning in my 1980 Chevy Blazer, talking with my friend Chance Turner. I remember the quarter-mile hike down the closed section line road in the dark, cold mornings to the blind carrying my gun and a bag of decoys slung over my back. There were always the arguments with Chance about what pattern we would use for arranging the decoys. I can picture the details of the hunts—the gadwalls, teal, and mallards coming in, Chance shooting my decoys and both of us laughing, and his dog "Goober" shaking off water on us. Chance was my friend, and I'd just patch the decoys later. We shot a lot of ducks out of that blind and off the north end of Oologah Lake out of my fourteen-foot semi-v boat.

Of course, there are also memories with a few other good hunters during the time from 1978 to 2005 when I hunted with Lorn Rohr, Bob Newlon, Terry Whitfield, Mark Rouk, Don Brown, and John Hoover, hunting in many locations. I can picture those mallard drakes with their metallic green heads twisting down through the trees into the decoys. Those hunts have many more memories of calling and watching ducks circle and come back with wings set for our decoys in an open hole of water. Many limits of greenheads, woodies, teal, widgeons, and gadwalls were brought home with those men. Thanks to all the other men: Lindel Adair, Del Nutter, Frank O'Donnell, Ben Bradford,

Brian Adair, Mike Brown, Doug Wagoner, John Boren, Byron Jasper, Jason Jones, Jeremy Jones, Danny Cotner, Brad Swan, Richard Swan, Norm Russell, T. M. Harrison, Steven Deem, Mark Huberty, Jim May, and Randy Shoeman for contributing to my memories and keeping me in good spirits with fun while either duck hunting, pheasant hunting, dove hunting, quail hunting, fishing, or working in the Claremore Area Ducks Unlimited chapter for thirty-five years.

I have listed below some experiences that bring back good emotions while listening to music that I purposely used to make memories over thirty years ago. Memories were created with the help of a tape named "Cusco 2000." I listened to this New Age music, while I was on a Caribbean cruise to Cozumel in February 1994 with my wife. I played only one tape on my portable Sony Walkman cassette player during the four-day cruise. I selected the tape in advance for its rhythms and instruments, which I thought matched the mood of the trip. Instrumental songs like "Islands of the Galapagos," "South America," "Africa-Afrika," "Sarengeti," "Flying Condor," and "Rhythm of the Wilderness" were perfect for enhancing the exciting time I experienced on the cruise.

These energizing tunes composed by Cusco will always remind me of the pleasant experiences I had while walking and jogging at midnight on deck seven of the Royal Majesty with my wife. They remind me of leaving the harbor at Miami on a sunny Monday afternoon, cruising past Havana, Cuba, on a cloudy, Tuesday morning, and arriving at San Miguel on Cozumel Island at sunrise on Wednesday. The tunes bring back emotions of activities on the ship like shooting trap off the stern of the ship. I feel as if I'm lying in the cabin looking out the window feeling the Gulf wave motion or leaning on the railing of the tenth deck feeling the soft Gulf breeze blowing in my face in the warm nights. "Cusco 2000" creates a mood of relaxation, pleasure, and excitement.

The clear, crisp, energizing music of Cusco brings back

memories of the snorkeling trip on Cozumel, the colorful fish and coral, and basking in the sun on the sandy beach drinking a Corona. Shopping around San Miguel and stopping off at Carlos'n Charlie's while listening to UB-40 is unforgettable. Although we were only in Carlos'n Charlie's for about ninety minutes, the UB-40 music I heard during that time made a memorable imprint. I bought three UB-40 CDs/tapes when I returned home and added them to my energizing music collection.

Without going into detail about each trip/event, here is a list of some events associated with music. Sometimes it was harder to hear the birds taking flight, so I would only put in one earpiece. The music is as follows:

Music	Associated with these events
---Ann Murray	Dove hunting in Galveston, TX
"Snowbird"	In 1970
---"Mr. Bojangles"	Living in Galveston and going to Mardi
---"The Entertainer"	Gras with Charles and Lorraine Allain
--- John Denver	Fort Yates, North Dakota in 1972
"Country Roads"	With Jim and Jackie May
"Rocky Mountain High"	
--- *Cool Runnings*	Watching daughters win OK State HS Tennis Championships, '94, '95
--- Ottmar Liebert	Striper fishing trips to Lake Texoma
--- Johannes Linstead	In '94, '95
--- Ace of Base	Trip to Newport Beach, CA in 1995

173

Music	Associated with these events
--- *Top Gun* songs	Walking the beach and the Boardwalk on Balboa Island
--- Mannheim Steamroller	Technical QA Evaluations
--- Save the Wildlife	In IHS dental clinics in 1990
--- The Pointer Sisters "Jump," "Neutron Dance"	With Dr. Chuck Grimm
---Corona	Goose hunt on Foss Lake, OK in 1996
	With Dr. Steve Deem and John Hoover
--- This is Techno, Vol 4	Pensacola Beach, 1996
--- Two Unlimited	Puerto Vallarta, 1994 with family
---Ottmar Liebert	Watching grandson Hudson play in
--- Shahin & Sephr	MO Valley tennis tournaments
--- Johannes Linstead	In 2014—2016
--- "Macarena"	Grand Lake, Dr. Deem's dental staff '96
--- The Judds and	Duck hunting 1993--1995
--- Crystal Gayle	
--- Clint Black	South Dakota pheasant
--- Alan Jackson	Hunts 1994—1996
--- Lorrie Morgan	
--- Upbeat New Age music	South Dakota pheasant
--- Patrick O'Hearn	Hunts 1994—1996
--- Yanni	

Music	Associated with these events
"Walkabout"	South Dakota pheasant hunts
"Everglade Run"	
---Bluegrass music	Dove hunting 1995—1996
	Teal hunting 1995—1996
--- Neil Diamond,	ATOD Use Prevention to
---"Pot Smoker's Song"	Fifth- and nineth-graders in 1996
---Cheryl Crow	Duck hunting in South Dakota
"A Change Would Do You Good"	With John Hoover in 1998
"Maybe Angels"	

One thing that I wanted to try was pairing some gospel quartet music with my Cancun trip in 2014 with our friends Jeff and Joyce Hagen from Yakima, Washington. It's not typical tropical island, beach, or Mexican music, so I thought I would see what kind of emotional memories I would make with this. Most of the groups and songs were upbeat, peppy, had good bass parts and meaningful spiritual lyrics that I enjoyed. It was great. Some examples are as follows:

Artists	Songs
---Dove Brothers	"Anything but Ordinary"
	"He Came Walking"
---Gold City	"Turn Your Back"
--- Greater Vision	"My Name Is Lazarus"
	"He Is to Me"

Artists	Songs
---Inspirations	"Give the World a Smile"
--- Kingdom Heirs	"Mighty Deep Well"
---The Good News Quartet	"Just Over in the Gloryland"

As it turned out, the same kinds of emotions associated with trips to the beaches in Mexico made with other more traditional beach, Mexican, and dance tunes could be made with the Christian gospel quartet music.

My most recent playlist made after my third depression contains choruses that we sang at Bible Church of Owasso services. These are songs that remind me of the greatness of my Lord and His grace. Here are some of the uplifting songs:

Artist	Songs
--- City Alight	"Saved My Soul"
	"All My Ways are Known to You"
	"Grace"
	"Yet Not I but Through Christ"
	"Home"
	"Nothing but the Blood of Jesus"
	"The Love of the Father"
	"God Is for Us"
--- Sovereign Grace	"Behold Our God"
	"O Great God"
	"Now Why This Fear"
	"How Great You Are"
	"Our Song from Age to Age"

Try making music memories. You'll like the emotions and memories recalled some day after many years if you haven't played the old tunes repetitiously too many times while experiencing excitement in some new environment. Just relax and enjoy!

In a recent article by Sari Harrar in the June/July 2020 issue of *AARP Magazine Real Possibilities*[22], I read about one of the benefits of making music memories. "People who study the brain have shown that listening to music you enjoy can cause a release of dopamine, a chemical that increases feelings of happiness," says Sarah Lenz Lock, AARP's senior vice president of policy and brain health and Global Council on Brain Health (GCBH) executive director.

Thirteen

MY MOST MEMORABLE
HUNTING AND
FISHING TRIPS

MY FIRST DUCK HUNTS WHILE
STATIONED AT GALVESTON, TEXAS

My first duck hunt was with Charles Allain from Franklin, Louisiana. Charlie was a commissioned officer who worked in the medical records department at the USPHS Hospital in Galveston, Texas where I was stationed for my dental general practice residency (GPR) in 1970–71.

Charlie and I went on a hunt at Lake Livingston located east of Huntsville near Livingston on the Trinity River. I'd been reading in the Houston newspaper about the possibilities of some good duck hunting on the newly constructed lake that was filling up. Charlie was interested in going, so we looked up a marina on the east side of the lake where we could camp out and rent a boat. We loaded up and took off early one Saturday morning in my 1970 Toyota Corona at four thirty. When we arrived, we found a place between the marina and the lake to set up our tent and went to the marina to rent a boat for two days. We decided we could go up the Trinity River channel to the bridge across the lake not far from the marina; there we planned on finding some shallow water in flooded weed fields that I had read about being good places to hunt. We set up our tent and loaded our gear, guns, and decoys in the boat we had rented.

On the way up to the bridge we could hear shooting in the woods across the river channel from our tent. That was a good sign, but I was keyed in on the Houston paper's article about the good hunting in the newly flooded weed fields. When we passed under the bridge, we could see the flooded weed fields and some teal flying over them. We found a shallow area and put out our decoys. Some teal came near us, and we knocked down two, but there wasn't as much action where we were compared to the green timber we had passed on our way up the river from the marina. We kept seeing flights of mallards over the trees and hearing shooting coming from that area. Being new to duck hunting I didn't know the value of the availability of flooded green timber for duck hunting. I thought only wood ducks went into the timber. Oh, this rookie had a lot to learn.

I guess Charlie didn't understand that either, or he would have surely said something about going into the timber when we passed by the first time. After an hour of waiting for more ducks while hearing and watching the activity over the flooded timber, I said, "We've got to go check that out and maybe hunt there tomorrow morning." Charlie agreed. We picked up our decoys and headed down the river channel back to the timber.

We went into the timber straight across from our campsite. The place was a solid light-green mat of duck weed. We saw some colorful wood ducks get up and could hear wood ducks screaming as they flew through the trees with some hanging Spanish moss. We shot one wood duck passing over us. We kept hearing duck calling by a man giving his dog voice commands as well as using a whistle between some infrequent shooting. Flights of mallards were seen with their metallic green heads, blue speculums, and gray backs, which were visible in openings through the trees as they banked in a turn while circling above us. I was getting excited about tomorrow. It was too late to set up and hunt that day, so we went back to our campsite and prepared dinner using my small single-burner Coleman stove. That night we hung our three ducks on the Toyota radio antenna as we camped in our small tent.

It was a comfortable, cool evening, and we had plenty of time to discuss our anticipated hunt. We discussed why we thought mallards were in the woods—maybe eating the plentiful duck weed. I didn't know then that mallards liked the flooded timber because of all the small acorns from the oak trees. Now that I know this, I'm surprised that more experienced hunters weren't around the marina area. Maybe we were just lucky to be some of the first to hunt that recently flooded area. But why hadn't the Houston paper mentioned the flooded timber? Charlie never said anything about hunting mallards in the woods—just wood ducks—and I was discussing with Charlie how big clumsy-looking mallards could fly down through the timber. He said he thought they could do it, but he didn't have any experience hunting them in the timber. I went to sleep anticipating a good hunt the next morning.

When we got out of our tent the next morning it was dark and colder, but still not bad for a November duck hunt in Texas. We ate some pastries and fried some eggs and bacon for breakfast. We waited until sunrise so I could see my way around in the woods. I could hardly wait to get into the woods and put our decoys out in a place where there was an opening in the trees for the mallards to see us and come down. We found an opening with trees to hide behind. Someone was already shooting deeper in the timber to our west, but not very close to us.

I can still remember the first flight circling over us as if looking for a place to come down. When they banked in the turn close to the treetops, I could see their blue speculums and emerald green heads plainly in the bright morning sunshine. I tried calling, but I thought less was better in my case, so I stuck with a soft feeding chuckle, which I could do well because I had learned how to double tongue playing my trumpet for ten years. The first flight plummeted into the hole over our decoys—in a graceful manner for clumsy mallards. We let them start backpedaling before we started shooting. Man, they got out of the hole quickly, but we got three drakes. One was a cripple and I shot him again. We didn't have a dog, so I cranked up the motor, and we retrieved the ducks. We had just returned to our hiding spot when two wood ducks lit in our decoys and immediately took off when they saw us; we got one when they got up.

While we were waiting for the next flight, I was just enjoying the beautiful environment with the solid-green carpet of duck weed and the clear blue sky with sunlight coming through the trees with Spanish moss. It was a comfortable day for duck hunting. The wind was calm, and I had thought bright, sunny, calm days were bad for duck hunting—but not true for timber hunts I guessed! Then I saw another flight of five mallards through an opening as they banked in a turn off to one side of us. I gave a comeback call and some single quacks, and they circled again. Next time around one drake broke off and came down in the hole and landed; we remained still—hoping the others would follow. Before the others could come in, the drake got up. This time we were ready and let him have it. I guess a bird in the hand is worth four in the air. We picked him up and waited for more. We could hear some woodies screaming through the woods and it sounded as if they were getting closer. We were allowed to shoot two wood ducks each, so we decided we would take them if they came in. Sure enough, two came zipping through the woods and splashed down in the duck weed near our decoys, but as soon as they landed, they took off. This time we got one of the two.

We were allowed one more duck. I told Charlie he could shoot the next duck that came in. It was about ten and the other hunter's shooting had dropped off considerably. We were still hearing wood ducks in the woods. I heard a wood duck coming and told Charlie, "Get ready; here they come." I could see two or three weaving through the trees. Charlie quickly shouldered his gun for a reflex shot, and a colorful drake woody splashed in the duck weed. I yelled, "Good shot!" Charlie was pleased and maybe surprised also. We had about a three-hour drive back to Galveston and were ready to leave. It had been a successful hunt for two rookies.

One of the physicians at the USPHS Hospital in Galveston was from Beaumont, Texas; Dr. Tom M. Hayes was also a duck hunter and had a duck-hunting lease near the intracoastal waterway south of Beaumont. When Tom found out that I was just a rookie duck hunter, he invited me and Donna to visit his family for a Thanksgiving holiday to go duck hunting. It was always fun visiting with someone's family, especially for Thanksgiving dinner. When we arrived Wednesday evening, we visited for a while and then went to bed so we could get up early for the morning hunt.

We were up at 5:00 a.m. so we could eat a bite and get on our way for a thirty-minute drive to the marsh. There was a guard house at the gate, but no one was there that morning. Tom unlocked the gate, and we drove to a parking spot where we began walking a couple-hundred yards to the blind. It was a good-looking marsh with ducky-looking vegetation in two feet of water north of the intracoastal waterway. Tom complained about the damage to the marsh vegetation by the nutria that we could see swimming around us on the way to the blind. It was a foggy morning, and I wondered how Tom could find his way to the blind. He had a well-built blind with some open water in the vegetation. We put out the decoys and got ready for shooting time.

We heard duck wings and some quacking, but visibility was

limited to about thirty yards, and we hadn't seen any ducks. The ducks evidently could see our decoys better than we could see them because four teal came in and landed in our decoys. We got two of them. Tom was calling and soon some ducks passed in our view and quickly disappeared in the fog. Tom kept calling with his pintail whistle. A flight of several ducks showed up coming straight to our decoys from the right side. We got three of them. My old Crescent Davis double barrel 20 had done well; I got one and Tom got two pintails—one a beautiful full-plumaged drake.

The fog was lifting slowly, and I could see more of the marsh—in every direction it was marsh as far as I could see. We talked about the marsh and the kind of hunting Tom had there; he said mostly pintails, gadwall, teal, shovelers, and some mallards. We waited. We heard wings go by, and Tom started calling his mallard call. We saw four mallards with their wings cupped and orange feet splayed; they were dropping fast out of the fog. When they began backpedaling Tom said, "Take 'em!" We knocked down three. One was crippled, and Tom shot again. We retrieved our three drakes, and Tom seemed glad to have some mallards in the bag; he said they weren't commonly seen there. While waiting awhile, we kept hearing some ducks calling a moderate distance from us. Since we weren't seeing any, Tom said he was going walking to jump some up while I remained in the blind.

Tom hadn't been gone long, and I had two pintails circle the blind. When they came back, I shot one hen pintail. The duck was crippled, and I had to reload and shoot again. This time the duck dived under the water but stayed there with her short tail sticking up about two inches out of the water in some thin grass. I decided to wait and see what would happen next. While I was waiting, I glanced at something that looked like a log floating in the water. I thought, *I don't remember seeing any log* and turned to look again; this time I saw that it was a five-foot alligator. The duck in the grass would have to wait, and I marked the location of the duck well and waited for Tom to come back. I hadn't heard him shoot. The fog had lifted partially by now, and I still couldn't see anything but marsh. I heard Tom coming back. When I looked around, the alligator was gone. When Tom got to the blind, I told him about the alligator, and he said, "Some are around here, but no one has ever been hurt by one."

I showed Tom the tail feathers sticking out of the water before stepping out of the blind to retrieve the mysterious pintail hen. I found the tailfeathers and gently lifted the dead duck out of the water with no resistance. I wondered what had kept the duck submerged. I lost my balance and fell on my way back to the blind—just like a rookie. I didn't get much water in my waders, but my gun had been submerged. I hopped up and shook the water out of my gun. It wasn't freezing that morning so I could probably still shoot.

The pintail behavior was a mystery. This event happened long before I read an English poem that described in poetic verse how ducks go down under the water and hold on to a plant or stick and die. I would observe this phenomenon a few times more in my duck-hunting career. I have also seen crippled ducks swim off in trashy water with only their eyeballs above the water almost undetectable. I thought that event has probably happened to many hunters who thought their duck dived, died, and didn't resurface, but this time in the marsh I had evidence that it was a real phenomenon.

Tom and I had a few more small flights come in, and we shot three more gadwall and left for home. Tom and I talked about the pintail that died submerged under the water; he had never seen that happen before—dead ducks usually float! But he had seen ducks slowly escaping with only their eyeballs above the water.

I told Tom that I was concerned about my gun getting rusty from the briny water; it was an old gun that my grandfather had given me, and the bluing was mostly gone. My grandfather had shot a banded March Hawk in Kentucky with the gun in February 1940 and sent the information to the US Department of the Interior, Bureau of Biological Survey. He received a letter back from them reporting that the hawk had been banded July 1, 1939, at Toronto, Canada. He saved the report and gave it to me when he gave me the gun. The old gun was special to me for that reason. Tom told me we would dry the gun off well and oil it down when we got home.

When we got back to his house, we didn't clean the ducks; instead, Tom hung them up by their heads without gutting them to "let them cure for two or three days—an old English custom," he said. After cleaning and oiling my gun we enjoyed a tasty Thanksgiving dinner together with all the trimmings that his mother had prepared that day. Donna and I thanked Tom and his family for their hospitality and good food. It had been a very enjoyable time for both of us.

On the way home I told Donna that I was going to make Tom a gold piece that could be inlaid into his gunstock. We had a casting machine at the hospital dental clinic and all the wax and investment material to make a mold for the casting that we used for casting gold crowns. In 1970 I could buy gold from a jeweler for $35 an ounce—an ounce today is worth $1,900. An ounce would be plenty for the inlay and the casting button. I began waxing the inlay soon after we returned. It would have his name, T. M. Hayes, with a flushing mallard above and one below the name— all embossed above the surface. I used a quarter-sized piece of pink denture wax and waxed the embossed ducks and name on its surface. I placed three sprues on the back side. Then I poured investment plaster around the wax just like we did for casting gold crowns, burned out the wax in a small furnace, melted and refined the gold with charcoal dust in an asbestos-lined crucible, and when the purified gold was glowing orange and shiny on top I cast it with a centrifugal casting machine. It was a beautiful piece after I had polished it. I believed Dr. Hayes appreciated the art. He thanked me and said, "I didn't know you could do this!" I don't know if he later had it inlaid in his gunstock; if not, he still has a beautiful memento, worth about $900 now, demonstrating my gratitude for an outstanding hunt as a rookie duck hunter.

PARTY BOAT FISHING IN GALVESTON

In the summer and fall of 1970, Donna and I also went several times with two good friends, O. B. and Susan Jackson, party-boat fishing on the *Texan* about thirty miles offshore. Susan worked at the University of Texas Medical Branch in Galveston as a physical therapist with Donna, and O.B. was completing a medical residency there.

We made several trips in the gulf fishing for red snapper. On the way out, O. B. and I used clothesline cords with large jigs trolling for bonita and ling; we often caught bonita but rarely caught ling. The lines were tied to a rear rail with a piece of tire tube also tied to the line, which would stretch and decrease the sudden jerk when the fish struck the jig. We would pull in the line wearing gloves preventing blisters on the hands and fingers.

My brother, Terry, and a friend visited from Kentucky that summer and we all went out on the *Texan*. I advised him to wear gloves while pulling in the fish, but he thought his hands were tough enough from putting up hay in Kentucky. When he had his first fish about halfway in, he said, "I need some gloves," but it was too late; he already had blisters. We went to the captain's cabin, and I asked the captain if he had anything for treating blisters. He pulled a small brown bottle from a medicine cabinet. When I put some on my brother's blisters, he turned pale, winced, and groaned with severe pain. I thought he was going to pass out. I looked to see what was in the bottle, and it was mostly alcohol. I didn't know that he was already seasick. He had to lie down in one of the bunk beds. That ruined his fishing trip before we even got to the red snapper beds.

When we arrived at the snapper beds where the water was clear

and green—as opposed to the murky water along the shoreline—
the captain would tell us when to drop our lines baited with squid
and how deep to go. He was usually right, and we would begin
pulling in some medium-sized red snapper. Sometimes we would
drop down our lines and begin to catch hardheads, which looked
like small catfish to me, and the captain would say, "Hardheads,
reel up your lines; let's move to another spot." We moved from one
spot to another while catching snapper each time. We repeated
this routine until the captain was ready to return to shore, which
was usually fine with us. Being in the hot sun and trying to catch
fish on a rocking boat was tiresome work—and I'm sure it was fine
with my younger brother.

When we arrived at the dock, usually the *Buccaneer* was
already docked with medium to large red snapper, some weighing
twenty pounds or more, hanging from an upper level around
the front and sides of the boat. It was a beautiful sight to see the
colorful red snapper hanging there. The *Buccaneer* always had
more and bigger red snapper than the *Texan*, but we liked the
Texan partly because it was a smaller group, and we could troll
with the hope of catching a ling on the way out and back.

The bonita had dark red meat. There was only one time that
we cut the meat into small pieces and ate it raw after dipping it in
mustard sauce when we went back to O. B. and Susan's apartment
after the trip. It was just okay.

One day when we were returning from the docks everyone was
leaving town, going out Galveston Avenue to the causeway toward
Houston. Windows were being boarded up, and we knew what
that meant. But we hadn't heard about any hurricane coming.
Well, all PHS commissioned officers had already been warned
by the hospital director during orientation that we couldn't leave
Galveston because of a hurricane. He told us about the last time
some officers went to Houston, and he sent the military police
(MP) after them and brought them back. We were fortunate that
the hurricane changed course and went east of Galveston during

the night. It was difficult to believe we had gone fishing in the gulf with a hurricane coming.

The next spring, we spent an adventuresome weekend in Nuevo Laredo, Mexico, with O. B. and Susan. Living in Galveston was very much like being on a one-year vacation since we were just out of school, living on the beach, and had some spending money.

THE RETURN TO NORTH DAKOTA
FOR HUNTING PHEASANTS

Mike Brown, an IHS pharmacist, and I both transferred from Fort Yates, North Dakota, to Oklahoma; he in the fall of 1972 to Stillwater, and I in February 1973 to Tahlequah. In fall 1973 we decided to go back to North Dakota for a two-week goose and pheasant hunt.

The first week of goose hunting at Devils Lake near Penn we stayed with the family of Don Striffel, a Bureau of Indian Affairs (BIA) teacher that we had known in Fort Yates. The goose hunting was futile; we experienced what the term "wild goose chase" meant. For three days every time we hunted on one side of Devils Lake the geese flew out the other side. We would drive around to the other side of the lake after not shooting anything, and hunters would be walking from the lake with geese draped over their shoulders.

We put out decoys in fields at two other locations with very little success. At the first place we encountered a white van that showed up about three hundred yards from us, and four men dressed in white suits got out of the van and started putting out their goose decoys and white rags. They had a large spread, and we were lucky if a few geese flew high over us on the way to their spread; we didn't want to sky-bust and ruin their hunt and we never killed a goose that day. We hunted another morning in a winter wheat field on the Striffel's land but without any luck. We never killed a goose that week.

We were ready to shoot some birds when we arrived near Fort Yates on Friday before the opening day of pheasant hunting. We camped out on some private land in a windrow near our friend's ranch house within the Standing Rock Sioux Indian Reservation; we were about ten miles north of Fort Yates.

While stationed at Fort Yates in 1971 and 1972, Mike, Jim May—another pharmacist—and I had good success hunting sharp tail grouse and Hungarian partridge (Huns) within twenty miles of Fort Yates. However, pheasant hunting was a different story; we could only find a few pheasants on the Silk's small farm two miles south of Fort Yates, which had good cover around an old shed and along a wet-weather creek below a bluff. Because a 1968 blizzard with snowdrifts up to the eaves of houses had killed most of the pheasant population, only a few pheasants remained in areas where there had been significant cover for protection.

Mike, Jim, and I were forced to drive three hours to Aberdeen, South Dakota, to hunt pheasants. We always had good hunts there but wondered where one of the physicians at the small local Indian Hospital where we worked always seemed to get his limit somewhere around Fort Yates. We found out that he had a Native American friend that he hunted with, but they would never tell us where they hunted.

It wasn't until after the second pheasant season when Mike and I were driving around on the Port Ranch that we saw about thirty pheasants congregated in a small alfalfa field, and we suspected that might be where the physician and his friend had been hunting. The Cannonball River flowed through the Port Ranch and had plenty of tall cottonwood trees and cover for pheasants to have survived the blizzard in 1968, and they had survived and repopulated that local area well.

We had some time on Friday to do some scouting at the Silk's land where we had shot pheasants when we lived in Fort Yates.

After we found some birds, we drove to the Port Ranch to ask permission to hunt on Saturday. The next morning, the opening day of pheasant season, we hunted the Port Ranch about ten miles north of our campsite.

As we were parked in the dark on a hill at the Port Ranch waiting for sunrise, who else but the physician's Indian friend pulled up and parked beside our truck. It was quite a coincidence, because the Port Ranch is very large, and he could have stopped at any number of other locations. In our brief conversation with him, we could tell that it was a surprise for him to see us there at his honey hole. We found out that his physician hunting buddy had been transferred to a clinic in Sisseton, South Dakota. We left our spot at sunrise and headed for the Cannonball River, where lots of weeds and cover were available for pheasants. We hunted with Mike's Brittany and Shorthair for two hours along the Cannonball River that morning and got our limit of four birds early.

We went to the ranch house, and Mrs. Port came to the door. We asked her if she would like to have four pheasants. She said, "Yes, and you're welcome to come in and have some coffee cake." We thought that was very gracious of her, and we gladly accepted the offer. She took the untagged birds to her basement and returned to seat us around a large round table covered with names embroidered in many colors all over the white tablecloth. She said, "If you'd like to sign your names, I'll embroidery them on the tablecloth also." We thought that was unusual, but we were glad to have our names among all the other guests at the Port Ranch. We had a pleasant conversation while we finished our coffee and cake. We thanked her for her hospitality and went back out hunting some more.

It was a beautiful, sunny day and a pleasant temperature for North Dakota in October. It was warm enough that crossing the shallow river hunting birds flying on both sides wasn't too bad that day when we got a little wet. We had another enjoyable hunt along the Cannonball and even shot a few Huns on the way back to our campsite. We reasoned that shooting more than our limit of pheasants that day was okay because we had given the first four away, which is still no justification for breaking the law. We cleaned the four tagged pheasants and four Huns. We stored the birds in a basement freezer of the ranch house and drove into Fort Yates for dinner at the Pelican restaurant.

The next day we hunted at the Silk's farm beginning with the large vacant barnyard lot full of tall, thick, dried weeds. Dogs were a necessity there. We shot three pheasants and moved across the creek and climbed a steep hill to the edge of a bluff. Walking along this bluff one of Mike's dogs pointed a pheasant in some short grass near the edge. I could see the pheasant just hunkered down in the grass ready to fly off the bluff; I told Mike to be ready; I was going to catch the cock. I got down behind the bird with my hand no more than six inches above his back. When I made my move the pheasant was gone out over the edge of the bluff without me touching him. Mike shot him, and we had our limit of four birds. We spent time the remainder of that morning visiting old friends in Fort Yates and giving them the untagged pheasants that we shot that morning. After eating in Fort Yates, we hunted for sharp tail grouse in an unpicked corn field on the Silk's farm. It was hard hunting, but we saw some grouse fly into the corn field from a bluff and jumped those. We shot three grouse and went back to our campsite to clean birds.

The next morning was cold, in the teens, with a light snow. Camping out in a tent had become a bit more uncomfortable. We fried some eggs and bacon before returning to hunt at the Port Ranch again. We had another good hunt along the Cannonball, but the river was deeper where we crossed that day, and we stepped in the water more. We went back to the campsite, and after changing our wet socks and boots, we cleaned and stored the tagged birds in the basement freezer.

That afternoon we hunted for sharp tail grouse and Huns in the surrounding rolling prairie lands. It was always hard hunting up and down the hills. The grouse were wilder later in the season and wouldn't hold for the dogs; it was a matter of trying to sneak up on them in the prairie or find them feeding in a cornfield on the Silk's land where we had a chance of getting closer to them. We would find Huns in the draws where there was lots of cover. We found an alfalfa field with hay stacks to hide behind where we did some pass shooting of grouse coming off a prairie hill into the alfalfa field to feed. We did get five sharp tail, but only two Huns that afternoon, and went back to the campsite to clean and store the birds. It was still another cold night in the tent.

The next morning, we went to another place on the Cannonball River, but not on the Port Ranch. It was a sunny day and much warmer—in the fifties. We got four more pheasants and then went into Fort Yates to eat lunch and refuel our truck. At the service station in Fort Yates the local reservation sheriff's fifteen-year-old son was pumping gas. He saw our pheasants in the back of the pickup and asked how we had been doing hunting. We bragged to him about the good luck we were having, which later we thought might have been a mistake.

After lunch we visited other friends in Fort Yates and gave them the four untagged birds. Then we went hunting for more grouse in the cornfield at the Silk's. The grouse were in the cornfield later that afternoon, and we had an exciting hunt just like old times when we used to get our limit with Jim May in that field. I still have a picture taken in 1972 of the three of us on Mike's front porch with a limit of nine sharp tail grouse. We headed back to the campsite and cleaned six grouse and stored them in the freezer. We also penciled in slash marks for four more pheasants and six more grouse to our bird count that we were keeping on the side of my trailer's wooden box that hauled our camping equipment and hunting gear. Mike had a dog box in the back of his small Toyota pickup.

On Wednesday morning, our last day, we went back to the Port Ranch. We had a pleasant hunt that morning, bagging four more cocks. We continued to hunt in the prairie for grouse and Huns on the way back to our campsite. We got a couple more Huns and one grouse. By about four o'clock we were in a field within view of the ranch house. I was so tired that I just lay on the ground to rest for five minutes. The temperature was in the fifties, but it was cloudy and looking like rain. It felt so good to just lie on the ground for a few minutes. Our hunt was finished, and I made sure that the last four cock pheasants in the back of the pickup were tagged before we headed to the house. We now had twelve tagged pheasants—our legal possession limit for the trip.

When we pulled into the drive at the ranch house next to our campsite, I saw a car coming around the house. On the side was a large round logo: "North Dakota State Fish and Game Department." It stopped, and we parked near it. I was feeling pretty good because I knew we had tagged all four pheasants. We got out of our vehicle and began to talk with the two men about the hunt we had that day. Then they asked to see our birds, and we showed them our tagged birds in the pickup. I don't think Mike had noticed the logo on the side of the car, and he didn't know who they were. They introduced themselves, and I recognized one name as the head of the North Dakota State Fish and Game Department. I thought it unusual for the head man to come from Bismarck seventy miles away. I thought maybe it was because we were on privately owned land within the Standing Rock Indian Reservation, and maybe the reservation sheriff had no jurisdiction over non-Indians staying on private land.

I was still feeling very confident that everything was okay until one of them asked, "Where are you keeping all the rest of your birds?" Then I suspected that they had already looked in the freezer in the basement. I knew that we had one cock having both legs and back blown up so badly that we had not been able to keep the legs. It could not be identified as a cock pheasant without an attached spurred leg. We told them our birds were in the basement freezer. They said they had already looked in the freezer.

They also said, "We believe you've killed about thirty pheasants," which was more than we had recorded on our trailer. One said, "We have the evidence. We know what the score is." That made me wonder if they had already seen our pencil marks on the trailer at our campsite. I couldn't tell for sure if they had talked to any of our friends in Fort Yates to whom we had given pheasants, but I could think of someone they might have talked to that could provide evidence—Mrs. Port.

I remembered what a friendly relationship our family had with the game ranger when I was growing up in Kentucky. I figured the Ports, having a large ranch with deer hunting as well as excellent pheasant hunting, also had a friendly relationship with the rangers and the sheriff. Then I remembered that we had signed the tablecloth. That was evidence that it was us who had left untagged birds with her. Mike and I talked and agreed to confess that we had killed over our limit of birds. The rangers were very cordial and requested that we ride with them to Fort Yates to the sheriff's office and sign a confession.

By now a light rain was falling, and it was a cold, dark, dreary drive to Fort Yates. Even though I felt like a criminal, which I was for having broken their game laws, we were having a friendly conversation with the rangers. One of them said, "We're not trying to railroad you and could charge you with more than over the limit and untagged birds—maybe a charge for each bird over the limit."

I asked, "Why did you have to call so many people asking about us?"

One of them—knowing that I was a dentist—replied, "It's just like checking teeth, you want to find every cavity you can." That humor was a little bit of a relief. He then asked if we shot any hens.

I said, "No, we don't shoot hens!" Maybe he was referring to the blown-up untagged pheasant breast with no spurred legs to identify it as a cock.

We arrived at the sheriff's office, and the sheriff was waiting for us. We signed a statement that read, "I do hereby state and admit too exceeding the season limit of pheasants by North Dakota Law as per Governor's proclamation" dated 8:40 p.m. on October 25, 1973. The Sheriff of Sioux County, Kenneth Snider, told us it would be $100 each.

Mike looked at me and asked, "Can you write a check for me? I don't know if I have enough money in the bank to cover it."

The sheriff said, "We don't extradite for game law violations, but we do for bad checks." I told Mike that I'd be glad to write a check for $200. I knew he would repay me. We were thankful that they hadn't fined us several times more than that for each bird over the limit. I'm sorry that I violated the hunting laws of North Dakota. Hunting is much more than shooting a lot of birds. We could have spent more time hunting sharp tail grouse and Huns and had just as much fun without killing over the limit of pheasants. We chalked it up as an embarrassing learning experience; we learned that bragging to others about our good hunting was to be avoided. We accepted the fact that our hunting trip had cost us about one-third more than expected.

During the drive back to Oklahoma, we couldn't avoid a discussion about the mystery of how the State Fish and Game Department had been made aware of our hunting trip and why they had made such an effort traveling seventy miles to confront us. We thought about the possibility of the sheriff's young son making an innocent comment to his dad after talking to us at the gas station and seeing the pheasants in our pickup. The sheriff had always been watching our hunting when we lived in Fort Yates but never caught us doing anything illegal. The sheriff could have contacted the State Fish and Game Department because we had been there hunting for five days and our possession limit was only twelve pheasants, which we could have killed in three days. Maybe it was the Native American who found us parked at his honey hole one morning. However, I later worked with his wife at the CIH in 1978 after she had separated from her husband and moved to

Claremore. She told me that she wasn't aware of her husband being involved in the sting, and I had no reason not to believe her.

However, the best piece of evidence that we could think of was that tablecloth we had signed. We suspected that the Ports had been through the process of documenting other hunters, because they had lived there many years and had a good relationship with the State Fish and Game Department and sheriff. They owned such a popular hunting location for both pheasants and deer along the Cannonball River. That event with Mrs. Port seemed all too conveniently orchestrated to be coincidental to me. We didn't know if Mrs. Port had initiated the call or the sheriff had contacted her about our visit. It didn't really matter; we weren't angry at anyone, but it is still a mystery until this day.

THE DUCK HUNT THAT CHANGED
MY CAREER IN THE USPHS

In 1975 while stationed at the Tahlequah W. W. Hastings Indian Hospital I was duck hunting in Long Bay of Fort Gibson Lake near Wagoner, Oklahoma. A friend and I stumbled onto a well-constructed floating blind in a small cove on the southwest side of the bay. We decided to hunt there for the rest of the morning since no one was using it. We put out some decoys and hid my small boat in some willows. No sooner than we were situated in the blind the first flight of mallards came over the willows about eighty yards away along the north side of the cove and set their wings for our decoys. We shot three. There was no calling or anything; they just seemed to like the hole as if they'd been there before. They had surely been feeding somewhere near the north side of the sheltered cove and landed for water. The cove was ideal for hunting, with solid ground for wading; it was in a calm area out of the wind protected on the north and south sides by tall willows with the sun to our right on the east side. It wasn't long until another flight of about ten came in. This time we got four—all greenheads. It was like shooting that I had seen on videos and TV shows—almost too easy to be true. We got our limit in a short time and headed back across the bay to the ramp, loaded up, and returned home.

Fortunately, we were able to repeat that scenario several times because no one was ever hunting there when we returned. I don't remember seeing any name posted in the blind, and I never knew who owned it, but someone had gone to a lot of trouble to build such a fine floating blind on Styrofoam blocks, loading it on a trailer, hauling it to the lake, and pulling it across the lake. I told my friend that next year when it came time for the duck blind drawing, I was going to try getting that spot.

The next year in September when the annual duck blind drawing for Fort Gibson Lake rolled around, I was there. The drawing was held east of Wagoner at a wildlife refuge within a mile of Long Bay where the blind had been located. I had never been to a duck blind drawing, but a large crowd of hunters had shown up. When they drew the first name it was mine, and I got first choice of all the blind site locations on the lake. How unbelievable was that! The next week my friend and I began constructing our blind from T posts and chicken wire in which my boat would fit. We cut willows and brushed the blind well.

It was about this same time that I received a call from my IHS Oklahoma City area dental officer, Dr. Bill Hussman. He called to inform me that the IHS dental director in Bethesda, Maryland, Dr. Robert Mecklenberg, had called him and requested that he call me about coming to the Bethesda headquarters to assist him for six months while his deputy chief was reassigned to work on another project. My discussion of the request included informing Dr. Hussman of my desire to continue my career working as a clinician—not as an administrator in the IHS dental program. I had seen short-term requests like this turn into career assignments after getting a Master of Public Health (MPH) degree. I also couldn't resist informing him that I had just drawn the best duck hunting blind on Fort Gibson Lake and didn't want to miss hunting there that year. He said, "Why don't you call Dr. Mecklenberg and tell him what you've told me."

Dummy me, I did just that. My conversation with Dr. Mecklenberg did not go well. When I told him what I had told Dr. Hussman, I qualified it by saying, "If you can't find anyone else to do it, I would be willing to come." He immediately responded, "Well, (colorful words) if I could find someone else to do it, I wouldn't be calling all over the country." Right then I thought, *I've ruined my career and chances for my promotions in the USPHS.* I was aware that administrative dental officers stationed at headquarters were the dental officers who made the rank of admiral, and clinicians in the field were usually limited to the rank of captain.

I wasn't asked to transfer for that temporary position. I am grateful for Dr. Mecklenberg allowing me to be very successful at doing what I enjoyed most for the rest of my USPHS career—remaining a clinical general dentist and managing a large clinic and service unit dental program at CIH. I found out later that Dr. Bill Maas, who was stationed in North or South Dakota, had gone to Bethesda to help Dr. Mecklenberg.

At the next annual IHS continuing dental education and administrative meeting that was for dental officers with at least five years of experience in the USPHS, I was approached by several dental officers who commented, "I heard you are a serious duck hunter." They enjoyed kidding me about my reputation for turning down a chance to work at the IHS headquarters for the duck hunting. But that's not the end of this story.

In 1994 I was nominated to be inducted into the American College of Dentists (ACD) in Washington, DC; the convocations traditionally occurred in conjunction with the annual American Dental Association meetings. There I met Dr. Maas, also being inducted into the ACD, sponsored by Dr. Mecklenberg. My sponsor for the ACD nomination was a periodontist from the University of Pennsylvania, Dr. Tom Rams, with whom I was working on a periodontal research project at CIH.

When I mentioned the duck hunting story to Dr. Maas, he said, "Oh, I see, there go I but for you." We had a good laugh, and all enjoyed visiting that evening. Dr. Maas later became an admiral (RADM). Although I didn't become an admiral—and by the way I only shot two little teal from that best blind site on Fort Gibson Lake that year—I enjoyed being a successful USPHS career captain as God had planned. During my third depression I had learned to believe the answer to one of *The New City Catechism*[23] questions: "What is God?", which we had been memorizing at Bible Church of Owasso since September 2017. The answer is, "God is the creator and sustainer of everyone and everything. He is eternal, infinite, and unchangeable in his power and perfection, goodness and glory, wisdom, justice, and truth. Nothing happens except through him and by his will." Like the ending of the catechism notes, "Nothing happens except through him and by his will." I believe the last sentence of this catechism applied to me, as it was God's will in this case.

A COLD, SCARY EXPERIENCE ON OOLOGAH LAKE

After calling five of my hunting friends, I could find no one who would go hunting with me on the next day when the temperature was to be seven degrees with twenty-five to thirty-five mph winds and a wind chill of eleven below zero; I decided to go by myself. I would be hunting over decoys in a safe shallow-water blind in the spillway bay of Oologah where the ground was firm and had no old dead tree stobs sticking up off the bottom—*a safe place*, I thought. Soon after setting out my decoys, I knocked down three greenheads, and one was getting away. I jumped out of my blind and was moving fast as I could in water above my waist when I tripped over a stob while chasing the wounded drake. As I fell forward, my waders began filling with water, my feet floated upward, and I was floating on my stomach. In order to regain my footing, I had to prop myself up with the butt of my gun; my gun and gloves were instantly covered with ice when they came out of the water. I was scared because I had four hundred yards to go to the car; I grabbed the two dead drakes and headed to the car. I couldn't catch my breath to go more than fifty yards without resting—not realizing it was because my waders had an extra twenty-five pounds of water in each leg.

I did get home with frozen feet, legs, and hands. I realized when I stepped out of the car how much water was in my waders, because the adrenalin had worn off and I could feel the weight as I walked to the back door of my garage. After removing the waders. My wife thawed me out in a tub of lukewarm water for thirty minutes. After another hour, while eating and trying to dry my gun out, I went back to get my decoys.

While waiting in my blind, there was a group of gadwalls that lit in my decoys. I tried to shoot, but my gun was still frozen. After trying several times while blowing my warm breath in the chamber it fired; I got one on the water and two going away. I picked up my ducks and decoys and went home as if it had been a normal hunt.

GOOSE HUNTING WITH DR. STEVE DEEM AND JOHN HOOVER

In 1997 I talked Dr. Deem and T. M. Harrison into going goose hunting with an experienced goose hunter, John Hoover, and his friend. I had been to Foss Lake in western Oklahoma before, but was really a rookie goose hunter compared to John. John and I had drawn for two goose blinds on the refuge adjacent to each other 250 yards apart. Our blind was surrounded by tall grass and was near the lake by some trees with the sun at our backs; John's blind was about thirty degrees to our right at the end of the wheat field. His blind backed up next to some large eastern red cedar trees. I had about seventy-five Canada goose decoys and six snows with a plastic flying Canada on a stick five feet tall. I just expected that John, with his expert goose-calling, would shoot more of the smaller five- to six-pound prairie geese than we would. The limit was three Canadas per person.

As it turned out we were having good success calling that clear, cold morning, and more geese came off the lake into our spread than into John's. We were killing geese nearing our limit when John wounded one, which went down in our spread. That day I sky-busted at a snow goose about eighty yards straight up, and it fell like a rock near our blind, which seemed unusual for such a high-flying shot. The goose was bleeding from a chest hole the size of a .22 rifle bullet. Everything was going our way that day, and we had nine geese. When I cleaned the snow goose, I found two tungsten BB shot welded together the size of a .22 slug lying near the heart.

All that John would say was, "I don't think they liked the cedar trees!" John was not celebrating; he was quiet after being outhunted by three rookies.

DAN'S ORAL SURGERY AFTER DUCK HUNTING ON THE ELK RIVER

It was a cold, brisk, dark morning when I let Bob Newlon's chocolate Lab, Dan, out of the Blazer. He took off running wild; after a couple of minutes we heard a loud yelp, and Dan returned with heavy bleeding from his mouth. We had no clue as to what had happened and couldn't see any cuts but suspected maybe he had run full steam ahead into a tightly stretched barbed-wire fence and cut the inside of his mouth. As we hunted that day, the bleeding and clots from Dan's mouth slowed, but he continued to have some light bleeding. We were having good luck hunting across from the boat ramp on the Elk River in eastern Oklahoma within a mile of its confluence with Grand Lake. Ducks liked the shallow water with Japanese millet. Bob and I got our limit of greenheads and took off to the vet's office in Claremore, Oklahoma, where we lived.

The vet showed us that Dan had suffered a deep laceration into an artery under his tongue as well as broken off the top third of his lower right cuspid with a red dot visible—indicating pulp exposure. The vet called another vet who did dental work on animals and came back with a quote of $1,500 for a root canal and crown. Bob said, "I can't afford that," but I don't want to lose Dan. I suggested removing the tooth, but the vet said that was not advisable due to expected poor healing in a dog's lower jaw and potential infection. I suggested a root-banking procedure that I had read about in my dental journal, a procedure that involved cutting off the crowns of the remaining lower front teeth and suturing the gums over the roots and letting it heal before making a full lower denture.

The vet said he didn't have a drill, and I said I could cut the tooth level with the bone using a fiber cut disk with my Dremel drill if he could put Dan to sleep. He said go get it since I only lived five minutes from the vet's clinic.

When I returned, he was giving Dan a general anesthesia using Ketamine. I wrote about a cousin of Ketamine, esketamine, being used as a successful antidepressant in Chapter 4. Ketamine is an abused drug used with opioids having a much higher risk of overdose than opioids alone. Ketamine produces a dissociative anesthesia, and Dan's big golden eyes were open the full time I worked on him. I laid a gum flap on both sides of the tooth and peeled back the gums exposing the bone. After cutting off the tooth at the crest of bone and beveling the edges of the tooth, I sutured the gum back tight to cover the pulp and tooth using resorbable sutures. Dan never flinched, and the procedure went well.

Dan recovered well and never missed a day of hunting that season. Years later when I would ask Bob about Dan, he would say, "Dan never complains; he eats well, and he's doing fine, I guess."

KANSAS PHEASANT HUNTING WITH LINDEL ADAIR

My first trip to Norton, Kansas, for pheasant hunting was in early November 1978 with Frank Odonnell, Bryan Adair, Lindel Adair, and his brother—Joe Bob—and friends from Wichita. Opening day was always around Veteran's Day, and the weather was usually sunny and dry with pleasant temperatures for running the dogs and walking the fields. We would stop in Wichita and pick up Bob and Brett, Bob's son, and their friends. The old tennis courts on the south end of town by the rodeo grounds were an ideal place to park our campers because they had an electrical box on a utility pole that supplied electricity for our campers. The high school football field was next to us, and we could walk over and watch a game on Friday night.

We always got up early, because in Kansas the season opened at sunrise—contrary to South Dakota, which opened at noon. Lindel and the Wichita group had been hunting in Norton for several years, and the routine for opening day was eating a good meal early at one of the church-sponsored breakfasts. Some other mornings Frank would fix coffee, bacon, and eggs, with toast and jelly; most of the time we would go to our favorite breakfast restaurant on Highway 36 that ran through Norton on the north side where we could also have biscuits and gravy with bacon and eggs. Lindel also knew the best places to open season on the public land around nearby Keith Sebelius Lake and where we needed to park early to stake out the best spots.

We started hunting each morning where the pheasants roosted

around trees and weed patches along the lake and surrounding hilly grasslands. I've seen Lindel come out of a low-lying, thinly wooded area between the lake and the cropland with pheasants hanging all over him. Lindel liked separating himself from the group and hunting there with Fred, his Brittany, every opening day early in the morning before we started driving the long milo fields. Bryan, Lindel's seventeen-year-old son, preferred starting with the grassland on the hillside above the milo fields. After he got some birds off their roosts, he would already be up there waiting for the birds we missed after being flushed out of the milo fields. Many of the pheasants would head in Bryan's direction when flushed, and he was a good long-range shooter.

After lunch we lounged around for an hour before going back out for the afternoon hunt. We would hunt weed patches, draws, sloughs, and dry cattail patches in the afternoons. The dogs were valuable in all these areas, and many men usually wound up with a limit by the end of the day. One evening every year we would go to the Ducks Unlimited annual banquets in Norton. We always had a good meal and enjoyed time there with the raffles and auction of prints, decoys, guns, and hunting gear.

One evening in the early 1980s while attending a fun Ducks Unlimited event I had too much alcohol to drink—knowing that God condemns drunkenness many times in the Bible. Anyone who drinks wine or other alcoholic drinks runs the risk of becoming drunk without restraint for moderation by the Holy Spirit. I was aware that I had too much to drink that night, so I asked my friend Lindel to drive our group back to the campsite in my 1980 Blazer; Lindel never ever drank more than his safe limit on hunting trips, but several others did.

I sat in the seat behind Lindel holding Boy, my black Lab, between my legs. We hadn't gone very far when I had the urge to vomit quickly. All at once the vomit went all over Boy's head and back, on my good shoes, and on the floor carpet. I never had time to roll down the window. This had never happened to me on any hunting or fishing trip. What an embarrassment!

I had to ask God for forgiveness that night. The next morning, I was embarrassed by having to get out in the twenty-degree weather and clean my carpet, shoes, and Boy with everyone in our group of about ten men watching. I felt guilty about this incident for the next thirty-five years; I learned from Terry Devitt, one of my BCO pastors, that it was possible to lose focus on God and grieve the filling of the Holy Spirit. You lose focus by not staying in the word, which allows a transgression like this to happen. According to Terry, five ministries of the Holy Spirit exist:

- The Holy Spirit regenerates sinners (Titus 3:4–5; John 3:5–8).
- Jesus baptizes believers in the body of Christ. (1 Corinthians 12:13; Luke 3:16).
- The Holy spirit indwells the believer. (John 14:16–17; 1 Corinthians 3:16).
- God seals us with the Holy Spirit. (2 Corinthians 1:22; Ephesians 1:13, 4:30).
- The Holy Spirit fills the believer. (Ephesians 5:18).

The first four of these ministries are fixed for an individual at the time of salvation. Only the filling of the Holy Spirit through God's Holy Word is a continuous process. It is the only ministry that is viable after the Holy Spirit has been grieved or quenched by transgression.

I am reminded once again of the answer to the question, "What is God?" in *The New City Catechism*.[23] "God is the Creator and sustainer of everyone and everything. He is eternal, infinite, and unchangeable in his power and perfection, goodness and glory, wisdom, justice, and truth. Nothing happens except through him and by his will." I believe now that God allowed this embarrassing transgression in my life to teach me a lesson and possibly using this experience for his glory in my book. After repenting and receiving His forgiveness, drunkenness has never happened to me again thanks to the filling of the Holy Spirit. I repeat what I have said in this book before; the only way to be free from any risk of drunkenness is total abstinence from using alcohol. The Holy Spirt, through scripture, tells us right from wrong and how to behave. However, I recommend if you don't drink, don't start. If you do, ask the Holy Spirit to help you keep it in moderation. Get your answer by continually reading scripture.

God could have made it easier for us if he had simply commanded us not to drink any wine, but he never did. He allowed us some leeway for personal choice. Jesus even turned a large volume of water into wine at a wedding ceremony where Mary, the mother of Jesus, and his disciples were there (find this interesting event in John 2 NASB). However, He commanded us not to be drunk in many passages in the Bible—too many to list here! He also admonished us not to be a stumbling block for those who choose not to drink, "But take care that this liberty of yours does not somehow become a stumbling block to the weak." (I Cor 8:9 NASB)

I would like to note that in all my forty years of hunting and fishing trips with Lindel Adair I never observed him drunk—a trait that a boyhood friend, Ben Bradford, explained to me how Lindel probably learned moderation from his father who liked to drink beer while playing pool, but never got drunk. Lindel, a proud Native American, was also a practicing Christian who enjoyed having fun in life and reading his bible each morning.

When Lindel passed away in December of 2018 I realized that I had lost a dear friend. Besides being a hunting and fishing partner for forty years, through all my seventeen years as Chief of the Service Unit Dental Program and Chief of Dental Services while stationed at the Claremore Indian Hospital (CIH) I sought Lindel's counsel and management advice on many occasions when he served as Personnel Officer and Administrative Officer at CIH. Personnel and management problems always occurred in a large service unit with a large fourteen-chair hospital dental clinic and five service unit field dental clinics serving a ninety-thousand-patient population. This involved staffs of twelve dental officers, twenty-seven dental assistants in the six clinics. No patient ever died on my watch. Praise God!

Although, never discussing the gospel, Lindel was a Christian example for me in dealing with others. Lindel did have a relationship with Jesus Christ and told me several times how much he enjoyed attending the local large Asbury Church on South Mingo in Tulsa. That surprised me because I had always thought Lindel belonged to a smaller church. He enjoyed life in all his activities, and glorified God through his actions.

He helped me pull a prank on Mike Brown, a USPHS Pharmacy Officer living in Stillwater while stationed at the Pawnee Indian Hospital for many years beginning in 1972. Mike was the one who went with me back to North Dakota in 1973 to hunt pheasants—a story that I wrote about earlier in this chapter. We later started a tradition of trading three days of excellent quail hunting around Pawnee for two days of duck hunting on Kerr Reservoir with me when I was stationed at Tahlequah. The duck hunts were continued on Oologah Lake after I transferred to Claremore in 1977. After one of these Thanksgiving hunts in the early 1980s I was telling Lindel about Mike's best quail dog being in the vet hospital on IV antibiotics with a severe lung infection for a week and unable to hunt that Thanksgiving.

Each year one week after Thanksgiving for several years, Mike had been invited to bring his dogs to the Grand National Quail Hunt at Enid, Oklahoma, which included several celebrities and politicians. Mike still had two other bird dogs, one a far-ranging older Brittany that had been trained in Texas with hunters riding horseback behind him, and another young Shorthair that had broken several coveys that Thanksgiving. Mike was concerned about the possibility of not having his best dog for the Grand National Quail Hunt that year.

Lindel and I concocted a scheme to pull a prank on Mike. Mike didn't know Lindel, but Lindel knew of Mike's reputation for being a very competitive quail hunter. Lindel also had good quail dogs and would represent someone on the Grand National Quail hunting committee in charge of assuring good quality dogs for the hunt. Lindel got on the phone and called Mike at work to tell him that he was calling just to check on his dog power before the hunt that week to make sure that he still had good dogs. After he told Mike this, I could hear Mike's tone of voice on the speaker phone becoming a little nervous and defensive about his dogs.

Mike said, "Yes, sir, I have good dogs this year. I have an older Brittany, and if he gets tired, I can run a young Shorthair in." Lindel put a little more pressure on Mike and said, "Well, you're sure they'll be as good as you've been having for the hunt in the past years." Mike said, "Yeah." Then Lindel said, "Okay I have another committee member who would like to speak with you."

Lindel gave me the phone, and I said, "Mike I was just wondering about your best dog that's been in the vet clinic for a week." After a short pause Mike said, "Hazle, I can't believe you did this to me." Lindel and I had a big laugh—at Mike's expense—because Lindel had done such a good job of fooling Mike. The sad thing was that Mike's dog died a few days later from complications of that lung infection, and I don't believe Mike went to the Grand National Quail Hunt that year.

One night in Norton it began sleeting about bedtime, and we could hear sleet hitting the metal top of the camper that night. It had been raining for part of the day and the gravel roads were slick already. I said to Lindel, "I'm glad I have my Blazer here with four-wheel drive."

He said, "Yeah, we should have no trouble getting to our spot in this nasty weather." It got very cold that night—in the upper teens. Everything was covered with ice the next morning. We ate a little bite, and I told Lindel that Frank and I would go out early and stake out a spot.

We left the campground, and the highway was slick, but the gravel road covered with fine grained pebbles—like pea gravel—was even slicker with the ice on top of frozen mud. Frank and I came to a hill with a slightly banked curve to the right. I thought I would stay left on the high side of the road so as not to slide off on the slope to the right side if my wheels began spinning. But I got up too high on the crest of the ditch where it met the embankment, and the front wheel slid off on the left side of the road; the front end of the Blazer started sliding down the fifteen-foot embankment. The more I tried to get out of the ditch, the farther I slid down the hill until I was almost high centered on the crest.

We couldn't do anything until Lindel came along with his pickup and hopefully pulled me out. I thought it was embarrassing when Lindel saw us stuck in the road. One problem was the street treads on my Blazer tires; they had very little traction. Of course, Lindel and the others had a big laugh since we had been talking about how good it was to have the four-wheel-drive Blazer. Just as Lindel was hooking up to the Blazer, we stopped and watched as a six-cylinder rusty old pickup passed us on the inside of the curve and slowly creep up and over the hill. That made it even more embarrassing, but I was laughing with the others. We made it to our hunting spots okay that morning, and I don't remember it interrupting our hunt that day.

A few years later, Lorn Rohr, Del Nutter, Ben Bradford, and Joe Miller began going to Norton and WaKenney with us. All these men were associated with the IHS except Ben, who had worked for Dow Chemical for twenty-six years. Pheasant hunting became more difficult around the lake after it filled up and covered all the good cropland; we had to find private land to supplement the lake hunting. It was in the late 1980s or early 1990s that we began hunting at WaKeeney. We had good hunts on some private land there for a several years. We tried Ness City, Liberal, Scott City, and Ulysses, Kansas, for a few years with moderate success. We hunted at Smokey Hill Air Force Range near Salina one year. But none of these locations were as good as when I first started going to Norton.

I recently talked to Ben Bradford just to have some reminders of our Norton hunting trips. Ben first reminded me of the time in Norton when he spent a cold night sleeping in the back of a pickup with a topper because he didn't like all the noise from the other men snoring in the camper; he had only a small electric heater for warmth. The problem was that the electric box where all three campers and Ben's heater were plugged into kept throwing an overload breaker. Ben said he never got any sleep because of getting up several times during the night and going out in the cold to turn the electricity back on. I could understand why he remembered that event.

Then he reminded me of the time we left Norton when the roads were already covered with four inches of snow, and it was still snowing hard. Lindel was driving his pickup with an aluminum dog box hooked on the rear of his large late-model Ford pickup. As we were going up a slight grade coming out of Norton, another pickup passed us and cut us off causing our truck to swerve and hit the left ditch while going fifty miles an hour. The ditch was eight-feet deep, and I thought his pickup was going to roll over, but Lindel kept going straight up the ditch with snow flying everywhere; somehow, he guided the truck back upon the road and straightened out without going into the ditch on the other side. Yes, God was surely watching over us that time.

I thought of the time we went back for a second hunt at the end of December since everyone already had their licenses for that season. This time we went to Wilson Lake where there was some public hunting only thirty-five miles west of Salina. When we arrived at the campsite the temperature was in the teens, the lake below us was frozen, no electrical hookups were available, and the wind was blowing about twenty-five miles per hour with a light snow. That night two of the men slept in the back of a pickup with a topper without any heat. Our camper was parked on the edge of a bluff; I could look out a side window of the camper at the frozen lake one hundred feet below. That night I worried that the camper was going to be blown off the bluff and into the frozen lake, because the wind gusts rocked our small camper all night.

The next morning the two guys in the camper were complaining about it being so cold they couldn't sleep well, but I was just thankful to still be alive. We ate breakfast, and six of us went out to hunt well past the sunrise time we usually began hunting. We hunted in some good-looking weed patches and grassy draws. We shot only one bird that morning and decided to leave for home at noon. That was the worst pheasant hunting trip that I had ever been on; we never went back for a second hunt in the same season again.

Eventually Lindel, Ben Bradford, and I started going to Murdo, South Dakota, in the late 1990s and had some good hunting on private land. One morning we crossed a large pond dam in a deep draw and found a large group of pheasants at two grain bins on top of a hill on the other side where we had permission to hunt. We drove past the grain bins through some old rusty cars and through pheasants playing in the gravel road around the two grain bins, but not many flushed, so we turned our pickup around and approached the bins with two of us in the back and started shooting—killing five birds. Then we parked on the hill and walked down the hill to the draw below the grain bins where we had watched some birds go down. We got four more out of the weeds and cattails in the draw—our limit for the day. The attraction for the pheasants at the grain bins was spilled wheat around the grain elevators. No houses were within miles of that location, and many pheasants were in that area because there were round bales of hay surrounded with weed patches, many acres of grain, draws, and the large pond all with good cover. We returned several times that trip to have good hunting in that area. The Range Country Lodging in Murdo was an excellent place to stay because it also had a pheasant cleaning area where we could conveniently return and clean birds each evening.

I can't forget the game farm southwest of Murdo. It was a favorite place to wind up late in the day after some road hunting. We could line up in the ditch on the east section line across from the game farm. Several hunters would be lined up along the three-hundred-yard stretch waiting for the pheasants to fly out of the game farm into the Conservation Reserve Program (CRP) grass field behind us to roost. The pheasants were very cautious about flying this gauntlet as they had learned from experience. They would peer out of the grass and look up and down the gravel road for hunters waiting on the other side. If they saw us, they would go back in the grass and move down the road to another location and start coming across. It was good fast shooting as time neared sunset. Retrieving the birds was not easy in the CRP, so we tried to shoot them before they could fly across the road—being careful to stay out of range of other hunters along the line. We could usually kill four or five and have lots of shooting. It was a good way to end another successful day of hunting.

DUCK HUNTING WITH A BROKEN RIB

Jason Jones, my son-in-law, and I had hunted Fort Cobb Reservoir on Friday after Thanksgiving in 2000 before returning for a Saturday morning hunt. We had checked a map of the lake at a small bait shop near the dam on Friday to determine the boundaries for legal hunting because the main park office was closed on Friday. The map shown to us by a young lady indicated a line across the lower third of Fort Cobb Reservoir with state park land on the shoreline highlighted in yellow indicating no hunting was allowed. We'd had a fair hunt on Friday on the east side of the lake but had seen more ducks on the west side of the lake at a location that, according to the young female clerk at the bait shop, was in a legal hunting zone outside the park with a nearby boat ramp.

On Saturday we were having an extremely good hunt with the mallards decoying well and almost had our limit of greenheads before I decided to move over to the left a few yards. As I stepped off a large log the water was deeper on the other side, and I fell hitting my left torso on a stump. I immediately felt a sharp pain and had difficulty breathing. The pain was worse than when I had broken a rib on my right side by falling backward on a corner of a large rock while fishing a few years earlier on the Verdigris River near Claremore. I told Jason, "I think I've broken a rib!" I couldn't shoot any more, but he soon shot two more greenheads for our limit and began gathering up the decoys.

A man in a green uniform---a game ranger I supposed---approached us from the south along the shoreline. After briefly talking to us he said, "The reason you've had a good hunt is that you've been hunting in the state park." The ranger looked at me kneeling on the ground and asked, "What's the matter with you?"

I said, "I think I've broken a rib."

He asked, "How's that?"

I explained what had happened and then began to explain how we had visited the bait shop, which was a certified deer hunter check station for the Oklahoma Department of Wildlife Conservation, and a young lady had shown us a map and assured us we would be safe hunting in this area. He showed no sympathy and said, "You can bring the young lady and the map to court with you." After that he wrote us citations for $125 each.

Jason hauled both bags of decoys and ducks to the boat and then loaded the boat on the trailer, and we headed for Mercy Hospital in Oklahoma City. Every breath and bump in the road made the trip painful. At the hospital emergency room, they did an x-ray and a CT scan to confirm there was no ruptured spleen; they placed an elastic strap around my rib cage, which I was to wear for a week. The doctor prescribed some pain meds. We did not go to court; instead, we just avoided the hassle and mailed in our fines.

OPENING DUCK SEASON TWO WEEKS EARLY

I was an associate in practice with Dr. Steven Deem in Claremore in 1999 after retiring from the USPHS in 1995. Dr. Deem was eager to go on a duck hunt. It was the end of October, and members of the Claremore Area Ducks Unlimited (DU) Committee had been discussing building their duck blinds for the coming season. Somehow, I got the idea that maybe duck season was opening at the end of October as it had done sometimes in the past.

One day when I was in a hurry to get to work at the dental office, I opened the sports section to Sam Powell's hunting article in the *Tulsa World* for that week to see the headlines, "New Duck Season to Open This Weekend." I thought, *Good, they've moved opening day back to the last weekend in October.* I closed the paper and arrived at Dr. Deem's office telling him we were going hunting that weekend on the upper end of Oologah Lake. We arrived early Saturday morning before daylight at an old oxbow, Kester Creek, on the west side of the lake that led to the Verdigris River and unloaded the boat.

As we approached the end of the oxbow where it opened into the river, we couldn't get through because the lake was down a foot and the oxbow had silted in. The lake was low enough that we had to unload our decoys and take off the motor so we could push the boat over the silt through a beaver channel into the Verdigris. There was just enough daylight that I could see a deer hunter in his stand at the edge of the river within twenty-five yards of our commotion—probably an unhappy deer hunter by now. We loaded everything back in the boat and headed south two miles down the Verdigris to some open water. We were having a good hunt, but only heard a few other shots. I mentioned to Steve that other hunters surely had difficulty getting into the lake that morning because we weren't hearing much shooting. I turned around and saw a boat with two men and a black Lab up to the north about three hundred yards in the Verdigris watching us.

After getting our two limits of a mixed bag of pintails, gadwalls, teal, and greenheads by nine, we loaded up and arrived at the slough where we had to repeat the process unloading and loading again in front of the deer hunter still there. After pushing through the slough, I recognized my friend Mark Rouk and one of Chance Turner's sons with their Lab thirty yards ahead of us. These two men were on the Claremore Area DU Committee. Mark asked, "What are you doing out here today?"

I said, "Duck hunting, what did you think?"

They laughed and said, "But duck season doesn't open for two weeks!"

I said, "I saw Sam Powell's article in the *Tulsa World* this week, and the headline read a new duck season was opening this weekend." Before they could say anything, I realized my mistake. I had that sinking feeling in my stomach when I realized that the article—if I had only read it—was referring to the opening of duck season in western Oklahoma, which always opened two weeks earlier than eastern Oklahoma. I asked, "What are you doing out here?"

Mark said, "We're snipe hunting." I remembered that Mark always took his Lab on some practice hunts for Wilson's snipe before the opening of duck season.

I asked, "Did you get any?"

Mark said, "Three."

I was ready to take one in case we were checked. What ranger or judge would believe my story about the article in the paper? If we had a snipe, maybe a warden could believe we had been hunting snipe. On the way home Steve said, "Let's stop at a convenient store and get something to drink."

I said, "I'm not stopping anywhere and draw attention to the two bags of decoys in our boat.

BIRD HUNTING ON THE VONEYE'S LAND IN SOUTH DAKOTA

A normal routine for a sunny cool autumn day of pheasant hunting went like this. Hunting began at noon, and the first stop was the honey hole, a small one-acre wet-weather slough with a few cattails. Four men with dogs walked up the shallow drain toward a large willow tree where four other men had the hole surrounded. It was like an English hunt when the pheasants busted out of their cover in all directions. We usually could get six birds before moving across the road to hunt a small creek bed with a cattail slough. Then we might walk the tall grass forty-acre Conservation Reserve Program (CRP) field adjacent to the honey hole. It was a productive way to start every other day. The Voneye's also had corn fields and shelter belts that were very productive. When we had our limit, it was back to the assembly line for cleaning the birds in a cleaning room with tables, concrete floor, and a drain and then soaking them in saltwater. We could clean twenty-four birds in thirty minutes.

To give you an idea of how many pheasants lived in that area, we saw about fifteen sitting in a dead tree along the road near an old abandoned homestead—looking like Christmas ornaments hanging on a tree. I have a picture of thirty-three pheasants running up a snow-covered hill. Because pheasants were so plentiful, John Hoover convinced us all to hunt with 410 shotguns one year, and we got our possession limit for the trip using 410s.

John and I would duck hunt some mornings in the nearby sloughs, prairie potholes, lakes, and ponds. We had plenty of shooting, but the ducks weren't as easy to hunt as I had expected. Maybe many had already been shot at in Canada. We took pictures holding our ducks while kneeling in front of an old mule-drawn-single-bottomed plow that was painted red. Corn shocks were tied to a light pole surrounded by white and orange pumpkins and colorful gourds on the ground. One morning we sat at the edge of a three-acre pothole in my Suburban waiting for sunrise while periodically turning on the lights to see if any ducks were coming in. I played "A Change Would Do You Good" by Cheryl Crow repeatedly. We were having fun talking but were seeing no ducks even though we waited thirty minutes past sunrise, so we made the change to another smaller slough. There we had ducks decoying well and had a good morning hunt. We made a memory with that song, and I gave John a cassette with the song to stimulate a good memory recall. He says it still reminds him of that morning.

One day I asked to block a cornfield strip with two other hunters so I could video the action while five men walked through the corn rows with dogs. That wasn't a productive filming session. When the pheasants began flying out over us, I couldn't stand it, so I dropped the camera hanging around my neck—still running—and I started shooting. All I caught on the film was the noise of my gun going off and shells being ejected on the ground by my feet. I got three pheasants—my limit for the day. They never let me block and film a drive again.

One day we pulled a prank on Jerry, who lacked two birds having his limit. John Hoover and I took two heads and feather pelts from the cleaning room and staked them at the edge of some tall grass along the driveway around the corner from the ranch house. This was in an area between two shelter belts and pheasants were often seen there crossing the road. Jerry was told that he could shoot the next two pheasants we saw. As the pickup with everyone else in it rounded the corner coming from the house a pheasant flew across the road near the two dummy birds. He spotted the two cock dummies and hopped out of the back of the pickup in a hunched-over-low position sneaking up the ditch toward the birds about fifty yards away. As he approached the birds, he was close enough to tap one of the heads before he saw they were fake; then he kicked them into the tall grass. That was a trick that worked well. Jerry later got his limit!

It was October 23, 1995, that we hunted in a blizzard that dumped twelve inches of snow in eight hours. By hunting the shelter belts and CRP near the ranch house we still got our limit though—barely able to see. Mark grilled some pheasants in the garage that day, and it all worked out well. We always topped off the trip by attending a Ducks Unlimited banquet at Woonsocket where we enjoyed a good dinner, the raffles, and auction.

While driving to and from South Dakota, relaxing around the ranch house, and hunting in the fields I used a Walkman with earphones listening to the same music repeatedly to remind me of all the good hunts in South Dakota. I would leave one earphone out when in the fields so I could hear the birds flush. Now when I listen to Clint Black's "Life Gets Away," "Summer's Comin'," "No Time to Kill," and "A Change in the Air" I can recall the emotions of the hunts. I also listened to "Five Minutes" by Lorrie Morgan, "Walkabout" and "Everglade Run" by Yanni, "Halley Came to Jackson" and "Down at the Twist and Shout," by Mary Chapin Carpenter, along with songs by several other artists. I haven't been hunting at the Voneye's since about 2006, but I still have some powerful memories of many trips over a period of fifteen years when I put in my earbuds and listen to the songs.

THREE HUNTS WITH BRYAN ADAIR

I took nineteen-year-old Bryan Adair on his first duck hunt. His dad was Lindel Adair, the CIH administrator, also my hunting and fishing buddy. Bryan was an excellent pheasant hunter, which I found out on a few trips to Norton, Kansas, with his dad and others. We put in on the east side of the Oologah Lake west of

New Alluwe. We went about one hundred yards off the shoreline, which was bordered by willows. I had built a portable blind for my fourteen-foot semi-V aluminum boat that would unfold and with additional netting provide cover while we hunted in open water.

The south wind was moderate that sunny day, and we had our backs to the sun, but it was cold. We had about three dozen mallard decoys divided into two groups. It was cold enough that even with our hot coffee my toes were beginning to hurt after about two hours, and we had not had any ducks look at our decoy spread. I'd begun to be disappointed that I had taken Bryan on such a poor duck hunt for his first experience.

About that time, I saw a flight of twenty or so mallards far off coming from the north headed down the lake our way, and I gave a few loud hail calls. I was using the hail call trying to encourage them to keep coming. I told Bryan to keep his head down and not move till I said, "Shoot—and don't shoot any brown ducks!" As they passed in front and turned back to our left heading east, I could see through the netting as they circled wide behind us, and I gave some single quacks and feeding chuckles. They made a wide turn out on our right side heading west; after a loud come-back call, they banked straight toward us with their wings cupped, locked up, orange feet splayed, and only sixty yards out headed straight for the opening between our two groups of decoys. I waited until some were backpedaling ready to land and I shouted, "Shoot!" We unloaded our guns and six ducks were lying on the water—amazingly with no cripples.

Bryan jumped up and said in an excited voice, "This is the easiest hunting I've ever done!" I looked on my side at three greenheads, but on Bryan's side I saw three hens—brown ducks.

I asked, "What do you see?"

He said in a hesitant voice, "Three brown ducks."

I asked, "Why did you shoot the hens?"

He said, "They all looked alike."

I'd been there before when I first started hunting ducks, so

I told him, "That's okay; it happens." I said, "I see two limits." We were still using the point system at that time, which allowed a one-hundred-point limit, and at seventy points each for the hens and twenty points for each drake; one hen and three drakes equaled 130 points—which was okay if the last duck shot was a hen. As far as we knew, it could have happened in that order. The two remaining hens totaled 140; although the second hen caused the total to exceed the one hundred points, that was okay. Bryan later said he was afraid we might be in trouble with so many hens. If the game ranger pulled out his rectal thermometer and the temperatures of all six ducks were all about the same, he would realize that we shot all the ducks at the same time. If one hen had been colder it would mean that the hen was probably shot before the drakes—leaving us with one extra drake over the limit. We didn't really know the order in which the ducks had been shot, so I didn't believe three hens would be a problem, but Bryan never forgot that he had shot three hens.

We picked up our six ducks and decoys and headed home. I was glad Bryan at least got to shoot some ducks on his first hunt. He later began hunting ducks on Fort Gibson Lake and told me about some very successful hunts he had when the water level was up. I was glad to have taken him on his first duck hunt.

A few years later I rode with Bryan to Ulysses, Kansas, to meet Lindel and his brother Joe Bob with others from Wichita who brought their camper for the pheasant hunt. We met up at a city park and spent the night with Frank Odonnell in Lindel's camper before hunting the next morning. I can't remember why Bryan and I hunted at a different place than the others that day, but we were separated from the main group. All we did was hunt pheasants along the graveled section lines, tanks, and around a feedlot. The land is flat in that area with many wheat fields and some milo fields.

There was not much cover for birds in the flat cropped fields. Some fields had enough cover from standing wheat stubble or harvested milo row crops that could have been walked and blocked, but the birds were wild, and with only two of us and no dogs or blockers that didn't seem to be a practical idea. We found most of our birds by stopping at intersections and watching for pheasants coming out of the tall dried weeds along the bar ditches. When we spotted one, we would begin walking that bar ditch and usually found several pheasants each time we repeated this process. There were not many houses and minimal road traffic to prevent us from hunting like this. I once shot a pheasant flying out of the bar ditch weeds that went down in an open wheat field about 150 yards away. We saw a large long-haired gray dog leave a small farmhouse and run across the wheat field toward my pheasant. He picked up the bird and returned to the house as if he had done that routine before. When we finished walking that bar ditch, we turned at the intersection and drove in front of the farmhouse, which was about one hundred yards off the road. The big dog was sitting on the front porch eating my pheasant.

We found several small tanks containing water with mounds of embankments covered with the same dried tall weeds. These were productive, but sometimes a bird would fall into the water, and we would have to wait for it to drift to the bank. One feed lot had areas with weed patches on adjacent land that was not near any cattle and not posted. Pheasants liked these areas, and we shot some there.

When we had our limit of eight birds, we returned to the campground and hung out while waiting for the other hunters to return. The other six men returned with only one bird, and several were complaining that there were no birds; they—especially Frank Odonnell—were ready to move on to another area. Bryan and I just laughed and showed them all our birds. I can't remember what happened after that, but Bryan and I felt very good for having shot so many birds. I believe we ate and moved on to another area.

Bryan did take me on another pheasant hunt to North Dakota near the town of Braddock about forty miles southeast of Bismarck. Leaving on Halloween and returning November 7, 2013, Bryan flew his dad, Lindel, Ben Bradford, and me eight hundred miles in his Cessna 210 Turbo from Tulsa, Oklahoma, to Bismarck. The four-hour plane ride from Tulsa was exciting with Bryan flying near the large propellers of the wind farms we encountered on the way up. We stayed in an old farmhouse belonging to Betty McLish near the tailwaters of Braddock Lake. We met Brett Adair with his two friends, Jeff and Mark, who drove up from Wichita, Kansas, with their bird dogs.

The city of Bismarck was booming compared to when I was last there in 1973. The Bakken oil fields boom in northwest North Dakota near Williston has created $16 billion in state assets to pay state bills totaling only $7.5 billion. This compares to neighboring South Dakota, which had a debt of $3.3 billion in 2015. The median household income for North Dakota has risen to $61,843 in 2017 for a median age of only 37.1 compared to a median US household income of $60,336 in 2017. North Dakota had become a wealthy state! The median household income for residents of Bismarck was $66,087 in 2017.

Staying in the old farmhouse reminded me of the comradery I had with a small group on a relaxed duck-hunting weekend northeast of Bismarck near Pettibone in 1972. A private dentist in Bismarck had graciously invited me on the hunt with his group who owned an old farmhouse as a hunting lodge. All we did was eat well, lounge around, and do early morning pass-shooting off roads crossing long prairie potholes followed by jumping small cattail slews loaded with mallards during the day—no decoy shooting. They knew all the good small cattail slews in the area that we could drive near, park, get out, and shoot. After eating lunch and lounging around for a couple of hours we jumped more slews in the afternoon until we were worn out.

At the farmhouse in Braddock huge clouds of low-flying snow geese were rising and falling above nearby combined cornfields until landing in a long three-hundred-yard by seventy-five-yard area. Numerous ducks also were on nearby pothole lakes. There were daily late evening goose and duck-hunting shoots down a hill three hundred yards from the farmhouse to the tailwaters of Braddock Lake where waterfowl were plentiful. Lindel and I went duck hunting on a nearby lake early one morning; without decoys we had only some unsuccessful pass shooting but saw thousands of ducks. I surely wished we had a decoy spread that day for some good calling and shooting.

Pheasants had repopulated North Dakota well since I had last hunted there in 1973 after a 1968 blizzard had destroyed much of the pheasant population. Plenty of corn and wheat fields were in the area and good cover with some tree rows holding lots of pheasants. We had very good pheasant hunting considering it was our first time hunting the area.

Another bit of excitement for me was the return trip to Tulsa. We had not stopped to refuel on the way back, as we had done going up to Bismarck, and Bryan said we were running low on fuel when we were crossing the Kansas-Oklahoma border—seventy miles from Jones Riverside airport. The Cessna Turbo 210 has an eighty-gallon tank and at cruising speed of about 190 mph used fifteen gallons per hour—that's sixty gallons at least and more with a south headwind returning. Approaching the lights of Tulsa, Bryan could not locate the runway lights at Jones Riverside Airport. We had circled above the lights of Tulsa—maybe for ten minutes. But it seemed longer to me because I was worried about running out of fuel while looking for the runway. He decided to call the airport tower for help with his location and bearings to the runway. He said he had landed at night a thousand times and had never lost the runway. The controller in the tower at Riverside guided Bryan back on track for the runway before we ran out of fuel. It felt good to be on the ground, and that ended an exciting trip about ten that night.

GOOD DUCK HUNTING ON OOLOGAH LAKE

Oologah Lake had the best duck hunting of all the lakes I had hunted in Oklahoma, and it was only ten miles from my house in Claremore to the lower end of the lake where I first began hunting in 1977. However, the best hunting was thirty-five miles to Nowata and five miles east to the upper end of the lake. I had so many good hunts at Oologah after hunting my way up the lake to Highway 60 over a period of almost three seasons. When there was enough rain to raise the lake level three to ten feet, the upper end provided outstanding hunting in the hardwood timbers on the east and west sides of Old Highway 28. In the 1980s the Oklahoma Department of Wildlife Conservation improved the good duck hunting on the upper end with a project that flooded a 277-acre rectangular strip of hardwoods along the east side of Old Highway 28 just south of Highway 60. We didn't have to depend on flooding for the hunting to be reliably good. They created several holes down the middle about seventy yards in diameter, with the timber stacked around the edges, which made good cover for hiding. The water was one to two feet deep and usually had Japanese millet sown in the holes with an airplane by the wildlife department.

I can still picture in my mind the many days of circling mallards responding to our calling with their emerald metallic green heads and blue wing speculums of the drakes shining in the sunshine before dropping into the holes to our decoys. In one of those holes I yelled at one of my friends, Jamie Keith, on the other side that a drake was coming his way, but he didn't see him in time to shoot. When the drake made the circle again to my side, I got a good shot and dropped the bird. When Mark Rouk's dog brought the bird back to us, it had a band on its leg—my good luck again. I had many good hunts in the green tree area with Richard and Brad Swan, Mark Rouk, Jamie Keith, Larry Dalvine, and others.

However, that good green tree hunting only lasted about three years, and the beavers dammed up the water control structure in the dyke across the south end. Additional rains and very high lake levels throughout the fall, spring and summer kept the green tree area flooded for longer than a year. No matter how hard the wildlife department tried to destroy the beaver dams they couldn't stop them from quickly rebuilding them. The wildlife department finally made a V cut hole in the dike and the water drained, but the damage had been done. The hardwoods were all destroyed.

Jason and Jeremy Jones hunted with me at the V-cut in the dyke a few years later for a super hunt with Jason's nine-month-old female yellow Lab named Mazie. We used the sides of the V cut in the dike to hide from the ducks under some small trees and weeds on the bank. For some reason the ducks liked that area where a large pool of water formed in front of the V and was bordered on the east side by some trees. The water in the pool was a good depth for placing some decoys, then hiding the boat under some tree limbs hanging over the dyke. We shot fourteen ducks that day, and Mazie retrieved all of them. It was just an enjoyable sunny day for a super hunt. Even by 2019, no mature hardwoods were in the green tree area.

Before I started hunting mainly on the north end of Lake Oolagah in 1980, I had taken my hunting and fishing buddy, Lindel Adair, to the blind site that I had drawn in 1979. My blind was located west of New Alluwe and just north of Plumb Creek in the stickups of an old fence line about fifty yards from the shoreline in three feet of water. The blind had a metal framework, which I had spent several hours constructing, and required a ladder to get into. This was a location that I thought looked attractive for ducks, even though I hadn't seen any ducks there. I still hadn't learned the importance of hunting where ducks had been seen using the area—not just what looked good to me.

Lindel and I walked to the blind on a cold, windy day, and oh that blind was cold. We stood there for two hours, and all we saw were cormorants flying up and down the middle of the lake. I'm telling you this to let you know that every duck hunt that I've been on has not been successful; that's what makes this hunt memorable—one of my worst duck hunts ever. But I did take Lindel on a good duck hunt a few years later at the north end.

Lindel and I arrived near the old Salt Creek abutments where I usually launched my boat off the west side of Old Highway 28 about 1.5 miles south of Highway 60. When we got out of my Blazer, the wind was blowing snow in our faces at about twenty mph, and it was about twenty degrees. We loaded up the boat with all our gear and decoys and backed it off the shoulder of the road into water that got deep fast down the sloping old roadbed embankment. I had Lindel hold the boat while I pulled the blazer forward thirty yards out of the way of other hunters launching there. It was a good place to launch, and many hunters used it because there was no other access to that part of the lake without going over open water, which was dangerous on windy days.

Several hunters had capsized in the cold water and died coming from the west side of the lake out of a Double Creek boat ramp. John Hoover told me about rescuing two hunters near death from hypothermia clinging to their boat in Double Creek. We didn't have to get in any open water that day with Lindel, because my hunting spot was near the confluence of Kentucky Creek and Salt Creek just north of any open water.

We saw several flights of mallards on the way to our spot; that was encouraging. We pulled beside a large log that was already covered with snow, and I set out the decoys. It was still snowing. I had never hunted ducks in snow like that, but it didn't seem to bother the ducks that day. I saw a flight of ducks and began calling. Some ducks circled once, cupped their wings headed for our decoys, and we shot three drakes. We continued shooting ducks in the snow and had ten drakes before we left. When we got back in the Blazer, I think we both were relieved to be out of the cold, snowy weather. I had finally taken Lindel on a successful duck hunt even if it was a nasty day.

I had an unusual hunt on Oologah lake around 1988 with two dental coworkers. Dr. Mark Huberty was a young USPHS commissioned officer from Sheboygan, Wisconsin, who worked with me at CIH, and Dr. Steve Deem who had a private dental practice in Claremore. Neither had been duck hunting before. We also took Dr. Huberty's wife, Heide, and Dr. Deem's two young sons, Charlie, thirteen years old and Jerry, eleven. We drove south on Old Highway 28 from Highway 60 to the old concrete abutments in Salt Creek to launch the boat.

I made two trips in the boat through a thin sheet of ice carrying everyone to our hunting site near an old square concrete structure on dry land just south of the confluence of Kentucky Creek and Salt Creek. I had hunted in this area south of Salt Creek recently and suspected that the ducks were still there because there was Japanese millet in the area. We could see ducks flying south of us over the open water loaded with stickups. We set our decoys up on the south side of the concrete structure, and everyone but me hid in the weeds around the concrete; I stood in shallow water by a large seven-foot-tall tree stump. We were seeing hundreds of ducks to the south over the open water and expected to have some shooting soon. I was calling, and ducks would come near us but remained just out of range; we shot at a few and hit one lucky shot, but we couldn't stand seeing them circling and landing about one hundred yards in front of us in the dead stickups. I had hunted out there earlier that season and stood next to another very large tall stump in four feet of water.

Because we weren't having much success, I suggested that Mark and Steve go stand behind the tall tree stump for cover and shoot some of those elusive ducks. They went out there and dragged six decoys with them. As soon as they got there and set out the decoys, they started shooting mallards. They were wading in water almost to the top of their waders when retrieving the ducks.

Heide, the two boys, and I were enjoying watching the show, but the young boys wanted to shoot their three-inch twenty-gauge gun. I picked out a target, the large stump to the east of us, and asked Charlie, the older one, to load up the gun with one shell and shoot at a knot on the stump. I didn't look at the shells his dad had brought, but when he pulled the trigger and the gun went off it knocked him back six inches. I said, "You must be shooting the heaviest loads possible for a 20-gauge gun to kick that much. Let me see your shells." I looked at a shell, and it was a three-inch heavy load with one ounce and an eighth shot. I said, "Yeah, that's the heaviest load you can shoot in a 20-gauge."

Charlie looked at his younger brother and said, "Yep, Dad did it to us again!" Heidi and I laughed at what he had said. I never did know what he was referring to when he said that, but I couldn't wait to tell his dad about that.

Heidi had been sitting on top of the concrete structure watching Mark and Steve with binoculars, commenting on what was happening. Then she said quietly, "He's under!"

I asked, "Under what?"

She said, "Mark went under the water." The first thing I thought about were the large roots of the stump that stuck up out of the slick mud and had made walking difficult for me when I had hunted out there.

She said, "He's up. He looks like he's okay." I thought okay but wet and cold, and he probably would be coming in soon. They had already shot several mallards, but they continued hunting for ten minutes longer. They came in packing the decoys and mallards. When they were near us, I couldn't keep from laughing, and I asked Mark what happened.

He said, "I lost my balance because the tree roots were slick, and I slipped down." I asked if he was okay, "He said yes, but I'm getting cold."

I took Mark and Heidi back to the Blazer first so he could get out of the cold. I started the Blazer and turned up the heater. When I brought Steve and his two boys in, I asked Steve to hold the boat while I turned the Blazer and trailer around; there was just enough room to back the trailer off the old roadbed and turn around on the narrow road. We got everything loaded up and went home. Everyone seemed to have enjoyed the adventure.

Bob Newlon and I had many good hunting days in 1992 on the north side of Highway 60 when the lake was up ten feet, especially at the north end of Kentucky Creek. We found a bend with an open pool in the creek just before it narrowed to an undetectable channel. Other hunters, including a group of men who started in North Dakota every year and worked their way south—always hunting Oologah Lake—would come to the edge of the hole, turn around and leave. Bob and I figured we were in one of their best spots. The hunters who started up north had a blind that fully covered their large boat, and they told us Oologah Lake was one of their favorite stops. I have a picture of their boat and pictures of us having some good mallard hunts there.

I once hunted with Buck Vest in a small open field on the

north side of Highway 60 bordering the west side of Old Highway 28 where the woods ended and at the edge of a small wheat field. Once, when the water was up eight feet, Buck and I were standing at the edge of the woods on the west end of that field and shooting out over decoys to the north. Buck and I were having a fun hunt together; we were shooting many greenheads on a cold sunny day—on our way to getting our limit early. The temperature was in the teens, and Buck dropped his gun in the icy water. He retrieved his gun, but the ice in it ruined his hunting that morning. What a stroke of bad luck for Buck. I had to help him finish his limit. We got a good laugh out of that one.

That location was within ten yards of where on another hunt with Bob Newlon my glasses were pulled off my face by a tree limb as we were leaving after getting our limit of greenheads. I tied a rag on the limb and went back after the water receded the next spring and found my glasses mingled with some leaves and covered with silt—what a surprise.

A similar event happened when I dropped a small flashlight that I was holding in my mouth while putting out decoys in a place Bob Newlon called the "little hole." The flashlight was a small 2.5-inch red Tekna Splash-Lite with a lithium battery that I had dropped. The spot had a firm bottom, and I could see that the light was still on, but I didn't want to bend over and retrieve the flashlight because I couldn't reach it without getting my coat wet as well as having water come into my waders; I would be wet and cold before we started hunting. But I hated to lose my favorite light with an O-ring for waterproofing that I had bought in Saint Louis five years earlier. I stuck the paddle end of a short aluminum oar into the firm mud to mark the spot so I could come back when the water receded. Three months later after the water went down, I went back and found it—with the light still burning. Ha! Just kidding. I still have the flashlight hanging on my lanyard with a duck call, and it still works well after thirty-five years.

I began hunting with Bob Newlon more often in 1991 in the

little hole. The little hole was west of Kentucky Creek and was best entered from the south through a beaver trail. This entrance was hard to see from Kentucky Creek, and not many hunters knew about the spot. The only other way into the little hole was navigating through some timber when the water level was up a few feet, but the hole of water couldn't be seen through the timber from Kentucky Creek. We were always having to bust through the beaver dam and drag our boat over it to get into the hole. Whatever we tore out, the beavers would build back by the next morning. The sound of running water attracted them to the break in their dam.

The best hunting in the little hole was when we planted Japanese millet (beginning in 1993) with rotating hand spreaders during the hot July and early August months while there was a wet sheen on the mud, which helped the millet sprout faster. The crops formed a beautiful green mat after a few weeks and produced plenty of millet. I took pictures of our deep footprints in the mud and later of the green crop. We usually had our best hunting on the southeast end of the hole when we had a good millet crop and some trees to hide in and shoot out of our boat. That was hard work when it was hot and humid walking through the mud, but it always paid off with many limits of greenheads and was worth the sweat.

Bob and I were in the northwest corner of the hole one day when a single mallard drake landed about fifty yards from us along the willows. I told Bob I was going to take a shot, and Bob said, "You'll never kill him that far away especially on the water." I took the shot, and when Bob's Lab retrieved the duck, it had a band. I have records of five banded mallards, one gadwall, one goose, plus a banded widgeon with no record because I had the duck mounted. This is a total of ten bands because two mallards had two bands each—extra $20 green-tinted aluminum bands.

The little hole was divided by a peninsula on the north end. We often hunted on each side of the peninsula as well as the south point. One day Bob and I hunted together with Tony Cloud and John Hoover in another boat on the northeast side of the little hole when the water was up eight feet above normal. We put out about eighty decoys and shot our limits on a sunny day.

A little farther south of the little hole was a large open hole with water two to three feet deep without much vegetation; it held mostly shovelers unless we sowed millet. We called it "the mud hole." It was more visible, surrounded by grass and weeds, and had easier access from Kentucky Creek, so more hunters knew about it but didn't hunt there because it lacked vegetation to attract mallards. Mark Rouk, Bob Newlon, and I hunted over millet that we had sown in July. It was opening day November 7, 1997, when we got our limits of mixed bags of mallards, teal, gadwall, and pintail. T. M. Harrison, Jason Jones, my son-in-law, and I camped out along the Verdigris River and hunted there in December 1998, the first weekend after the break, where I had sown a good millet crop that year. We killed our limits two days in a row.

Lorn Rohr and I had several good hunts in a large flat east of Old Highway 28 and between Salt Creek and the old southern east-west dyke of the defunct green tree area. I also hunted with Lorn in "horseshoe lake" between Kentucky Creek and the Verdigris. Decoy strings had to be at least fifteen feet long to hunt there, but at times mallards decoyed well there, and we could shoot limits. We also hunted with Mark Rouk several times for a few years on a point south of Winganon bridge and west of Winganon ramp when everything in the north end was frozen; we shot mostly mallards, common mergansers, and goldeneye there. Mark and I once hunted on the west side of the lake along Will Rogers Point after launching off Goose Island; we shot ten large common mergansers one day when icy sludge was floating in large clumps in the lake.

The wildlife department did develop some large acreage of shallow-water pools north of Highway 60 along the west side of the Verdigris River in an area called the overcup bottoms that provided some decent hunting and wasn't very crowded. That was the last location I hunted with Lorn before he passed away with lung cancer. He was short of breath and struggling to keep up while walking on the dykes to our hunting spot one morning. Lorn never talked much about the status of his cancer and never complained, but I knew that day he was not well. Lorn passed away not very many months after that, and I lost my last duck hunting partner.

Lorn once told me that I had influenced him to start attending Memorial Heights Baptist Sunday school and church services. I was humbled and glad for Lorn. I had known Lorn for many years through his attendance at DU banquets and his association with Dr. Byron Jasper, my deputy chief at Claremore Indian Hospital (CIH). Lorn and Byron bass fished in tournaments together. Lorn was a hard worker at the IHS Oklahoma City Area Office and drove from Claremore to Oklahoma City—an hour and forty minutes one way—daily for several years until he obtained a position in procurement at CIH.

As I got to know Lorn more, I found out that he and Linda really enjoyed western swing dancing. They had even entered competitions for several years. Donna and I went out to eat with Linda and Lorn on several occasions. I was at Lorn's house just a few days before his death with Brother Paul Simpson, pastor of Memorial Heights Baptist Church in Claremore. He discussed with Lorn his spiritual condition; he professed being a believer in Jesus Christ as his Lord and Savior and believed that he was going to spend eternity with his heavenly Father.

I had given Lorn a charcoal Combe Herringbone English Ivy driving cap to wear after he lost his hair from cancer chemotherapy. I went to Tulsa with Lorn on a few occasions to get his chemo. Lorn wore the cap everywhere, and it was on him in the casket at his funeral home viewing. When I saw him, that made me cry to think Lorn felt such a close friendship that he was wearing that cap. I thought he looked classy in it with his characteristic prognathic jaw.

When Brother Paul preached his funeral he said, "Lorn had a life well lived and had finished well." I agreed. Lorn and I rarely discussed the gospel of Christ in all the years of hunting and fishing, but he became a believer. Lorn taught me another thing—that is, you can be involved in leading a person to Christ without having discussed the gospel. Of course, Lorn received the gospel message from the good preaching of Brother Paul.

After losing Lorn in 2004, my duck hunting slowed considerably. Some seasons weren't so good for the next few years, and the upper end of Oologah had become more crowded. I was fortunate to go hunting with Don Brown a few times in his shallow-water projects, but duck hunting really ended for me when we moved to Broken Arrow in 2013. With a smaller yard and living in a gated community, I had no place to keep my duck-hunting boat; I sold it and all my one hundred duck decoys. I gave Don Brown my remaining seventy-five goose decoys.

GRAND LAKE AREA DUCK HUNTS

The person most responsible for me being able to hunt Grand Lake and the Afton area was a good friend, Terry Whitfield from Vinita, Oklahoma. I met Terry as one of my dental patients. Terry and I became best friends and went hunting and fishing together for the next fifteen years. Terry was more of a fisherman and quail hunter than a duck hunter. Oh, he had jumped ducks on ponds for years but never hunted ducks that were called in over decoys. Terry was a very likable, easy-going man without much extra money. He lived within his means and did some painting and finishing cabinets when he needed money. He did unusual things like always wearing tennis shoes and a flannel shirt while hunting and fishing—even when the temperature was in the teens. He was just a fun person to be around. He fished much of the time below Grand Lake dam and Big Cabin Creek for crappie, white bass, and catfish. He had permission from most of the owners of the ponds around Vinita and Afton to jump ducks.

I finally got Terry interested in hunting over decoys. On one of our first pond hunts over decoys, I saw some ducks coming, so I handed my cup of coffee to Terry and said, "Hold this while I shot some ducks." I shot three widgeons, and he never got a shot. What a dirty trick that was—but funny for both of us.

One of the first places he took me was the Cowskin Elk River near where it empties into Grand Lake northeast of Grove. His brother owned a lot on the lake with a concrete boat ramp on the south side of the Elk River. The water was crystal clear there, and the ducks had plenty of millet to eat because the GRDA would lower the lake three to four feet each summer and sow millet in the mud flats all over the lake. The Elk River area was a beneficiary of this process for restoring habitat for fish, waterfowl, and other wildlife.

When we arrived at his brother's ramp, we first saw ducks three hundred yards away directly across from the boat ramp. When we went over there, ducks were getting up out of some millet. It was an excellent place to hunt, with some willows for hiding the boat nearby and some shallow water where the millet was planted. At that time, I had Boy, a black Lab, for retrieving the ducks, so we could hunt from the boat. We shot a limit of mallards the first time we hunted there. More patches of millet were in flats around islands a few hundred yards west on down the river where the lake widened. Not many duck hunters used the Elk River area at that time. We went back several times over the next few years, sometimes with Danny Cotner and Bob Newlon, and usually shot lots of ducks—mostly mallards. But after a few years that place became more popular, and we hunted less there.

I also hunted on Grand Lake a few times with Terry and others, on Weed Island about two miles south of the old sailboat bridge; we could launch my boat at the Bear's Den boat ramp near the bridge if the lake wasn't too rough. Weed Island was a roost for hundreds—maybe thousands—of African egrets that came there at sunset every day. I've been out there in my Tahiti jet boat and taken pictures of them flying about a foot above the water against a backdrop of beautiful orange sunsets. Bird droppings had defoliated all the trees on the island, which was maybe 150 yards long from east to west and eighty yards wide. White droppings were everywhere and were unavoidable under the trees; it was a mess to tolerate for some good hunting. We usually set up on the west end away from the droppings facing west toward the open water; that way we could hunt whether the wind was out of the south or the north with the sun behind us. It was always a fun shoot watching the ducks coming from far out over the lake and circling before they cupped their wings and came into the decoys in the bright sun coming up from behind us, which made the emerald metallic green heads and blue speculums of the drakes with bright orange legs stand out. Weed Island provided some pleasurable, comfortable hunting.

I went boating in August 2019 with Donna on our fifty-second anniversary vacation when Grand Lake was up four feet. I was surprised to see that all the tall trees that had been on Weed Island had fallen over and washed away; the island had only weeds and grass growing with a few young willows on the east end still covered with the white egrets.

Another favorite place Terry and I hunted was near Grand Lake east of Afton. This large horseshoe-shaped pond had tall oak trees on the dam, and at both ends of the U. In the middle of the U was a mound about twenty feet high with a few large trees on it also. The pond could not be seen from any road because it was located between two hills. We climbed a fence where a railroad track intersected the section line on the northwest side of the pond and walked about four hundred yards. We usually put the decoys out at the north end of the east arm of the U, which was shallow enough for wading and placing decoys. The ducks apparently liked getting out of the wind and eating acorns on that side. We sat on the mound between the two ends and shot down at the ducks when they came up the U and tried to land behind our decoys—the only place I've ever shot down at ducks. I can remember Terry sitting next to me with his flannel shirt and tennis shoes on when the temperature was in the twenties. He was a tough Native American. Sometimes we could jump ducks that landed on other parts of the pond. The trip back to the truck was more difficult because we always added a limit of ducks to each decoy bag.

One day after it had been raining several days, Terry took Frank Odonnell and me to an area of wet weather sloughs that bordered a section line between Vinita and Grand Lake where we shot five drakes on January 18,1985. One drake had two bands, a regular aluminum band on one leg and a green-tinted aluminum one that read "$20 reward" banded near Flaxcombe, Saskatchewan. The next day I shot three more drakes in the same area, and one drake had the same kind of bands as the one shot the day before; this one was banded in Harrisburg, Arkansas—that made four bands in two days with pretty low odds of that happening.

In the same area was a small spring-fed pond surrounded with trees off the road about 150 yards. Terry and I had jumped the pond for several years when other ponds in the area were frozen before we finally decided we should ask the landowner, Mr. Story, if we could hunt. We drove past his pond about half a mile to his house. When we asked if we could jump ducks on the pond he said, "No, I'd rather you didn't because the ducks keep the pond from freezing for my cattle to get water." We thought it was the other way around—that the ducks were there because the pond was spring fed and it didn't freeze—but we didn't argue with the farmer and thanked him.

The other location that provided some of the best duck hunting was of all places appropriately named Duck Creek on the west side of Grand Lake where Spinnaker Point and Arrowhead Marina were located. The upper end of Duck Creek fanned out for a short distance in north, east, and south directions after going under a low Highway 85 bridge. I hunted with Terry, Frank Odonnell, and Lorn Rohr at different times in all three of the small coves with very good success. One time after getting our limit of mallards in the south cove, Terry and I were leaving and shot two Canada geese as we surprised three geese getting up along the bank.

One day the game ranger, Keith Green, came by to check us when we were in the north cove, because he could walk to us from the west side of Highway 85 near the bridge. Keith was the one who on several occasions, when Chance Turner and I were hunting geese in maize fields around Afton, would get out of his truck and come running toward us to check us. I supposed he was always running to catch us before we had time to change anything---like plugs in our guns or something. That day in Duck Creek, Lorn, Bob Newlon, and I were hunting with Terry standing on a small point with some brush and tree laps around us. Lorn was getting wet and cold because he had little protection from the light drizzle that morning. Terry had on his usual flannel shirt and tennis shoes but didn't mind the drizzle because he was a tough Indian, and we were all excited because we had been shooting some ducks. Green walked over to us and checked us out a little bit; then we talked for a while before inviting him to use one of our guns and shoot some ducks with us. I let him use my gun so I could keep calling the ducks; he shot several ducks and appreciated the good time we had. That was a different and unusual but pleasant experience.

Another hunt near Duck Creek involved several of us; Norm Russell and Richard and Brad Swan all spent the night with Dr. Byron Jasper and his son, Bobby, at his condo on Spinnaker Point where Duck Creek opened into Grand Lake. Dr. Jasper had purchased the condo in the early 1970s when he was stationed at the nearby Jay Indian Health Service Dental Clinic. He was later transferred to a clinic in Hollywood Florida, but I had recruited him to come back from there to be my deputy chief of the Claremore Service Unit Dental Program in 1980. Byron enjoyed having Donna and me over for the fireworks display in Duck Creek on the Fourth of July and on other occasions. He had tennis courts, and we all played tennis plus fishing and boating in my 455 Oldsmobile Tahiti jet boat.

One December I arrived at the condo with my duck-hunting boat Friday afternoon before anyone else. It had been cold for several days and was predicted to be about fifteen degrees on Saturday. We were planning to hunt in the upper end of Duck Creek if it wasn't frozen over. There had been a good wind on Friday, and it wasn't frozen yet, but if the wind died down it probably would be frozen by morning. I started a fire in the fireplace and made some stew before the others arrived. I had time to lay down and rest for a while.

When they all arrived, we had a good meal, talked about our plans for hunting, and watched some duck hunting films before going to bed; we had to get up at four thirty for fixing breakfast, eating, and getting all our gear ready to hunt. If Duck Creek was frozen, we would use plan B and drop off the two boys, Bobby and Brad, at the minnow ponds while the rest of us traveled to Byron's deer lease in the direction of Vinita. Byron had seen ducks in a slough in the woods on his deer lease. It was only a few miles as a crow flies from Grand Lake.

We loaded up on a cold, still morning. We drove down the lane to Highway 85 and turned right to go north over Duck Creek. It was no surprise that Duck Creek had frozen over during the still night; we had to use plan B and drove to the minnow ponds. The minnow ponds were a group of six small spring-fed rectangular ponds below a hillside; they never froze in the winter. Terry Whitfield had shown them to me, and we had jumped gadwalls there several times. They were good places for mallards and gadwall when so many other ponds in the area froze over. We dropped off Brad and Bobby with some decoys and drove over to the woods on Byron's lease.

We climbed a locked gate with our waders on and walked about one hundred yards across a grassy field to get to the woods. It was an unlikely looking place for ducks, but we could hear several hens quacking as we approached the slough in the woods. It was already shooting time, but we didn't shoot when a large group got up—hoping that they would return in small groups. Oak trees provided small acorns for the ducks to eat. The water was only about one foot deep, so we broke some ice and put out about fifteen decoys. I had my camera and was anxious to get some video of the mallards coming down through the trees. Richard, Norm, Byron, and I stood against the largest trees we could find around one side of the seventy-five-yard-diameter hole. I was calling a small group of ducks circling several times before weaving their way down through the trees. I think we all shot and wound up with four ducks—Norm still says it was three hens and a drake. He said the first thing I said was, "I didn't shoot a hen!" He still believes I did. It was Norm's first and only duck hunt, but he enjoyed that hunt.

The action wasn't very fast, but some small groups kept coming, and we were picking off one or two each time. I was getting a few good videos of the mallards weaving around the tree limbs, although the colors were not very bright because it was a cloudy day and shady in the woods. But I hadn't had a chance to do much filming in wooded areas, so I was glad to have the videos of our hunt with us talking and having fun. We didn't get our limits that morning but had a good hunt horsing around and talking in the woods. We packed up and went to pick up the boys.

They saw us coming and soon came up the hill to the entrance where we had parked. They had no ducks, and we asked them what happened. They said all they saw were hens. They described how flights of brown ducks kept coming into their decoys and with their tails almost touching the water before they would take off. I knew that hen mallards didn't gather in flights and immediately suspected that the ducks were probably gadwalls. The boys were only sixteen years old and hadn't duck hunted much. I just asked if they remembered seeing any white speculums, and they said, "Yes!"

I asked, "Didn't you think about them being gadwalls?" We all started laughing because they had several flights of ducks that came in and could probably have shot their limit if they had been shooting at the gadwalls. The boys couldn't believe it and were a little embarrassed. We all loaded up and returned to Byron's condo for sandwiches before leaving for home. It had been an exciting adventure for everyone.

FABULOUS DUCK HUNTING AT
DON BROWN'S WETLANDS

I believe the first time I met Don Brown was at the first Claremore Area Ducks Unlimited Chapter Banquet in 1977. Don was an annual Ducks Unlimited (DU) sponsor and a generous donor. It wasn't long after talking with him about his duck hunting experiences that I realized it was his excellent floating blind on Long Bay in Fort Gibson Lake in 1975 that had changed my career in the USPHS. Don and his wife Brenda have always been friendly, compassionate and generous people who had been successful in their home health equipment businesses in Arizona, Tulsa, Claremore, and other locations in northeastern Oklahoma. He had made some successful local real estate investments after he sold his home health equipment businesses. He also has developed, with the assistance of the US Fish and Wildlife Department, several shallow-water projects for waterfowl hunting on most of his one thousand acres along Dog Creek five miles south of Claremore Lake. One year we took Greenwings (members eighteen and under in DU) to Don's place for constructing wood duck boxes and placing them along Dog Creek on his property. Don had several holiday parties at his house with a pool and trophy room containing mounts from Africa, Alaska, Colorado, New Zealand, Montana, and Arizona as well as local waterfowl.

Don began his land development in the early 1980s by constructing a fifty-acre lake just about seventy-five yards behind his house. Don uses the lake to flood the surrounding shallow-water pools after sowing milo and millet in the summer. Two years ago, he drained his lake and hired someone, with the help of the US Fish and Wildlife Department, who worked all summer to redo the dams around the lake and sow switch grass to prevent erosion—quite an expensive job costing over $200,000. He has always had to fight beavers upsetting his maintenance of water-control structures in the shallow water pools around the lake. It is a continuous job maintaining the projects: brushing seven blinds every year with oak tree limbs, working the ground and sowing seed for food in the summer heat, mowing the dams and berms, maintaining the banks of his lake preventing erosion, pumping water out of Dog Creek to his projects on both sides of the creek, and doing whatever he could to continue improving the projects.

I remember John Hoover helping him with many of these things, and Don now hires three men to help him. The last thing I can remember John helping with was in 2012—while I still lived in Claremore—when they built a pit blind in the flat between Dog Creek and northwest corner of the lake and buried a large tank of some kind large enough for four men. That pit blind was the last place I hunted on Don's land before moving to Broken Arrow; four of us, including Don, John, and Allen Lee had a tremendous hunt on a beautiful, cool, sunny morning.

I can remember that hunt because in 2013—after not hunting much for several years—I was out of shape and had lost much of the leg strength and balance I had developed from many years of duck hunting. I had fallen once the year before when hunting with Bob Newlon. At Don's pit blind, I was using the bag of floating decoys to maintain my balance while walking in deep mud from the berm where we had parked the Mule. Little did I suspect that the other three men would have all the decoys set out and come back to get my bag of decoys before I reached the pit blind. Man, I only had about twenty yards remaining to reach the pit blind; the mud was deep enough that I almost fell more than once getting there. I was thinking how embarrassing that would have been. That's the kind of thing that happens to rookie duck hunters, but I felt better when Don told me later that he had fallen in the mud at that blind.

After a good hunt and getting our limit with several difficult shots, I was able to use a bag of decoys and get back to the Mule without falling. What a relief! Allen took a picture—probably my most favorite of all duck hunting pics—of John, me, and Don in front of the Mule with all the ducks hanging over our shoulders. That picture is in the collage on the back of my book in the upper left-hand corner. I had another similar picture of the three of us from another hunt at Don's, but this one was even better since it was in bright sunlight. Don surely liked it also because he has it posted on the wall in his clubhouse.

I helped Don with his project on a few days. One of my lasting accomplishments was planting some honeysuckle around a blind built into the lake dam on the northwest side. I dug large holes and used some good potting mix to plant them. I even came back a couple of times during that dry summer to water the plants and make sure they survived that first year. They did survive well and within in a few years covered the blind well and kept their foliage during the winter months, which meant that Don didn't have to spend time brushing that blind every fall. However, that blind burned while doing a three-year controlled burn and killed the honeysuckle in 2018—after surviving twenty-five years. This blind was where I had shot a beautiful drake pintail with long perfect pin tail feathers. It hangs on my wall in a flight position in my office to remind me of a good hunt that day. Another day I was hunting in that blind, and the cap came off my Browning Gold magazine allowing the spring to shoot out fifteen feet to the edge of the water; I somehow found the two caps, plug, and spring. I helped Don plant more honeysuckle on that blind in September 2019 after it had been rebuilt. The last time I helped Don was with four other men brushing five blinds on two beautiful days in October 2019, which required cutting down four small oak trees to supply the brush.

Another memorable hunt with John and Don was on a cold day with freezing drizzle. We were in a blind on the south end of the same hole as the honeysuckle blind; John had named it the "death hole." Don always planted milo in this hole, and the ducks loved it. I had to walk across the pool from the berm to the other side where the blind was located and had no problem walking then because I was still hunting a lot and in good shape. We had to break some light ice in the freezing drizzle to put out the decoys. It was a challenge trying to track the ducks without being seen when they would fly around behind the blind and then getting a shot off if they were close enough when they reappeared at the side or straight up over the blind. Other shots were easy when a group came in directly in front and started backpedaling their wings to land. Surprising enough, I didn't always hit every one of these easy shots, and it was difficult to believe when one survived three shots as it climbed and flew away—and sometimes more shots when John and Don joined in the shooting. These are the kind of shots that are not hard to hit—just easy to miss.

There was also an interesting twist to this hunt. Some mallards were landing out of gun range behind our decoys. As soon as they landed, they ducked under the water and came up shaking their wings. Of course, they would fly off after doing this a few times and getting close enough to detect the presence of decoys and men in a blind. After watching this happen to more than one group, we decided that they must be shaking the frozen drizzle from their wings. None of us had ever witnessed this strange behavior before.

The usual routine when hunting with Don was to pull up beside the barn about sixty yards to the south of his house and wait for him to come out. Don's championship quail hunting dogs, or a few years later when he had just a Lab, located in a kennel near the barn would begin barking. That began the excitement and anticipation of another good duck hunt. Don's hunts were pretty much a sure thing because of his excellent habitat. Even when no ducks were to be found at my regular hunting sites, Don always had ducks. When Don would come walking to the barn and begin loading the Mule for another hunt, I often wondered if he ever got tired of duck hunting. It was always a tiring routine for me getting up at 3:30 or 4:00 a.m. and hunting three days in a row. Fighting the winter elements, sitting in the sun all day, walking through the mud, making things happen the desired way, and sleep deprivation took a toll on me. I believe Don somehow was hunting five or six days a week.

After not seeing him for six years since moving to Broken Arrow, I called recently inviting him for dinner at Hammett House to discuss the hunting stories about his place to be included in my book revision; he was enthusiastic as ever about duck hunting and taking care of his projects. That morning he'd been out tearing up beaver dams, which they had rebuilt overnight for several days, trying to drain his shallow-water pools so he could plant milo and

Japanese millet. He said that he almost had them drained. Don also wanted to invite John Hoover to lunch because John often helped Don with his projects. This was fine with me because I also wanted to talk with John about some of our hunts together, and I hadn't seen him for six years either.

It was when I called Don to set up the lunch meeting at the Hammett House in Claremore that I received some good news; he was having a youth duck hunt October 5, and he invited my grandsons on the hunt. For many years I had thought I'd like to take my grandsons duck hunting on Oologah Lake or somewhere, even if it had to be a paid hunt. Teaching my grandsons to hunt was important to me since my grandfather had taught me how to hunt rabbits and squirrels in Kentucky. Two grandsons who live in Georgia have hunted deer with their father, but the two who lived in Broken Arrow have never hunted anything.

I had taken the two from Broken Arrow clay pigeon shooting twice, thinking they would do well with good hand-eye coordination from playing tennis many years. On the first clay pigeon shoot I was surprised two times—first when out of twenty-five pigeons the thirteen-year-old hit seven clay pigeons and second when his sixteen-year-old brother hit only two. They both did much better on the next shoot at Bryan Adair's place. I was able to take both boys on the youth hunt October 5, but only Brady could shoot because Hudson had turned seventeen and was too old to shoot that day. Brady shot eight times and got one blue wing teal on his first hunt. I also took Brady to a Claremore Area Ducks Unlimited Banquet on October 17 hoping to spark more interest in duck hunting. As a Greenwing, he was given a fine DU double-reed duck call, which he needed to replace the old one I had given him. I'd bought them new chest waders and hunting jackets planning to hunt more during the regular season. I was planning on letting them use my two Browning Gold semiautomatics, and that would leave me with a trusty old 870 pump. I bought twelve new decoys with weights and a Lucky

Duck decoy with battery-operated spinning wings and a pulsating mallard. We were ready to hunt.

Cleaning out the beaver dams was a repetitive process for Don because many times after he almost had the pools drained it would rain. Sure enough, it rained four inches the night John, Don, and I ate lunch together on April 30, 2019. We had record-setting flooding in May and June. All the lakes on the Arkansas River and around this area in northeastern Oklahoma experienced the worst flooding in three decades. Don couldn't work the ground and sow any grain, but he said he had plenty of three-foot-high smartweed and sedge grass for food when season opened November 2, 2019.

The time finally came when Don invited me to his place to hunt with my grandsons on November 30, 2019. I had been praying and preparing a year for this hunt—taking them clay pigeon shooting twice, buying us all new waders, buying them camo hunting jackets, buying a dozen new decoys, and two six-slot full-body decoy bags as well as a Lucky Duck greenhead spinner and a pulsating mallard. Originally, we were to go early that Saturday morning, but Don called just fifteen minutes after my grandsons had arrived Friday evening at my house to spend the night before the early-morning hunt. He said, "We can't go hunting in the morning. I have eight deer hunters coming for opening day." Don leases his property on the east side of Dog Creek for deer hunting, and he hunts deer on the west side, and we were supposed to duck hunt on the east side; we were all disappointed. However, Don called back thirty minutes later and said we would hunt ducks beginning at eleven and shut down at three. The deer hunters would be gone by eleven. Don said, "Be there at 10:45." We were all excited again, and on top of that, the boys could sleep in instead of getting up at 4:00 a.m. and not have to go to bed early as their mother had requested. Grandma would not have to get up so early and fix us the sausage, eggs, and biscuits with jelly and honey as she had planned.

We arrived at Don's at ten thirty in time to get our waders

on and all our gear unloaded ready for Don to pick us up in his Mule. Don picked us up and got Dan, his black Lab, out of the kennel and headed for the blind—the same blind Brady had shot one teal out of on his youth duck hunt October 5. On the way we saw hundreds of ducks getting up in large groups around the marshes, which had accumulated water from recent rains. Large flights of pintails, mallards, gadwall, and some teal were there. Brady, Hudson, and I placed the decoys while Don took the Mule to a concealed spot. We also had two Lucky Duck spinners and a Hibdon pulsating mallard, a mallard tail that moves like a tipping feeding duck with a pulsating water pump creating lots of action and small waves. We all got into the blind.

Don stepped back out of the blind holding Dan while he shot a couple of times to get the ducks up again, but Dan escaped when Don shot. Many ducks were flying over us, but Don and Dan were still out of the blind. After Dan was back in his hiding place on one end of the blind, it wasn't long until a gadwall came across from the right to left within range. Brady made the first shot and dropped the duck. I said, "Very good shot, Brady, but how did you manage to shoot over the front of the blind without the eight-inch stool you used to stand on during the youth hunt."

He said, "I was on my knees on the bench." The bench consisted of two two-by-six boards in the back of the blind.

I said, "How did you do that and keep your balance?"

He said, "It wasn't easy, but I turned sideways."

I said, "Now that really made it a spectacular shot! Way to go, Brady."

The action was slow on a very windy day. Don thought the ducks didn't like flying in the wind that day. Don and I were calling the few that were flying, but they weren't responding well. It was also a beautiful bluebird day with the temp fifty-five degrees. Hunting from eleven until two, which is usually their time for loafing in safe places, was working against us. They had too many large groups attracting them when some did get up and fly around briefly.

But we had a flight of about eight pintails circle us two times, and Don was giving them short peep-peep pintail calls on his dog whistle turned upside down. Although they weren't as close as we would have liked, on the third time around Don thought we should shoot while we had a chance. He said, "Take 'em!" The closest ones were on Hudson's end, and he shot one hen and had a shot at a drake but forgot to pump his 870. I had never let them put more than one shell at a time in their guns for safety reasons when I had taken them out on two practice runs shooting single clay pigeons. Guess they could have used a third time with some doubles. The rest of us just missed our longer shots.

Then we had a single greenhead come in and land about thirty-five yards out to the left on Hudson's end, so we let Hudson take a shot on the water. The drake disappeared under the water for a few seconds. He surfaced and took flight immediately. Hudson knocked him down, and Don finished him. Dan did a wonderful job retrieving all the ducks, and Hudson took a very good close-up picture of him with the drake in his mouth swimming back to the blind.

The boys had three ducks, but old grandpa had none. Within the last ten minutes before we had to leave in order to get the boys back home by four as their mother had requested, I was gathering my things in the blind preparing to leave when Don said a mallard hen had landed. "Wait for the drake to land," he said. I never saw either duck until they were getting up after Don pushed the blind flap forward. I made a kill shot on the drake and shot once at the hen escaping up and away before Don yelled, "Don't shoot the hen!" I guess when you have that many ducks around it's more sporting not to shoot hens even when we only had four ducks. I have been in places many times where we didn't have to shoot any hens to get our limit. It's also good conservation planning for the next year. Don's a very good shot, and I think he gave us a break letting us shoot more than he did while he did most of the calling. It was appreciated.

We had finished—not with twenty drakes—but with a good hunt for the boys' first duck hunt. I was glad it had been pleasant weather rather than a cold, freezing day for their first time out. We finished picking up the decoys while Don went for the Mule. When he returned, he took a good pic in the sunshine of the three of us and Dan, with the four ducks hanging on the blind behind us. It had been a good way to finish something I had been planning and preparing ahead for a year—grandpa taking two grandsons on a duck hunt. Thank you, Don!

We were able to return to Don's two more times during regular season that year. I also took the boys to Scott Grubs' hunting lease at Ketchum near Grand lake for a good hunt when it was in the low 20s and spitting ice pellets in a thirty-foot-long blind with four others. But the boys never complained about the cold weather and enjoyed the hunt. I knew they would be okay duck hunters after that. Hudson made wader hangers out of dowel pins and two by fours so we cold hang the waders until next season.

DUCK HUNTING ON KERR RESERVOIR

I had four years of fabulous duck hunting on Robert S. Kerr Lake from the fall of 1973 to February of 1977 while stationed at the W. W. Hastings Indian Hospital in Tahlequah, Oklahoma. I would make the one-hour drive down Highway 82 on the east side of Tenkiller Lake to Vian and continue south under I-40 to the Sequoyah National Wildlife Refuge (NWR). I would be waiting at the main gate ninety minutes before shooting time, hoping to be in front of the Fort Smith hunters. We had to wait for the federal ranger to open the gate sixty minutes before shooting time. When we entered the main gate, on our left we passed the waterfowl refuge, a large mile-wide no-hunting area for three-quarters of a mile south before the waterfowl refuge boundary extended into the reservoir. Here is where we had to turn west for a mile and then go south for half a mile to our launching point.

This hunting area consisted of several irregular-shaped islands surrounded by cattails and shallow water. Each year after Thanksgiving I would take Mike Brown, from Stillwater, to this area for duck hunting two days. Mike reciprocated with a three-day quail hunt with him during the Thanksgiving holidays. Mike was an IHS pharmacist at the Pawnee Indian Hospital and had permission to quail hunt on thousands of acres near Pawnee owned by a rancher named Waters where we usually got our daily limits with Mike's two bird dogs.

Mike was a very competitive quail hunter, and he was also always anxious to shoot as many ducks as he could. We usually hid in the cattails and shot widgeon, gadwall, pintail, teal, and mallards over decoys out of my boat. This was when most smaller ducks, widgeon, gadwall, and green-winged teal, were only ten points and mallard drakes were twenty points with mallard hens and pintails 70-point ducks; with a one-hundred-point limit, hunters could possibly have a daily bag limit of ten ducks.

One morning Mike, John Boren, a pharmacist at W.W. Hastings, and I were parked in our boat blind in shallow water surrounded by grass and brush piles. We had been shooting all the usual ducks on a bright, sunny day until about nine when there was a lull in the action. We were just talking in my boat blind when suddenly Mike turned and shot a bird that had flown in low from our right side. It was an excellent reflexive passing shot on a fast-flying bird. He looked at me and asked, "What was that?"

I said, "That was a $500 bird! You'd better hide it in some brush and mud behind us before a federal ranger comes by to check us." John's dog had retrieved the bird and explained to Mike that it was a cormorant, which was a protected bird; hunters and fishermen hated them and had tried to get the wildlife department to declare a season on them to reduce their large population.

Mike said, "It looks like a cross between a duck and a goose but had a five-inch sharp beak." Mike was an experienced quail hunter but weak on duck identification. He hid the bird about twenty yards behind us in mud under some old tree limbs. He hadn't been back in the blind two minutes when we heard a loud airboat crank up. Most likely this was a federal ranger about two hundred yards away on the other side of some cattails around another island. We thought for sure he had seen the cormorant shot and was coming to give a violation citation. The boat zoomed around some cattails, came straight to our boat blind and stopped about fifteen yards out. The ranger had a black Lab sitting in his boat that could have been useful in finding the hidden bird. I could see Mike shaking in his waders. I did all the talking so Mike wouldn't have to expose his quivering voice.

The ranger was cordial and asked how we were doing; we talked for a short time. I thought Mike was thinking the same as I was—that maybe he had seen the cormorant shot. But he never asked to see our ducks, didn't check for licenses or signed duck stamps, and didn't check our guns for plugs. He left as fast as he had come in. I told Mike that was highly unusual. I'd been approached several times by federal rangers when hunting on Kerr—always in airboats—and they always checked everything they could. I even saw a ranger give citations to two hunters who had too many ducks; they hadn't known that blue-winged teal were twenty-point ducks instead of ten like the green-winged teal. I hadn't known about that either before that incident. Mike was lucky that day.

That same day after we had finished hunting and before we picked up our decoys, we were standing in the water talking when I saw a high, dumb greenhead falling out of the sky toward us with wings folded close to his body like a jet fighter. I quickly shouldered my gun and did another reflex shot as Mike had done earlier on the cormorant. The mallard fell like a rock near our feet.

Everyone thought that was a fabulous shot, and it was the end of a perfect hunt. We packed up and got out of there.

There was also good hunting in slews north of that launching point and in nearby Sally Jones Lake. I once jumped a single mallard drake on one of these slews that flew very slow and low to the ground. I shot the duck and picked it up, noting how light the duck felt and how emaciated his breast was—more than any duck I had ever held in my hand. I could only conclude that it was suffering from lead poisoning. At that time, rangers would take gizzards from our ducks to test for lead shot. They continued to do this testing when I moved to Claremore and hunted on Oologah Lake in the late 1970s and early 1980s. Several years later the whole country was using steel shot for migratory waterfowl based on their studies across the nation.

I had a few good goose hunts in fields west of Sally Jones Lake as well as in fields on the west side of the Arkansas River and south of I-40 after I had moved to Claremore.

However, my favorite hunting area at Kerr was what we called the "cattail islands," which could not be easily accessed from the west side of the waterfowl refuge without going across two miles of open water. Some hunters had died from hypothermia in the mid-1970s while duck hunting on Kerr after having their boat capsized by high winds. That area was more safely accessed by going east on I-40 from the Vian exit and exiting south at the first exit, Dwight Mission Road, and driving a few miles to a steep concrete boat ramp. The cattail islands, a strip of seven 100- to 300-yard-long islands fifty yards apart, could be seen from the boat ramp about four hundred yards to the southwest. The islands had surely been constructed for duck hunting—with strips between the seven islands.

Hunting there reminded me of watching taped videos of good duck hunting. There were mostly mallards that decoyed well in this area, and hunting was always good even with other hunters on the islands. We had no trees to obstruct our view and could see ducks coming from far away. One cold day the wind came up after a morning of hunting. While returning across the relatively short distance to the boat ramp in my fourteen-foot flat-bottom boat, waves started coming over the bow. My partner scooted to the back of my boat with me and my Lab—Boy—to shift the weight from the bow. We were glad to get back on dry land that day.

I once took two rookie duck hunters, Dr. Bob Partak, an IHS dentist, and John Boren on a hunt to the cattail islands. On the way to Kerr that morning I had been explaining duck identification and the point system. I explained in detail how to identify ducks by their size, speed of their wingbeat, shape of their tails, calls, and, of course, colors when it was light enough to see them. I told them not to shoot any high-point ducks like hen mallards, redheads, or canvasbacks.

That morning no sooner than we had set out the decoys and settled among the cattails on our stools, I saw a low fast-flying small duck zooming from the right side. I quickly raised up my gun and reflexively shot the duck dead before Bob and John saw it. I thought it was probably a hen wood duck or a teal. My black Lab, Boy, retrieved the small duck, and to my surprise, it was a redhead hen! I had never seen or shot any redheads—diving ducks—in the shallow waters of Kerr, but I had a ninety-point duck my first shot. This was what I'd just told Bob and John not to do. Man, did I catch some guff from those guys. I have never lived that down; I probably remember it better than they do.

On another hunt in that area I took Dr. Charles Gosnell, an IHS physician, who also brought his young black Lab that day. We were having lots of mallards come into our decoys, but there was just one thing wrong. Boy was retrieving every duck before Charles's dog could get to them. I felt bad for his young dog and thought I would help him out by tying Boy's short leader cord to my wader belt. Well, the next flight of mallards came into our decoys, and we dropped two drakes very close to us. Boy lunged, and I fell to my knees all wet, but Charles's dog got to retrieve the ducks.

Not liking being pulled into the water, I thought I would use a little operant conditioning on Boy and tapped him lightly on the top of his head with my gun barrel. Surprisingly, Boy immediately had a tonic seizure, his eyes rolled back; he was stiff and cold shivering. I had to carry him to a muskrat mound of cattails and let him lie there while I talked to him. I was so sorry. I wondered if he would be okay and if he would retrieve another duck that day. After he recovered and rested for ten more minutes; I then took him back to where Charles was waiting—this time without a rope tied to my belt. On the next incoming flight, we shot ducks, and Boy was off to the races retrieving more ducks. I learned not to tie a retriever like Boy to my waist if he wasn't broke to shot.

It is amazing how much the land topography of this outstanding duck-hunting area has changed in forty years. I can look at a satellite image of the area on my iPhone and see many good-sized trees on all islands in Kerr reservoir. It also appears that some of the water strips between the cattail islands has silted in. I'll bet the silty mud is deep and terrible for wading around the islands. I wonder if I was just lucky to have hunted in the glory years of a newly constructed reservoir and would like to know how the hunting is today. Well, on October 28, 2019, I talked to Paul Cook, a US marine from New Jersey working at Bass Pro Shops in Broken Arrow, who had hunted Kerr in 2018. He said he had seen thousands of mallards and done well decoy shooting east of the cattail islands, so I guess duck hunting remains good there.

Another favorite place to hunt in this area was a point on the southeast corner of the confluence of the Illinois River and the Arkansas River. The Illinois here, stocked with rainbow trout and having large striped bass, is the clear tailwaters of Tenkiller Lake. The point was below a Kerr McGee Plant that sat on top of a tall hill. I had to put in at Gore Landing on Highway 64 about 1.5 miles from the Arkansas. The water was shallow enough off the point to hold some decoys placed from my boat not too far from the bank. While hunting out of my camouflaged boat covered with propped up netting, we always had Boy to retrieve the ducks—mostly mallards.

One cold day with ice chunks floating down the river, I crippled a greenhead, and he was escaping to the other shore across the Arkansas with Boy about fifty yards behind him. Boy couldn't catch the drake but kept swimming about halfway across the half-mile-wide river. Fearing something bad might happen to Boy in the icy water, I cranked up my small Mercury motor and took off after them. Boy was about two-thirds across the Arkansas when I picked him up and went on to retrieve the greenhead. Boy was just fine, but I think he was glad to be in the boat that day. This was a good place to hunt with lot of mallards and without getting into open water—usually.

One more good mallard hunt twenty-five miles west of Kerr was on Eufaula Lake, which flowed into Kerr Reservoir via the Canadian River just south of the I-40 bridge. The huge Eufaula Lake was formed by the North Canadian, Deep Fork Canadian, and the Canadian Rivers. I was fortunate to have been invited by Dr. Jack Sellers, a dentist from Eufaula, on a duck hunt on the Deep Fork part of Eufaula Lake when the lake level was up four feet. We traveled north of Eufaula on Highway 69 and turned west on 266 toward Hoffman. We turned south on a section line south of Morris for a short distance to the water's edge. We launched off the graveled section line road and went south only about one-quarter mile, anchored the boat in a tree line, and put out our decoys in the comfortable two-foot-deep water.

It appeared that we were hunting in a flooded field with a firm bottom. It was a sunny day, and the emerald green heads of the mallard drakes were beautiful when they appeared with their wings cupped and sailing over another tree line one hundred yards to the north heading straight for our decoys with no calling needed. We shot four greenheads from the first flight! We continued shooting a few ducks, but I guess not enough for Jack and his friend. They waded out of my sight to the east on the other side of some short trees, but I stayed with the boat and decoys near the taller tree line where I knew it was safe wading with no holes. I didn't know at that time, but we were within a few miles of the Deep Fork NWR, which had a reputation for being one of the best places to hunt ducks in Oklahoma when the water was up in the hardwoods.

While Jack and his friend were gone, more ducks began decoying into my spread between the two tree lines. I was shooting a lot and had my limit of greenheads before they returned just in time to finish their limits. It was some of the easiest duck hunting I had ever done before 1976. I'll always remember Jack's gracious invitation for a fabulous hunt.

LAKE TEXOMA STRIPER FISHING

Each year at the Tulsa Boat and RV Show in February, Lindel Adair and I would start scheduling our annual Lake Texoma striper fishing trip. For several years we rented cabins at Vernon's Fishing Camp near Soldier Creek Marina at Kingston, Oklahoma. Lindel and I would drive down from Broken Arrow and meet Lindel's son, Bryan, and brother Joe Bob and his group from Wichita. After stopping in Durant for supplies and licenses, we arrived Thursday evening and went out to eat at a steakhouse near Kingston on Highway 70.

The next morning began early with a great breakfast at Vernon's with the guides. Then we all loaded in the two or three twenty-four-foot boats with fishing gear supplied by the guides for the short ride over to Soldier Creek Marina. Our guide, Mickey Rose, was in the boat with Lindel, Bryan, Dell Nutter, and me in 1994. In 1995, 1996, and 1997 Richard Swan, Dr. Bob Best, or Blake Adair was there instead of Del Nutter. Joe Bob and his group usually required two more boats. After launching, Mickey went around the marina area casting a throw-net for bait shad.

Catching stripers was always a sure thing with Mickey, using his experience and modern electronics for locating the schools of stripers. The guides went fast to their favorite spots, producing overspray, which felt good if I was dressed for it with protective clothing and a life jacket—not properly dressed meant getting wet and cold. When Mickey located some fish, he baited our lines and told us to drop to the bottom and reel up one or two turns. When we began hauling in stripers—sometimes with three men having fish on at the same time—Mickey was a busy man.

I always used at least one earpiece for my Walkman cassette player while listening to my favorite playlist for "Texoma Fishing." Some of the songs on my playlist included "Barcelona Nights," "2 The Night," and "Havana Club" by Ottmar Liebert; "East West Highway" and "Wild World" by Shahin and Sepehr; "Amazonica," "Djunga," and "Guitarra del Fuego" by Johannes Linstead, and "Will You Be There" by Michael Jackson and the Cleveland Orchestra.

Mickey was in communication with the other fishing guides, and if action slowed, he could quickly find another hot spot. Once we caught our limit, Mickey would keep us out till ten thirty that morning for catch and release.

Before the guides cleaned the fish, we took group pictures for each boat with the fish hanging in front of us. The guides cleaned and bagged the fish as we relaxed in the sun maybe drinking a beer and discussing the fishing that day. Then we loaded in the boats for the trip back to Vernon's for a light lunch because we knew there would be an all you can eat fish fry early that evening. Vernon would deep-fry some of the catch battered with his special mix of yellow cornmeal and seasoning; we also had coleslaw, fried potatoes, brown beans, and hush puppies—a real feast.

The 1996 fishing trip was the last out of Vernon's for us. Mickey Rose relocated to a new building in his Honeyhole Lodge near Kingston where we began staying on our trips. Mickey still uses the Soldier Creek Marina. Now, he owns a thirty-four-foot boat with a 350 V8 Yamaha motor that he uses fishing for bass, striper, catfish, and crappie year-round. You can check out his website at mickeyroseguideservice.com.

BCO MEN'S SPIRITUAL TROUT FISHING TRIP

I had been on a very successful trout fishing trip at White Hole Resort on the tailwaters of Bull Shoals Lake near Flippin, Arkansas in 2016. So, when Jeff Ferguson, one of our elders at our church, Bible Church of Owasso (BCO) told me in October 2018 that he was planning another trip to the White River in March 2019, I got excited and began preparing. Well you wouldn't expect a need to begin preparing six months ahead. However, I wanted my two grandsons, Hudson and Brady, to go with me along with their father, Bryan, who is also a deacon our church. I had always hoped to take them on a duck hunt—guess I would have to settle for a fishing trip first.

I went to Bass Pro Shops in Broken Arrow and bought them both fishing vests with some small clear polyethylene tackle boxes and clips to attach them to their vests—exactly like I used. I bought a new lightweight Pflueger President reel for Brady, who already had a rod, and gave Hudson one of my favorite Wally Marshal crappie rod and reel setups. I bought hooks, sinkers, corks, a few spinners, some power bait, and long forceps for retrieving swallowed hooks. Along with these things for stuffing their vests I gave them each a microfiber cleaning rag for holding the slick trout while removing hooks. Now all I needed was a practice run at John Boren's farm in Tahlequah, who had been inviting me for more than a year to come down with my grandsons and catch some channel cats he had stocked about six years earlier.

I called John and scheduled a trip the first of November—about two weeks out because he had some calves to sell. I asked him what to bring for bait, and he said he would just get some hot dogs—that's all he ever used. I also asked him if I could bring my shotguns and clay pigeon thrower so the boys could shoot some clay pigeons, which they had never done; eventually I wanted to take them duck hunting. He said, "Fine, I have a place close to the pond where they can shoot." The Saturday we drove down to John's was a perfect fall day—warm and sunny with very little wind. We stopped at his house and followed him out through the field to the pond. He explained the layout of the pond and picked the best place to start on the shallow end with a drop-off.

Brady hooked the first catfish before I got my line in the water; then Hudson hooked one. They were a nice size for filleting and eating—about two pounds each. I taught them about holding the fish with the rags while removing the hook with their forceps. They caught several larger ones. Brady hooked another one, and when he began reeling in the fish his reel fell off his rod, and the drag was whining as he held the reel in his hand. I was standing near him, and he asked in an excited voice, "What do I do?"

I said, "Hold on and I'll help put it back on your pole." We got it hooked up and he reeled in the biggest one for the day—about five pounds. By this time, we had six good-sized catfish, and I told them not to keep anymore because I didn't want to clean more than that out in the pasture. I also wanted them to shoot some shotgun shells. They caught a few more and released them so I could start cleaning the fish.

I came prepared to dress the fish in the field with a two-by-four board, vice-grip pliers, latex gloves, a sharp fillet knife, and a large nail to fix the heads firmly to the board. After nailing the head to the board, I made a slit through the skin into the soft flesh behind the sharp dorsal fin, extending the cut to just behind their ventral fins and across the belly. Then I began pulling the skin with the vice-grip plyers from the top behind the dorsal fin toward the tail, and it worked better than I had expected; it had been many years since I had helped an old friend, "Catfish" Frank Odonnell skin three large catfish over fifteen pounds each and fillet them. I let Hudson drive the nail, skin one, and fillet it, but Brady declined the offer. I kept the fish fillets cleaned with an extra bottle of water and bagged them in three one-gallon freezer bags that I had brought. Now, I thought they were ready for trout fishing on the White River.

Each boy shot a box of twenty-five shells at clay pigeons with my Browning Gold 20 gauge; Brady hit seven clay pigeons and Hudson, the oldest, hit only two. They took the fish home, and their dad grilled the fish that night and sent me a picture. It was a great ending for a successful fishing trip by also having the immediate gratification of eating the fish.

When Thursday, March 28, 2019, arrived, Bryan, Hudson, and I left Broken Arrow about 12:15 p.m. and traveled east on Highway 412 toward Flippin; Brady didn't go because they decided that he probably couldn't sit still in a boat all morning and afternoon. We stopped and picked up fishing licenses, trout stamps, and a little more bait at a Wal-Mart Super Center in Harrison, Arkansas. We arrived at White Hole Resort about 5:00 p.m. to see a wide strip of beautiful green grass behind the cabin along the river. The water had gone down about seven feet that evening after cutting off the generators at ten that morning. Everything was so green that it reminded me of Ireland. We went to the bait shop to see Steve, check in, and buy some of his four-pound test hand-tied-river rigs to use with the six-pound test line on our reels.

We went to the 178 Club about five miles down the road toward Bull Shoals Dam to eat while the other nineteen men arrived. When we returned, most everyone soon arrived except Jeff with the food. Bryan had picked up all the drinks, and Jeff had done an outstanding job of organizing and coordinating the trip. We visited for a while and discussed how the fishing might be the next morning with the planned full generation at the dam, which meant high and swift water where we were. We were about seven miles from the dam, so it would be ninety minutes after generators were shut off at 10:00 a.m. before our water went down to normal level, and we could expect better fishing conditions in a boat. We delayed our planned devotion by Adam Josserand to a little after 9:30 p.m. while waiting for Jeff and watching the NCAA sweet sixteen basketball tournament. After devotion, some of us finished watching Kentucky beat Houston; we turned in for an early rise and a 6:30 a.m. devotion by Adam again before breakfast.

Bryan, Hudson, and I were in a sixteen-foot aluminum boat with a reliable twenty-five hp Mercury motor. Bryan gave me the nod to man the motor. The current was swift enough to make the boat feel unstable if it was cut crossways to the current abruptly. Although we had a heavy drag chain, we couldn't keep our bait on the bottom because the boat drifted downstream too fast in the deep water; I tried going against the current using a small amount of power to slow our drifting speed. This required a lot of attention and distracted me from fishing; it also didn't seem to help the fish bite any better. We didn't catch any that morning, but after sandwiches for lunch we caught seven nice trout that afternoon—after the water receded—using chartreuse power bait balls with the river rigs. Hudson and I cleaned the fish at the resort cleaning station on the river by the boat slips.

We headed up to the cabins for dinner, consisting of a salad, smoked chicken, pulled pork, brisket, chips, baked beans, lasagna, and rolls. After talking and resting for a while we had devotion at eight thirty by Shawn Carnine using Hebrews 9. I felt it was an appropriate time to give my testimony praising God for giving me the adversity of depression over eighteen months that made me a more mature Christian. We watched a little more of the NCAA tournament and then went to bed for an early morning devotion again at 6:30 a.m. by Shawn using Hebrews 11.

That Saturday morning it began raining after a breakfast of pastries and yogurt. I am a Gideon, and I told those around me that the rain was my fault because the Gideon's State Convention was going on that weekend in Tulsa, and I was out fishing. I jokingly told them that they could throw me in the river, and maybe the rain would stop. Bryan, Hudson, and I had planned to go up the river six miles, within one mile of the dam, when the gates were closed and stopped generating; we would be at the lower water level with less current ninety minutes sooner.

While waiting for the rain to slack, I decided to go fishing behind the cabin on the jetty that protected the boat slips from the strong current. The jetty produced an eddy, and I thought that would be a good place to fish while the water level was high. I was fishing on the point, and it began a downpour. With my rain gear on I kept fishing and hooked my largest rainbow of the trip. I landed it on the bank, and when I picked it up with my rag, a stream of white sperm shot all over my jeans and boots. It was a nice male that had swallowed the hook.

Because it was raining so hard, I decided to walk up to our cabin and remove the hook under the covered back porch. I had someone holding a flashlight so I could see the shank and grabbed the hook in the curve with my long forceps. When I had the forceps in the right place, I pushed it down the throat and twisted; the hook came out without any bleeding. I took the fish to the cleaning station, gutted it, and removed the blood strip along the center of the rib cage. By this time the rain had slacked a little; Hudson and Bryan were ready to go upstream in the boat. I put the fish in a bag on ice and headed for the boat with my gear.

It took forty-five minutes to get upstream in the rain to the sign that read, "barbless hooks only, catch and release" within a mile of the dam. The water level was already receding, and we began a gentle drift along the west bank of the river. I expected to catch lots of trout that morning. The evening before, Fred Perry had given us a report on the trout stocking by the Arkansas Game and Fish Commission (AGFC)—over seventy thousand rainbows and thirty thousand browns below the dam in the White River.

This was fewer than in previous years but still plenty. In 2015 the AGFC reported 1,203,670 rainbow trout stocked throughout the year and 105,000 browns in December—more than half of all trout stocked in the state of Arkansas that year.

We drifted past many likely looking spots with eddies at a depth and speed we could feel our sinker bouncing off the bottom, a technique that usually caught trout, but we were catching no fish—not even a nibble. More than halfway down to White Hole Resort with Gaston's Resort in sight, Bryan hooked a nice rainbow. I saw the fish come in close to the boat on my right side, and I told Hudson to get the net lying in the bottom of the boat between us. He stood up in the middle of the boat but didn't seem to be moving toward the net fast enough, so I bent over to pick up the net. As I grabbed the net, I looked up just in time to see the fish flying over Hudson's head and out over the water on the other side of the boat. The fish wiggled and flopped off the hook into the water. Bryan said he was trying to land the fish in the boat when Hudson stood up; in order to avoid hitting Hudson in the head Bryan raised the fish higher in the air, but the momentum carried it out over the other side of the boat. It was a hilarious comedy of errors, and we lost the only fish we hooked floating down the river that day.

In front of Gaston's the water was much shallower, and Bryan began yelling, "Rock ahead!" I swerved to the right and missed the large rock, but the prop began hitting some loose gravel. I immediately tilted the motor up to avoid the gravel as we floated through the shallow water.

We fished a while longer, and I noticed it was after noon, so I told them I was headed for White Hole. One thing was nice about that day—we didn't have to clean any more fish before leaving for home. We packed up and left White Hole Resort, stopping to eat barbecue at Razorback Ribs in Yellville, Arkansas. It was a fun, relaxing, and spiritual experience for two days.

Notes

(Chapter 2)

1   J. J. Schildkraut et al, "Norepinephrine metabolism and drugs used in affective disorders: A possible mechanism of action." Am J Psychiatry 1967, 124:600–8.

(Chapter 4)

2   D. R. Hazle (1970). "Local Protein Synthesis in Peripheral Nerves-a Factor Influencing Recovery from Local Anesthesia" (Lexington, KY: University of Kentucky).

3   D. E. Knapp, S. Mejia, (1969). "Suppression of peripheral nerve protein synthesis by acetoxycycloheximide." Anesth and Analg 48:189–94.

4   J. J. Schildkraut, S. S. Kety, "Biogenic amines and emotion." Science. 1967, Apr 7;156 (3771):21–37.

5   I. Francisco, C. Alamo, "Monaminergic Neurotransmission: The History of the Discovery of Antidepressants from 1950s until Today." Current Pharmaceutical Design. 2009, 15, 1563–1586.

6   E. Ingersoll, "An integral view of antidepressants." Our Lady of Holy Cross Seminar, June 1, 2000. Available at URL:http://www.csuohio. edu/casl/NORD.htm.

(Chapter 6)

7   PDF available at URL:http://www.psnpaloalto.com/wp/wp-content/ uploads/2010/12/Depression-Diagnostic-Criteria-and-Severity-Rating. pdf or Google "Depression-Diagnostic-Criteria-and-Severity-Rating.

pdf" and under "Web Results" select "Diagnostic Criteria for Major Depressive Disorder and Depressive,"

(Chapter 8)

8   R. R. Fieve, *Prozac* (New York: Avalon Books, 1994).
9   R. Woolis, *When Someone You Love Has a Mental Illness.* (New York: Penguin Group, 2003), 147–49.

(Chapter 9)

10   Anxiety and Depression Association of America (ADAA). adaa.org.
11   Google "NARCAN" and select "NARCAN (naloxone)–Nasal Spray 4mg,"
12   National Suicide Prevention Lifeline (http://www.suicideprevention lifeline.org/).
13   "Neurobiology of Aggression and Violence," Am J Psychiatry. 2008 Apr; 165(4): 429–422.
14   Google "Alcohol, Sleep, and Why You Might Re-Think that Nightcap," *Psychology Today.* Posted Oct 28, 2013, Brain Babble Blog by Jordan Gaines Lewis.
15   I. Ebrihim, Alcoholism: Clinical and Experimental Research, April 2013 Also Google "Alcohol and a Good Night's Sleep Don't Mix," by Denise Mann from WEBMD archives.
16   Google "Alcohol and GABA" and select "Alcohol and GABA–Does alcohol increase or decrease GABA?".
17   "Sociodemographic Disparities Notes in Oral Cancer Screenings Rates," Decisions in Dentistry, Nov./Dec. 2019, Volume 5, Number 10:10. Tobacco Quit Line phone number
18   M. P. Bogenschutz et al. "Psilocybin-assisted treatment for alcohol dependence: A proof-of-concept study," Journal of Psychopharmacology, 2015, Jan. 13. Google "Psilocybin-assisted treatment for alcohol dependence a proof-of-concept study." for this article.
19   M. W. Johnson and Griffiths, "Potential Therapeutic Effects of Psilocybin," Neurotherapeutics, 2017, June 5, 14:734–40.

(Chapter 11)

20 "Help Win Others for Christ | Become a Friend of Gideons." The Gideons International. P.O. Box 140800 Nashville, TN 37214-0800.

(Chapter 12)

21 G. Highet, *The Immortal Profession.* (New York: Weybright and Talley, 1976).

22 S. Harrar, "Happiness in Hard Times," *AARP Magazine Real Possibilities,* June / July 2020, Volume 63, Number 4C

(Chapter 1 and Chapter13)

23 *The New City Catechism: 52 Questions and Answers for Our Hearts and Minds* (Wheaton, IL: Crossway, 2017).

Figure 1   (Chapter 4)
Figure 2   (Chapter 4)
Figure 3   (Chapter 9)

About the Author

D r. Darrell Hazle has dedicated his life to the service of others. He has known this was God's will for his life ever since being led to switch from majoring in agronomy to dentistry. After three years of agronomy at the University of Kentucky (UK) he was accepted into the UK College of Dentistry (UKCD) in 1966. It was there that God led him to do research on local anesthetics in the Honors Program which led to an interest in the brain which led to reviewing the literature in neurotransmitters, emotions, and antidepressants. With his family history of depression on his mother's side and his own bouts with depression and suicide ideation in 1975, 2004 and 2017 he felt he was uniquely qualified to write a book that would help others.

The author believes that there have been events in his life that have demonstrated God's protection and favored his development. The author was born in 1945 on a farm four miles from Abraham Lincoln's birthplace near Hodgenville, Kentucky. He graduated fifth "with distinction" in his dental school class of forty-five. He was awarded fellowship in the American College of Dentists in 1994.

Another service-oriented career decision was the choice to remain in the US Public Health Service (USPHS) instead of going into private practice. He became a Commissioned Officer in the USPHS in 1970. Expecting that he couldn't make as much money in the USPHS he stayed in because he thought he didn't need all of the extra things that money could buy. He enjoyed serving in the Indian Health Service, an agency in the Health and Human Services Department. There were many opportunities for development and advancement and good people to work with. He retired in 1995 as a Captain (0-6) with 15 PHS medals including the Out- standing Service and Meritorious Service awards.

He has a lovely wife who has always said "I'll go wherever you want to go" when they were transferred to Galveston, Texas; Fort Yates, North, Dakota; Tahlequah, Oklahoma and Claremore, Oklahoma. They have two daughters and four grandsons.

He has been a member of The Gideons Interntional since 2000. Of the people who have most influenced his life he lists his mother and father, his grandpa Hazle, uncle Red Hazle, his mentor at UKCD Dr. Donald E. Knapp, Terry Devitt and his fellow Gideons.

About the Book

D r. Hazle thanks God and those who have helped him have a happy, successful, and Christian life. He takes the readers through many events that he considers the providence of God in his life including the serendipitous discovery of the first antidepressant—imipramine marketed in 1957—which was used to treat his first depression in 1975. He describes in his book how at the age of seventy-five years he has had a successful career as a dental officer in the United States Public Health Service and an exciting retirement even with three bouts of depression and being maintained on medication since 1975 for bipolar disorder. Of particular importance is the adversity God gave him during his third depression---lasting eighteen months---and the spiritual changes which he credits with making hm a more mature Christ-centered Christian.

He also attributes part of his success in managing his bipolar illness with his understanding of neurotransmitters and emotions that began with a research project at the University of Kentucky College of Dentistry in 1968.

Described in the book is his family history of treatment for disabling depression in three generations including: one suicide and one suicide attempt, and three family members receiving electroconvulsive therapy (ECT).

He also challenges readers and demonstrates making

stimulating music memories with good emotions that they would like to recall for the rest of their lives.

He believes this book would be of interest to those exploring the science of depression, alcoholism, and addiction to nicotine and other drugs, as well as spiritual aspects of behavior.

In the last chapter read about the author's most interesting and memorable pheasant and duck hunting and fishing trips.

God has carried out his plan for Dr. Hazle. His sincere desire is that God would be glorified through this book.

Printed in the United States
By Bookmasters